Deleuze & Guattari
Emergent Law

Deleuze & Guattari: Emergent Law is a sophisticated, yet accessible, exposition and development of Deleuze & Guattari's legal theory. Although there has been considerable interest in Deleuze & Guattari in critical legal studies, as well as considerable interest in legality in Deleuze & Guattari studies, this is the first book to focus exclusively on Deleuze & Guattari and law. In Deleuze & Guattari's ontology there are two fundamental operations in the organisation of nature and the social: molecular and molar. Molecular processes of genesis and organisation draw upon the forces of the virtual, creating molecular emergent dissipative structures. By contrast, molar organisation draws upon the differentiating operation of a boundary that constitutes a division. After introducing and explaining this ontology, Jamie Murray situates Deleuze & Guattari's engagement with social organisation and legality in the context of their theory of 'abstract machines' and 'intensive assemblages'. He then presents their theory of law: as that of a two-fold conception of, first, a transcendent molar law and, second, an immanent molecular emergent law. Transcendent molar legality is the traditional object of legal theory. And, as explicated here, immanent molecular emergent law is the novel juridical object that Deleuze & Guattari identify. Developing this conception, *Deleuze & Guattari: Emergent Law* also draws out its implications for current and for future legal theory; arguing that it provides the basis for a new jurisprudence capable of creating new concepts of legality.

Dr Jamie Murray is Senior Lecturer in Law at Liverpool John Moores University specialising in Equity & Trusts Law. His research interests are Deleuze & Guattari, Complexity Theory, and Equity & Trusts Law.

Nomikoi: Critical Legal Thinkers
Series editors:

Peter Goodrich
Cardozo School of Law, New York

David Seymour
School of Law, Lancaster University, UK

Nomikoi: Critical Legal Thinkers presents analyses of key critical theorists whose thinking on law has contributed significantly to the development of the new inter-disciplinary legal studies. Addressing those who have most influenced legal thought and thought about law, the aim of the series is to bring legal scholarship, the social sciences and the humanities into closer dialogue.

Other titles in the Series
Judith Butler: Ethics, Law, Politics
Elena Loizidou

Evgeny Pashukanis: A Critical Appraisal
Michael Head

Niklas Luhmann
Andreas Philippopoulos-Mihalopoulos

Carl Schmitt: Law as Politics, Ideology and Strategic Myth
Michael Salter

Henri Lefebvre: Critical Legal Studies and the Politics of Space
Chris Butler

Bruno Latour
Kyle McGee

Deleuze & Guattari: Emergent Law
Jamie Murray

Althusser and Law
Laurent de Sutter

Roberto Esposito: Law, Community and the Political
Peter Langford

Deleuze & Guattari

Emergent Law

Jamie Murray

Routledge
Taylor & Francis Group
a GlassHouse Book

First published 2013
by Routledge
2 Park Square, Milton Park, Abingdon, Oxon OX14 4RN

Simultaneously published in the USA and Canada
by Routledge
711 Third Avenue, New York, NY 10017

A GlassHouse Book

Routledge is an imprint of the Taylor & Francis Group, an informa business

British Library Cataloguing in Publication Data
A catalogue record for this book is available from the British Library

Library of Congress Cataloging-in-Publication Data
Murray, Jamie.
  Deleuze & Guattari: emergent law/Jamie Murray.
    pages cm. — (Nomikoi: critical legal thinkers)
  Includes bibliographical references and index.
  ISBN 978-0-415-49601-8 (hbk: alk. paper) — ISBN 978-0-415-81750-9
(pbk: alk. paper) 1. Sociological jurisprudence. 2. Deleuze, Gilles,
1925–1995 3. Guattari, Félix, 1930-1992 4. Law—Philosophy.
  I. Title. II. Title: Deleuze and Guattari.
  K370.M88 2013
  340'.115—dc23   2013006500

ISBN 978-0-415-49601-8 (hbk)
ISBN 978-0-203-58420-0 (ebk)

Typeset in Times New Roman
by Cenveo Publisher Services

MIX
Paper from
responsible sources
FSC
www.fsc.org   FSC® C013604   Printed and bound by CPI Group (UK) Ltd, Croydon, CR0 4YY

For the schizo lawyers and vagabond lawyers
out there

Contents

Acknowledgements

In terms of the study of Deleuze & Guattari in relation to issues of legality, it was Kate Green, during the course of teaching a Legal Theory module together, who introduced me to *A Thousand Plateaus* and its potential for thinking anew issues of legality. Dragan Milovanovic's explorations of Deleuze & Guattari in relation to issues of legality have been particularly influential on me, as has generally his experimental theorisations and compositions of post-structuralist theory and issues of legality. Ronnie Lippens and Martin Hardie, in many ways, have encouraged and assisted me in the development of this project of the study of Deleuze & Guattari in relation to issues of legality.

In terms of the production of the book, my thanks to Colin Perrin and to Peter Goodrich who took on the book project for Routledge, and to Melanie Fortmann-Brown at Routledge for bringing the book production process through. In terms of the final production process of this book my thanks to Clare Weaver, Janet Roskilly, and Michelle Antrobus.

The planning and writing of this book project took place beside my lecturing work in Liverpool John Moores University Law School. Throughout this period the Director of Research was George Mair, and so thanks to George for supporting and encouraging this project. My thanks to Lorie Charlesworth for all her encouragement and support over the planning and writing of this project in her roles as long-time room mate, friend and co-conspirator. Above all, thanks to my partner Anna Carline, who had to put up with me immersed in the project at both work and at home, but who was always there with understanding, encouragement and support.

Key References

The four key Deleuze & Guattari texts are referenced as follows:

AntiOedipus	D&G (1984)
Kafka: Towards a Minor Literature	D&G (1986)
A Thousand Plateaus	D&G (1988)
What is Philosophy?	D&G (1994)

With *AntiOedipus* and *A Thousand Plateaus* referencing is complicated because of the existence of two English publications of each book with different paginations (both are the University of Minnesota translations). For *AntiOedipus* there is the 1984 The Athlone Press publication and the 2004 Continuum publication. For *A Thousand Plateaus*, similarly, there is the 1988 The Athlone Press publication and the 2004 Continuum publication. The Athlone Press publications have a font and layout that is easier to work from than the Continuum publications. In the references to these two books the first pagination is to The Athlone Press publication, the second pagination in brackets is to the Continuum publication.

Introduction

This project is concerned with the work of Deleuze & Guattari and its relations to issues of legality and social organisation. It is, thus, to explore their joint work as a social theory and to develop out from it their theory of legality and social organisation. The joint work of Deleuze & Guattari is comprised of the four co-authored books of *AntiOedipus, Kafka: Towards a Minor Literature, A Thousand Plateaus* and *What is Philosophy?* References will be made to sole-authored books by both Deleuze and Guattari, but by means of understanding or extending the jointly authored material.

The joint work of Deleuze & Guattari is marked by a number of distinctive features and thematic concerns that must necessarily inform and be reflected in any commentary on their work. This book is an introductory account of the joint work of Deleuze & Guattari, and a discussion of its relation to issues of legality and social organisation. However, it is also marked by an attempt to draw forward and dramatise these distinctive features and thematic concerns of Deleuze & Guattari and to produce a commentary that foregrounds their distinctiveness and novelty. Before providing an overview of the chapters of this book, the introduction will therefore first draw out some of the distinctive features and thematic concerns with the purpose of both introducing Deleuze & Guattari but also introducing what to expect from the concerns and composition of this book in so far as it seeks to draw out and dramatise these features and thematic concerns.

Two very significant features of Deleuze & Guattari's work are those that are carried in from Deleuze's prior work. The first is the ontology of the virtual, and the second is the critique of the State image of thought and the practice of nomad thought. These two features are crucial to an understanding of Deleuze & Guattari. Deleuze by *Difference & Repetition* had developed his own distinctive ontology that was absolutely central to all his philosophical thought, and which when carried forward was absolutely central to the joint Deleuze & Guattari work. This ontology developed a transcendental empiricism that elaborated a virtual ontological modality and an intensive ontological modality that were required to fully account for the actual and extensive ontological modality. This ontology thought through the virtual and intensive processes of self-organisation and emergence that account for the genesis and organisation of the extensive order of being. Deleuze specified particular processes and operations for the virtual, particular processes and operations for the intensive, particular processes and operations for the actual, and operations by which the virtual and intensive enter the actual but also by which the actual enters back into the intensive and virtual. The second key feature carried through from Deleuze's prior work and most keenly developed in *Difference & Repetition* was the development of a nomad thought thoroughly opposed to a representational State thought. Deleuze had set out against the line of European thought most closely associated with Kant and Hegel, and had instead taken up a line of thought that he saw running through Spinoza, Nietzsche and Bergson. This led Deleuze to pursue a nomad thought that explored difference and repetition in virtual and intensive processes of forces and affects that produced concepts as open but consistent multiplicities. Indeed, the univocal ontology specified an equivalence of being and thought that would bring philosophical thought to the processes and operations of the virtual and intensive. This very specific ontology and this very specific critique of State thought and pursuit of nomad thought are key central features that are carried forward to Deleuze & Guattari, and they are to be key features to this introductory commentary.

With the Deleuze & Guattari work itself there are perhaps four key features that are developed as thematic concerns; two of which take the two carried forward features from Deleuze and substantially develop them as thematic concerns.

The virtual ontology becomes a thematic concern throughout the joint work, being reworked and extended in many ways. A key development to the virtual ontology is the reworking of the ontology in terms of machining and schizo desiring processes, and the more refined and materialist reworking of the virtual and intensive processes in terms of abstract machines and machinic assemblages. The extension of this ontology that Deleuze & Guattari develop is the development of the virtual ontology as a social ontology of social machines and machinic social assemblages. Social organisation possesses a virtual plane and an intensive field where processes of self-organisation and emergence take place in relation to a respecifying problematic of social organisation to create various social machines and social assemblages. This thematic concern of the virtual social ontology is explicitly developed with a primacy of cosmic forces and cosmic lines of deterritorialisation in social organisation, thus marking Deleuze & Guattari's social theory as particularly expansive and ecological.

The critique of the State image of thought and the theorisation and practice of nomad thought is carried through, again, with reworking and development. Nomad thought is reworked as schizo processes of exploring the virtual plane and the operation of a machining of consistent concepts, then as the practice of a war machine that explores smooth space drawing lines of flight, and then as the philosophy of the drawing of planes of immanence, the creation of concepts and the invention of conceptual personae. Nomad thought as a thematic concern is also developed in a noology that is the study of images of thought; their creation,

genealogy and their transformations set against the brain as the plane of immanence for thinking. However, in whatever variation, the central thematic concern
of thinking in Deleuze & Guattari is always the creation of concepts.

The two new features of Deleuze & Guattari's work that develop as thematic
concerns and which need to be appreciated by way of introduction are the concern
for principles of composition and for ethical and political concerns of social
transformation.

In contrast to Deleuze's own books prior to the collaboration with Guattari,
which were academic philosophy, the joint books of Deleuze & Guattari, particularly *AntiOedipus* and *A Thousand Plateaus*, are composed on principles of
experimentation, desiring production, the pursuit of lines of flight, the creation of
concepts as transversal consistencies, the maximum proliferation of these
concepts in variation, appearing anarchic as against conventions of academic
philosophy. Guattari had little interest in the University as academic institution,
instead connecting his thought and writing to his experience with schizophrenia
as process in his psychiatric practice and to problems of organisation of transformational political groups. Deleuze with Guattari massively extended the scope of
material that could be worked around the machining of ontology and the noolo-
gising of nomad thought, and stylistically there was creation, experimentation
and dramatisation of concepts with affects and intensities. This thematic concern
of composition is, of course, entirely in line with the ontology and with nomad
thought. An introduction to Deleuze & Guattari's work should carry this thematic
concern.

Indeed, this book is compositionally and conceptually experimental. The entire
book is set out in Chapter 1 in Professor Challenger's opening three-line address,
and each chapter is an exploration of this central problematic, but from different
perspectives and with different development and concerns. The book does have a
level of linear development, but each chapter can be read relatively indepen-
dently, and a particular chapter that may be considered obscure or difficult will
have light shed on it by reading other chapters which address the same problematic but with their own different development and concerns. There is as much
conceptual proliferation and the putting of concepts in continuous variation as
I was able to develop, and every attempt is made to dramatise this conceptual
proliferation and variation. The representational route to introducing the thought
of Deleuze & Guattari is not taken, and instead every effort has been taken to
introduce the thought of Deleuze & Guattari on legality and social organisation
as experimentation. In particular, the book proceeds from a relation to commentary that does not forestall conceptual creativity and the introduction of new
concepts. In this, one key feature of compositional and conceptual development
of the book is the use of conceptual personae. Deleuze & Guattari employed
conceptual personae in *A Thousand Plateaus*, and in *What is Philosophy?*
conceptual personae emerge as the necessary operator for the creation of concepts
on thinking's plane of immanence. Conceptual personae are employed in the first
three chapters (three speakers from a Transfaculty of Deleuze & Guattari Studies),

and the invention of the conceptual personae of the schizo lawyer and vagabond lawyer become central to the development of Chapters 5 and 6.

The final thematic concern key to Deleuze & Guattari's work is for ethical and political concerns – issues of the injustice of capitalism, real problems of social transformation, and with ecological concerns also. The collaboration of Deleuze & Guattari was in the wake of the social movements of 1968, and Guattari, as much as he was a psychiatrist and writer, was a political activist. Much of the discussion in their joint work on social organisation was in response to direct problems in the organising of transformative political groups, and also directly linked to concerns of how to live and socially organise in a manner that did not risk falling into fascism. Across their joint work there is their own named thematic concern of capitalism and schizophrenia, and running through their work is the absolute commitment to the transformative forces of schizophrenia and the war machine in relation to the end of capitalism and the creation of a new earth. Forty years after the publication of their first joint work, this thematic concern feels still prescient.

Chapter 1 employs the conceptual persona of Professor Challenger borrowed from *A Thousand Plateaus*, and in turn borrowed by Deleuze & Guattari, where Professor Challenger appears as an expert on the ontology of the earth and an expert in clearing rooms. The chapter introduces the ontology of the virtual-intensive-actual that is so vital to any understanding of Deleuze & Guattari. It does so through framing the discussion of the virtual ontology in terms of the ontology of the earth (though more generally and much less extensively than the plateau 'Geology of Morals' (D&G (1988) 39 (44))). It does so because not only is the earth an interesting thing in which to frame the discussion of the ontology, but because the Deleuze & Guattari concept of the earth becomes progressively more prominent as the book develops. The ontology of the virtual is presented as a virtual modality of processes and operations of the plane of immanence, an intensive modality of processes and operations of the machinic phylum, and the actual modality of extensive time and space stratified things. There are operations of how the virtual enters the intensive, which in turn deposits the actual, with actual states of affairs then being taken up in intensive processes and operations that in turn enter into the virtual to reorganise the virtual. These operations were theorised in Deleuze's prior work as the quasi-cause and three passive syntheses, and in the joint work they become theorised in terms of virtual abstract machines, intensive machinic assemblages and extensive expression-content formed strata. In more contemporary language these operations can be understood in terms of the order from chaos, processes of self-organisation and emergence, and the creation of dissipative structures. The operation of the virtual is discussed in terms of differential relations, topology, manifolds, multiplicities, transversal consistencies of these multiplicities and virtual problematics. The operation of the intensive is discussed in terms of the progressive specification of intensive forces and elements in morphogenetic processes in relation to a problem field of intensive becoming that can be modelled as an assemblage of degrees of freedom in a phase space.

The actual is discussed in terms of the arrest of virtual and intensive processes in strata and states of affairs organised extensively near equilibrium in an expression-content closure, but which are in turn subject to operations of virtual and intensive sampling of the actual. The earth is, thus, discussed as existing as a virtual deterritorialised earth of the plane of immanence, the intensive morphogenetic earth of the machinic phylum, and the actualised earth of the territory, strata and plane of organisation. The chapter ends exploring further the relation between the virtual plane of immanence and the actual plane of organisation, but drawing out the primacy of the virtual earth, of decoded and deterritorialised cosmic forces, and of the eternal return, to the ontological becoming and being of the earth. This chapter, therefore, draws through Deleuze's virtual ontology, some of the ontological thematic concern of the joint work, and introduces the Deleuze & Guattari concept of the earth.

Chapter 2 employs a novel conceptual persona of Dr Brian Nome to operate as an obscure noologist and so to introduce the necessary material on thought and thinking from the perspective of a noology of images of thought. The chapter introduces noology as nothing less than the extension of nomad thought, schizo thought, and war machine thought to the study of the brain, the images of thought that can emerge and operate on the brain in relation to the problems of thinking on the brain, and the continual noological operation of engendering thinking in thought. In this noological approach, Dr Nome draws out from Deleuze & Guattari the nomad/schizo/war machine image of thought, the molar/Royal/State image of thought, and also something short of an image of thought but which nonetheless is a distinctive practice of thought of vagabond thinkers. The brain, just as the earth, is a plane of immanence, an intensive machinic phylum, and an actualised plane of organisation. Noology operates with the plane of immanence brain from which it takes up the image of the nomad/schizo/war machine image of thought and develops this image of thought in terms of working with multiplicities in manifolds, and creating consistencies amongst differences and intensive affects to create concepts. This image of thought becomes in *What is Philosophy?* the image of thought that draws a plane of immanence, invents conceptual personae and creates new concepts. In the schizo image of thought thinking engenders itself, which is to say it self-organises and emerges, always in relation to the plane of immanence as the virtual, as the specification and continual respecification of a problem and of problems. In noology and schizo thought the thinker always has the brain problem and brain problems. The creation of concepts in schizo thought is inseparable from the virtual problem that presupposes the engendering of thought and of problems that presuppose the creation of concepts. Noology, thus, studies the organisation, creation, genealogy and transformations of schizo thought, but also in so doing practises that schizo image of thought.

However, noology also studies other images of thought, together with their organisation, creation, genealogy and transformations, and in this noology has a critical task. There is also an image of thought that presupposes itself and thinks a plane of organisation that transcendentally organises a plane for thought that closes off the plane of immanence and intensive machinic phylum for thought. This is the State image of thought that organises itself through a transcendent operation of drawing a plane of organisation, unifying a plane and creating a distinction between the organised plane and a chaotic outside, establishing a transcendent organising principle which allows totalisations and distinctions on essences, an overriding principle of identity, the development of binarisation and hierarchical organisation of these essences and binaries, and the generalised development of a system of representation grounded in an operation of recognition. This is the molar-Royal-State image of thought that Deleuze bore down on in Chapter 3 of *Difference & Repetition*, and which Deleuze & Guattari continue to attack in all their noological joint work. What is added most significantly in this work is the exploration of the genealogy of the State image of thought in the social machine of the despotic Imperial State, and the continuing relation of the State image of thought to social organisation, legality and the State social machine. Also, already significant in their noological work is the issue transformation from images of thought into other images of thought.

Noology further, at least in the hands of Dr Nome, also studies a practice of vagabond thought. This is a thought that moves between the two limit images of thought of noology of the schizo thought image of the plane of immanence and State thought image of the plane of organisation. It is thought that is ambivalent between images of thought, and ambulant between the two images of thought. Vagabond thinkers are aware of the plane of immanence for thinking and can relate to schizo thinkers although they have no wish to think the plane of immanence. Vagabond thinkers think in the State image of thought when required and even may hold it in high regard, but vagabond thinkers do not share the complete occlusion of the intensive machinic field of intensities, affects, morphogenetic processes, incorporeal transformations and events of thought that State thinkers have. Vagabond thought is thus aware of schizo thought and the virtual to the extent that the vagabond thinker is the genius of the intensive machinic phylum of thought and of the intensities, affects, singularities, transformations, and incorporeal transformations that thinking can work with and effect at the loose edges of the State image of thought.

Chapter 3 turns directly to Deleuze & Guattari's social ontology of social machines, and develops a noology of legalities. Social organisation, like the earth and the brain, has an actual register but also a virtual register and intensive register. The Deleuze & Guattari theory of social machines is central to this study, with social machines drawing the plane of inscription of the socius and operating to connect the earth and the brain together with the forces of the cosmos in an abstract machine of social organisation. Social organisation self-organises and emerges in relation to the continually respecifying virtual and intensive problematic of social organisation. In relation to the virtual problematic of social organisation, a multiplicity abstract machine of organisation self-organises and emerges. In relation to the intensive social problem field, an intensive machinic social assemblage self-organises, piloted by the abstract machine of organisation, but also tapping material forces of self-organisation and emergence and actualised constraints. The abstract machine of organisation provides an answer to the problematic of social organisation, and the intensive social assemblage that develops in the intensive morphogenetic social problem field lays down and deposits the actualised social territory and strata. Together, the abstract machine of organisation, intensive social assemblage, and the actualised territory and strata constitute a social machine. A social machine develops to connect the earth and the brain in a socius and territory. The abstract machine of organisation is the abstract machine of legality of the social machine. One of the key tenets of noology is that images of thought have a genealogy that embeds every image of thought in a particular social machine. The multiplicity of an image of thought is also the multiplicity of a social machine's abstract machine of organisation. A legality has a virtual plane of immanence where the abstract machine of legality emerges in relation to a problematic of social organisation, an intensive morphogenetic problem field in which an intensive assemblage of justice and legality, and an actualised jurisdiction, system and set of institutional practices is extensively developed. The abstract machine of legality is the image of thought of a social machine. In answering the problematic of social organisation, and in connecting the earth and brain, there are many social machines that use very different abstract machines of organisation and many different strategies of multiplicities, coding and territorialising. In addition, there are many social assemblages of legality that self-organise and emerge on the socius, delivering functions of legality alongside that of the inscribing social machine.

The conceptual persona that focuses the discussion of social machines is Caprica Six. Caprica is ideally placed to discuss machining, desiring production, the problematic of social organisation, social machines, and the cosmic forces of social organisation that draw social organisation towards an eternal return in the search for a new earth and of a hybrid people yet to come. Machining in social organisation is as the machining of the earth and the machining of the brain, and it is the processes of social machining that account for the desiring production that creates and invests social organisation and the social field. Social machining is abstract machines of social organisation, intensive assemblages of legality, and a social territory and strata. A social assemblage is organised by its abstract machine in regimes of signs, regimes of organising bodies and technology, a social territory, and a means of relating to decoded cosmic forces of deterritorialisation. Many social machines organise themselves to close off the forces of decoding and deterritorialisation, but struggle to suppress these forces. Conversely, some social machines have an abstract machine that creates a transversal immanent social organisation precisely in cosmic decoded and deterritorialised forces. The cosmic forces of deterritorialisation are stronger than forces of coding and territorialisation, and social organisation emerges in deterritorialised cosmic forces, and social organisation tends towards an absolute decoding and deterritorialisation by which it becomes cosmic in the eternal return as a machinic opera pursuing a line of flight to a new earth.

Chapter 4 lays out the four social machines that Deleuze & Guattari discuss at considerable length in both *AntiOedipus* and *A Thousand Plateaus*. The four social machines are the territorial social machine, the State social machine, the capitalist axiomatic social machine and the nomad war social machine. The chapter explores these four modalities of social organisation in terms of social machines, abstract machines, abstract machines of legality, intensive and extensive social assemblages, and intensive and extensive assemblages of legality. Each social machine is considered in a constitutive relationship to an image of thought that it produces and operates. Each social machine is considered as an image of legality and abstract machine of legality (though there can be variations in the regimes of legality within the one abstract machine of legality). Each social machine and the instances that effectuate it are explored in terms of a genealogy of the social machines, together with consideration of social machines' relations of transformation in relation to other social machines, different social assemblages, and, indeed, to itself. The chapter is the noology of legalities in action, drawing a plane of immanence for the problematic of legality and surveying the entire social field in terms of abstract machines of legality and assemblages of legality, carrying out considerations and operations that are noological, diagrammatic, machinic and transformational.

The four social machines all relate to the real, relative, and absolute limits in the problematic of legality and social organisation, and make of each social machine a particular adventure in social organisation and legality. Some of these social machines emerge many times over, always different but sharing the virtual abstract machine of organisation. There are more social machines and new social machines can emerge, and there are many social assemblages that do not constitute social machines.

The territorial social machine is that of autonomous villages that through operation of alliance and filiation, a collectivisation of the organs, and the coding of all the flows, produce a primitive social organisation and legality. It is the territorial social machine that operates the fundamental action of social organisation of breeding man as an animal capable of social organisation and a memory of alliance and debt. There is carried out a profound procedure of the repression of the entire biocosmic intensive memory of the germinal flux, a coding of all the social flows, and the constraining of desiring production within the new bounds of social production. Though perhaps not directly related to contemporary conditions of legality and social organisation, the discussion of the territorial social machine sets out and illustrates in a fundamental way what is at stake in the problematic of social organisation and legality.

The State social machine is that of the rising up of a principle of transcendence in the milieus of the territorial social machines, whereby a despot imposes a reorganisation on alliance and filiation and unification and overcoding of all social production. The Imperial despotic Asiatic States typify the State abstract machine, but all States share the same abstract machine of organisation and even the modern nation States can trace their genealogy back to the Imperial despotic States.

The State social machine, and in particular the State image of law and abstract machine of legality, emerge as central to the discussion of the four laws and to the problematic of the entire book project. It is the State social machine that defines the very ideas of what it is to think and what it is to have a law, and draws a plane of transcendent organisation for legality that the noology of legalities will have to cross.

Both these social machines of the territory and of the State proceed by operations of coding, overcoding, territorialising and stratification in the register of the extensive and actual, and makes of these machines the adventures in legality and social organisation of the ecumenon earth.

The social machines of territory and State are overtaken by the emergence of a one-off social machine of capitalism with its organisation by arbitraging of the flows and a regulatory stabilisation through its axiomatic. This social machine emerges in the conjunction and arbitraging of two flows of decoded and deterritorialised labour and decoded and deterritorialised wealth as capital and the subsequent generation and extraction of surplus value from flow. This social machine has become global and has fully developed the financialisation present in the very inception of capital, and the State social machines are eclipsed to be recycled by capitalism as an operator of part of capitalism's regulatory axiomatic. Capitalism has pursued decoding and deterritorialisation very far indeed, and in so far as schizophrenic process is organisation through absolute decoding and deterritorialisation, the capitalist social machine at its relative limits and after the history of all the territorial machines and all the State machines, opens the social problematic and social field to the forces of absolute decoding and deterritorialisation. In this, capitalism is its own unique adventure, one which, though centred in the mechanosphere, ranges across the ecumenon and the planomenon, making its own adventure across all the ontological modalities of the earth.

Beside the territorial social machine and the State social machine, and aside from the capitalist social machine, there is another mode of social organisation that Deleuze & Guattari explore in terms of the nomad war machine social organisation and the planomenon as ethos. This is a social machine with an abstract machine of organisation that organises precisely in dynamic in variation transversal consistencies in decoded and deterritorialised flows. The nomad social machine is the social effectuation of a war machine abstract machine that is the abstract machine of immanent creativity and the image of thought of noology and schizo thought. The nomad abstract machine of organisation remains on the plane of immanence, and the social assemblage remains intensive mixing elements of signs and material organisation in a movement through a smooth space where territorialisation in strata is minimal to the point that the territorialisation of the nomad social machine is on deterritorialisation itself. Such social machines raise the issue of emergent law and a legality for a new earth, and raise the issue of an adventure in legality and social organisation adequate to the planomenon earth as ethos.

Chapter 5 turns to the concept of emergent law, and an extension within the Deleuze & Guattari noology of social machines and their abstract machines of legality to explore how a new concept of legality can be developed from Deleuze & Guattari work on social organisation and legality. This exploration starts with drawing out the fundamental distinction in Deleuze & Guattari treatments of social organisation and legality between the nomos and the logos. The nomos and the logos are not in any conceivable way interchangeable ways to talk about legality in Deleuze & Guattari. Rather the difference between the nomos and the logos goes to the difference in the mode of organisation of transversal consistencies in continuous variation and the plane of immanence and the mode of organisation of a transcendent molar fold and a plane of organisation. This fundamental difference between nomos and logos appears in Deleuze's ontology of the three passive syntheses in the second disjunctive synthesis of recording. Deleuze considers that there are two operations of this disjunctive synthesis in the processes of self-organisation and emergence. An inclusive disjunctive synthesis organises through establishing a dynamic transversal consistency in the disjunctive synthesis of the multiplicities in continuous variation and fluxing dynamic thresholds. The exclusive use of the disjunctive synthesis organises by making a distinction and organising a principle of ordering of a unity from a transcendent point. The concept of nomos legality is developed by Deleuze & Guattari in *Kafka* as schizo law and as immanent justice, and is explored in *A Thousand Plateaus* in relation to the war abstract machine, the nomad war social machine, and another kind of justice. These concepts of an immanent transversal consistency of decoded and deterritorialised social flows in continuous variation as an abstract machine of legality and an image of law are taken up and explored in the concept of emergent law. Emergent law encompasses the entire noology of legalities as part of its conceptualisation and practice, and develops critical and creative operations of the problematic of legality and social organisation. The critical operation is to 'have done' with the State social machine, molar law, molar lawyering, and all that comes with capture and investment in the State and molar law. In emergent law the first critical move is to 'do without' the State social machine, molar law and molar lawyering, on the basis of a *know how* of the problematic of legality, the plane of immanence of legality, multiplicities of legality, and machining of transversal consistencies of legalities. In short, it is to do without molar law and molar lawyering on the basis of the noology of legalities. The second critical move is to 'have done with' the State social machine and molar law, through a libidinal disinvestment of the State machine, molar law and molar lawyering, with a corollary investment of the machine and social field of the society yet to come and the social machine of the new earth. Emergent law will only ever be a minority practice. In its creative operation, emergent law, prolonging and developing the noology of legalities makes law in to a problematic of legality and makes the problematic of legality into a philosophical and ethical-aesthetic practice and paradigm (Guattari (1995)). Emergent law is a philosophical and ethical-aesthetic practice and paradigm of the problematic of legality, and is made up of an abstract machine of the creation of concepts of law and an intensive assemblage of ethical-aesthetic problem solving in relation to intensive problems of the case. The abstract machine of emergent law is schizo law and the operations of the schizo lawyer, deploying all of the noology of legalities and the practice of the exploration of the problematic of legality and the creation of concepts of law in continuous variation. The intensive assemblage of emergent law is vagabond lawyering, intensively exploring and intervening in the morphogenetic field of social flows and social problems, employing all the self-organising and emergent problem-solving resources of the machinic phylum, and developing of a practice of the creation of new rights as blocks of intensity-affect-event that are cases of solution to problems without precedent. Emergent law is the alliance of the schizo lawyer and the vagabond lawyer in a conceptu-alisation and practice of the problematic of legality that is the abstract machine and assemblage of the social machine of the new earth, and that draws a legality for a new earth. This concept of emergent law is developed solely from the work of Deleuze & Guattari. There are no references or links to historic and contempo-rary broader debates in analytical philosophy and systems theory of emergent law.

The final chapter considers the relation of the concept of emergent law to contemporary conditions. This is to consider the status of emergent law as a potential social machine. The chapter draws out two aspects of contemporary conditions that particularly touch upon the status of the concept of emergent law as a potential social machine. These two aspects are general processes of virtuali-sation of social organisation, and advanced crisis in capitalist social organisation. It was one of Deleuze & Guattari's persistent claims that at the exterior limit of processes of virtualisation and of the capitalist social machine that a new earth would emerge as a new socius. If processes of virtualisation and the capitalist social machine approach this exterior limit and the drawing of a new earth, the concept of emergent law can be evaluated as a social machine and legality for the new earth. The final part of the chapter turns to characterise how emergent law would develop as a social assemblage, and proposes that it would develop a legal-ity very different from that of the State social machine and the axiomatic of the capitalist social machine. Whilst the concept of emergent law makes of legality a philosophical and ethical-aesthetic practice and paradigm of the schizo lawyer and vagabond lawyer, the development of emergent law as a social machine would make law an ecology or ecosophy (Guattari (2000)). Emergent law would be the practice and paradigm of an ecology of the virtual and intensive earth, massively extending the reach of ecology presently understood, and opening up to a creative autonomy in relation to subjectivity, social organisation and the environment, heralding an ethical and ecological creativity and sustainability.

Chapter 1

Professor Challenger's Lecture on the Earth

The earth, the glacial, is Deterritorialisation par excellence: that is why it belongs to the Cosmos, and presents itself as the material through which human beings tap cosmic forces. We could say that the earth, as deterritorialised, is itself the strict correlate of D to the point that D can be called the creator of the earth – of a new land, a universe, not just a reterritorialisation.

(D&G (1988) 509 (561))

Introduction

Professor Challenger was here to introduce the Deleuze & Guattari ontology of the virtual, intensive and actual modalities of the becoming and being of the earth.

Professor Challenger began. The earth is planomenon, ecumenon and mechanosphere, and the only way to live now on earth is an ecology of the virtual and the intensive.

The planomenon is the virtual modality consisting of problematics and problems, becomings, abstract machines, multiplicities and the plane of immanence. As planomenon the earth is directly part of the cosmos and the cosmic plane of immanence. The ecumenon is the actual modality of extensive structures and entities, unified by molar machines whereby matter is submitted to identity and laws in a transcendent plane of organisation. As ecumenon the earth is the actual and extensive earth of stratifications, codings and territories. The mechanosphere is the intensive modality of the immanent operation of the self-posing problems, machinic phylum and intensive machinic assemblages in a morphogenetic field. The mechanosphere earth is the operation of self-organisation and emergence in materiality in far-from-equilibrium and non-linear processes. The intensive morphogenetic field operates between the virtual plane of immanence and the actual transcendent plane of organisation. The plane of immanence doubles the transcendent plane of organisation, and it is the virtual modality that has created the actual modality through the intensive morphogenetic field. The ecology of the earth connects the planomenon, mechanosphere and ecumenon of the earth together in a fractal line of becoming that is absolute deterritorialisation as the creation of the new in eternal return.

This Deleuze & Guattari theorisation of the earth would require an orientation of theoretical frameworks to ideas from mathematics and from physics. In particular, the virtual requires a theory of multiplicities in terms of manifolds, differential relations and singularities. The intensive register of the morphogenetic field requires an understanding of phase space and phase space portraits for modelling self-organisation and emergence in assemblages.

The fractal abstract machine and the cosmic plane of immanence earth

What is crucial to the Deleuze & Guattari philosophy is that their ontology is not simply of being and the actualised world. It is not an ontology of the actual and the possible. Instead, their ontology puts forward two further ontological registers of the virtual and the intensive. The virtual modality is developed in order to account for features of the actualised world and features of intensive processes that can sometimes intrude in to the actualised world. However, the virtual (and the intensive) is completely real. Thus, the virtual ontological modality is real but not actualised (D&G (1994) 208–9). There is a reality of the virtual that would need to be explored in order to follow Deleuze & Guattari. This earth is the cosmic earth, because the virtual ontological modality is how the earth participates in the cosmos.

The reality of the virtual is self-posing problematics and problems in differential relations and elements. There are many other key features of the virtual such as abstract machines, multiplicities and the plane of immanence. However, coming to terms with the virtual modality rests in the virtual as the problematics, problems, and differential relations as the virtual earth of the greatest decoding and deterritorialisation of the actual earth. In order to understand this reality of the virtual and the planomenon earth, the chaos from which the virtual self-organises and emerges requires consideration.

It is from a cosmic chaos that both the intensive mechanosphere and the actualised ecumenon have self-organised and emerged, but it is all through the virtual that chaos has become consistent chaosmos, with the virtual retaining a very close relation to chaosmos. The creative cosmic chaos is not characterised by disorder or a void of nothingness, and chaos is not 'a chaotic white night or an undifferentiated black night' (D&G (1988) 70 (78)). Rather, the creative cosmic chaos is characterised by a hyper-differentiation that is in infinite variation. In this chaos of hyper-differentiation that varies at infinite speed there is a movement in which continuously every potential form takes shape but which also vanishes instantaneously: 'chaos is an infinite speed of birth and disappearance… containing all possible particles and drawing out all possible forms, which spring up only to disappear immediately, without consistency or reference, without consequence' (D&G (1994) 118). Every permutation of the forces of the cosmos churn in this chaos, and every permutation of universes churn in this chaos of multiverses.

It is from this chaos of forces that the virtual self-organises and emerges in the drawing of a plane of consistency that renders chaos consistent (D&G (1994) 156). In this consistent chaos it is the differential relations and elements of the hyper-differentiation and the play of repetitions of the infinite variation that self-organise and emerge. The virtual operates with these differential relations and elements and their variations to connect flows of these elements, relations and variations that draw forward from the flows distributions of ordinary and singular points. In the instantaneous rates of change of the differential relations there are vectors that develop the virtual singular points and bifurcation thresholds (Deleuze (1994) 208–9). The singular points are those that operate as attractors in some manner for the connected differential flows or as bifurcation thresholds for the connected differential flows. These attractors and bifurcation thresholds are the organisation of difference in itself and continuums of pure differences (Deleuze (1994) 182). These singular attractors and bifurcation thresholds are virtual and are not actualised, and provide information about the connected differential relations and elements. Thus, 'the reality of the virtual consists of differential elements and relations along with the singular points that correspond to them' (Deleuze (1994) 208).

In addition, the connecting of the differential flows may develop multiple connections, relations and elements. These connections of multiple differential flows produce an aggregate of differential flows in which some flows will affect other flows, and in which some flows will be affected by other flows. These relations of affecting and being affected in the multiple differential flows are self-organising and emergent capacities of the connected flows and are virtual capacities (it is not an issue of emergent properties). Thus, the virtual differential relations operate not only with both singular attractors and bifurcation thresholds but also emergent capacities to affect and be affected. These self-organising connections and emergent capacities add information and virtual complexity to the related differential flows, together with adding virtual dimensions of degrees of freedom to the connected differential flows.

This reality of the virtual of differential relations in variation, singularity attractors, bifurcation points and emergent capacities are developed by Deleuze & Guattari in a theory of multiplicities that will be taken up in a little while, but at this point it is instructive to return to the connected reality of the virtual of self-posing problematics and problems: 'the virtual possesses the reality of the task to be performed or a problem to be solved' (Deleuze (1994) 212). The churn of self-organisation and emergence in differential relations in continuous variation of attractors, bifurcations and emergent capacities is the virtual self-posing of problematics and problems. For Deleuze & Guattari a problematic and a problem are defined precisely by a consistent distribution of the singular and the ordinary as the conditions of that problematic and problem. A problematic and a problem are the self-organising posing of a consistent distribution of singular and ordinary points, the thresholds at which the problematic and the problem changes, together with the problematic's and problem's problem space of the emergent capacities of the consistent distribution of singular and ordinary points. Thus, problematics and problems have a distribution of attractors and bifurcation thresholds, and have multi-dimensional problem space manifolds of these distributions and thresholds. The problematic of the virtual, and the basis of which it self-organises and poses all its virtual problems, is the problematic of how to hold things together, how to organise matter-energy flows, and the problematic of creation. The earth as virtual planomenon is the ontological modality of the earth cease-lessly writing in the real of the continuously respecifying problematic of how to create. The geology of the earth and the earth's massive exploration of evolution of organic life has been the ceaseless writing in the real of the problematic of how to hold things together and to create, with the earth's archaeological record merely scraps of rough drafts of the exploration of the problematic of creation. In this, the planomenon earth participates in the cosmic problematic of how to hold the cosmos together and of cosmic creation.

In the ontology of the virtual, the operation of the self-organisation in the connecting of differential flows and the self-organising of the distribution of the singular and ordinary points is the abstract machine. The virtual abstract machine is the operation of the virtual. The abstract machine connects the virtual attractors into virtual multiplicities, renders chaos consistent and drawing a plane of consistency amongst all the virtual multiplicities. As such, the abstract machine operates with unformed matters and nonformal functions, and connects diagrams for the organisation of processes of creation of actual entities. In addition, the abstract machines sample actual states of affairs and intensive morphogenetic processes to extract events to continually respecify the virtual plane of imma-nence and multiplicities. In terms of the reality of the virtual as the self-posing of problematics and problems it is the abstract machine that is the exploration of the problematic and of the posing of new problems.

It is the abstract machine that works on the differential flows to draw out attrac-tors and to connect them into multiplicities with emergent capacities. The abstract machine produces conjunctions of the flows and emits continuums of intensity so drawing out the singularities from the differential flows. On the basis of the instantaneous rates of change of the differentials flows, the abstract machine draws from the vector field the singular attractors of the flows. These attractors may be whole dimensionality point or cycle attractors, although the creativity and self-organising emergence of new capacities of the virtual is the result of chaotic fractal attractors immanent to the chaotic churn of the virtual. The abstract machine connects convergent and divergent heterogeneous series of these attrac-tors and operates to develop the distribution of those attractors in the new series (D&G (1988) 70 (78)). The emergence of virtual attractors is then developed by the abstract machine in connecting a distribution of singularities through the self-organising of an immanent dynamic consistency amongst the singularities by virtue of the immanent connections of the singularities. The self-organising consistencies of the singularities bring forth emergent capacities that are abilities to affect and be affected and degrees of freedom of the singularity distribution.

The abstract machine selects those distributions of dynamically consistent singularities and thereby produces the emergence of virtual multiplicities. The full definition of virtual multiplicities can then be put forward. Virtual multiplicities are abstract machine-produced immanently consistent distributions of singularities drawn from differential elements and relations, thresholds of transformation for that multiplicity, and emergent capacities to affect and be affected. The tendencies of the virtual multiplicity are the singularity distribution and the capacities of the virtual multiplicity are dimensions of the manifold of this distribution. The virtual multiplicities thus have dimensions in terms of their emergent capacities. However, these dimensions are dimensionally flat in that they occupy all the dimensions without being embedded in a higher dimensionality. Virtual multiplicities are also in continuous variation by virtue of their consistency of organisation as a dynamic immanent line of flight (D&G (1988) 483 (533)).

In this manner, the abstract machine operating with the forces of chaos immanently brings forth virtual multiplicities. However, the rendering of chaos consistent requires a second operation of the abstract machine of drawing a plane of immanence. The abstract machine further makes connections between all the multiplicities and draws a plane of immanence. To render chaos consistent the abstract machine connects a multiplicity to another multiplicity, and connects multiplicities to more than one multiplicity. The virtual is, thus, not a chaotic virtual, but a virtuality that has become consistent and an entity formed on the plane of immanence that sections chaos. This connecting of the multiplicities by the abstract machine is again through the machining of a dynamic immanent consistency between the multiplicities and selected on the principle of always connecting the multiplicities in a manner that increases the connections. The abstract machine draws the plane of immanence as the continuum of all the virtual multiplicities. The plane of immanence, therefore, has as many dimensions as all the dimensions of the virtual multiplicities from which it is dynamically meshed together as consistency. The immanent plane of consistency is a flat massively multi-dimensional plane that does not have a supplementary dimension to that which transpires on it (D&G (1988) 266 (293)).

The plane of immanence is connected together though a consistency in continuous variation. This meshing together of the virtual multiplicities into the plane of immanent consistency is in continuous variation organised on a fractal line of becoming which draws the plane and connects all the multiplicities. The fractal line connects the multiplicities as a line of flight and as the outside: 'The virtual earth is the plane of immanence as the Outside' (D&G (1988) 510 (561)). On the fractal line the multiplicities change, and connect with other multiplicities. The abstract machine operates as the fractal line that meshes all the virtual multiplicities in a point of survey of infinite speed and infinite range. In this the fractal line is a line forming a plane. Thus, all the virtual multiplicities flatten on a single plane of consistencies of exteriority (D&G (1988) 9 (9)). The plane of consistency is a 'flat multiplicity [that] is a line that fills a plane without ceasing to be a line' (D&G (1988) 488 (537)).

The organising fractal line of the plane of consistency selects only the virtual organisation of multiplicities that increase the connectivity of the immanent plane of consistency and leads to the development of the organising selection process of the eternal return. In the plane of consistency all the virtual differences and events are brought together and new connections machined between the differences and events, and old connections are continually dissolved. It is the selection of only that which creates an ever-increasing number of connections amongst the virtual multiplicities (D&G (1988) 508 (559)).

Thus, the three key features of the ontology of virtual are the abstract machine, the virtual multiplicities and the plane of immanence. The abstract machine and the plane of immanence operate with singularities, multiplicities, consistencies, and the fractal line of the eternal return. The virtual has many abstract machines working the plane of immanence, and the plane of immanence has many more features than a fractal consistency of multiplicities. The virtual is continually extracting events from the actual and intensive earth, and the abstract machines work with unformed matters as well as nonformal functions, and the plane of immanence is populated by more than virtual singularities.

Thus, the abstract machines combine emissions of particles and particle signs, and the virtual organisation of unformed matters and nonformal functions. The abstract machine, however, only works with deterritorialised traits of expression and traits of content. The traits of content are matter having only degrees of intensity, speeds or slowness; the traits of expression are only tensor operations akin to musical and mathematical writing (D&G (1988) 141 (156)). The unformed matters are intensities of capabilities and materials, and nonformal functions that are tensors, becomings, transformations, affects and traits of expression. With the abstract machine as pure matter-tensor, this is a writing at the level of the virtual that is a material writing of the real, 'it is no longer even possible to tell whether it [real writing] is a particle or a sign' (D&G (1988) 141 (156)). The abstract machine establishes connections and operates as a diagram for an assemblage made up of forms and substances, and expression and content.

Thus, the plane of immanence is the plane of the unformed and unorganised, the nonstratified and destratifed, subatomic and submolecular particles, pure intensities and free singularities (D&G (1988) 43 (49)). On the plane of immanence 'a semiotic fragment rubs shoulders with a chemical interaction, an electron crashes into a language, a black hole captures a genetic message, a crystallisation produces a passion, the wasp and the orchid cross a letter... all that consists is Real' (D&G (1988) 69 (77)).

As the abstract machines connect with matter-energy flows they pilot processes of self-organisation and emergence. Abstract machines are virtual multiplicity diagrams for intensive processes of organisation and emergence and for the creation of actualised organisation and entities. Abstract machines are 'engineering diagrams defining the structure generating processes that give rise to more or less permanent forms but are not unique to those forms' (D&G (1988) 40 (44)). To the real problems of creation undertaken by the earth, abstract machines are the virtual diagrams for the intensive processes of bringing an actual entity into existence.

Abstract machines further operate in the virtual to extract events and singularities from intensive far-from-equilibrium processes and actualised states of affairs. These are abstract machinic operations of sectioning and sampling the intensive and actual, and they operate to realign and inform the operation of the virtual plane of consistency and virtual multiplicities and inject events into the virtual to inform its continuous variation and respecification. The abstract machines operate a counter-actualisation, extract virtual events from intensive processes and the actual strata of expression and content, form and substances, in order to give them consistency. The extraction operation recovers a full multiplicity from a spatio-temporal actualisation, and extracts information in complex topological shapes. The abstract machine only takes from the actual causal event the dimensionality of the state space, and its topological invariants and distribution of singularities (D&G (1988) 70 (78)).

It is virtual abstract machines that explore and answer the virtual problematic of how to create something, how to organise something, and of what holds something together. The cosmos is the self-organisation and emergence in response to the virtual problematic of creation and the exploration of the virtual problem field.

Together with all these features of the abstract machine and the virtual, all molecular and supermolecular abstract machines are defined by their lines of flight. The abstract machine is the machining of an immanent consistency in continuous variations, and thus the consistency of the abstract machine is in its line of flight of decoding and deterritorialising. The consistency of plane of immanence abstract machines is in their transformations and novel connections with other lines of flight. The abstract machine of the plane of immanence is also defined by its line of flight. The virtual abstract machine is the fractal line of flight that connects all the multiplicities and which draws the plane of immanence itself as a fractal dimensional plane in continuous variation. This abstract machine of the fractal plane of immanence, which extracts events from the intensive and the actual to respecify the virtual problematic, selects only those new arrangements of events that create new virtual multiplicities that increase the connectivity of the plane of immanence. The intensive and particularly the actual are redundancy in relation to the problematic of organisation and creation. What does return from the virtual to the intensive and actual in the selections of the virtual abstract machine of the plane of immanence is experimentation on the problematic, the increase in connectivity of the plane of immanence, and the creation of the new in variation. The virtual is, thus, the ontological modality in which everything is in terms of becomings.

The planomenon enters matter with the emergence of virtual forces, virtual interactions, virtual time, virtual space, virtual matters and virtual particles.

Virtual time is of a simultaneity and co-existence where there are nothing but becomings and the time of the event: 'ordinal continuum unfolding into past and future, a time where nothing ever occurs but where everything is endlessly becoming in both unlimited directions at once, always "already happened" (in the past direction) and "always about to happen" (in the future direction)' (Delanda (2002) 107).

Virtual space emerges as a patchwork (D&G (1988) 474 (523)) of vicinities: 'vicinity is therefore like a shred of Euclidean space, but the linkage between one vicinity and the next is not defined and can be effected in an infinite number of ways'. Riemann space at its most general thus 'presents itself as an amorphous collection of pieces that are juxtaposed but not attached to each other' (D&G (1988) 485 (535)). It is a space of points, curvatures, and surfaces, all operating with purely local information. Virtual space emerges as the self-organisation of a set of points into a neighbourhood through relations of proximity. The relations of proximity are instantaneous rates of change in curvatures and surfaces in the differential relations.

In this virtual space and time the virtual abstract machines operate with unformed matters and nonformal functions to form virtual forces, matters and particles. The virtual particles operate at the level of the virtual prior to intensive processes and actual states of affairs, but which organise the emergence of these processes and affairs. Cosmic virtual space-time moves with dark forces, dark matters and supersymmetry subatomic particles.

The virtual earth as planomenon moves on a cosmic plane of immanence. The participation of the earth in the cosmic is the exploring of problematics and problems through immanent self-organising abstract machines that create and operate virtual multiplicities to draw together and mesh all the multiplicities into an immanent plane of consistency. The earth is, thus, the planomenon, and the earth as planomenon is the participation of the earth in the cosmos that is itself the planomenon. The earth moves upon the disc plane of the Milky Way in the disc plane of the cosmos. It is a cosmos that is a fractal line drawing a fractal plane in continuous experimentation and an expansion that is the eternal return of the novel against the backdrop of the redundancy of the actual.

The judgements of God: the expressionism of the molar fold and the plane of organisation earth

Thus, the earth is the eternal return of the cosmic multiplicities, and of a continuous and continuously folding and unfolding of consistencies. There is the abstract machine of the fractal line that draws the plane of immanence and there are the abstract machines of immanent consistencies that make up and operate on the plane of immanence. There is, however, against this plane of immanence an event of the arrival of God. The arrival of God is the arrival of the abstract machine of the expressionism of the molar fold, and the arrival of the molar abstract machine. The molar fold is a topological fold of continuous fractal five and above dimensional multiplicities with fractal attractors into discontinuous metric four-dimensional multiplicity with whole dimensionality attractors. It is the imposition of a four-dimensional expression upon fractal five-plus dimensionality multiplicities with fractal attractors. Thus, the operation of the molar fold is necessarily a five-dimensional topological fold. The five-dimensional topological fold constitutes and occupies a transcendent dimensionality to the metric four-dimensional discontinuous multiplicity. In this expressionism of the molar fold the organisational modality of the virtual and intensive is necessarily closed off in a hylomorphism of the expressionism of the molar fold and the occlusion of the genetic topological operations. Thus, the fifth dimensionality of the topological fold is constituted as empty, withdrawn, receding transcendent dimension that organises everything from above but which is nothing in itself, as the virtual and intensive topological operation is expelled from the expressionism of the molar. In the molar fold the virtual and intensive outside becomes the inside of the molar folding an operation of enclosure and transformation.

The transcendent expressionism of the molar fold is to code something. Coding is to impose constraints of whole dimensionality on a continuous multiplicity on fractal attractors, and to establish a fold discontinuity in the multiplicity closing it in on itself. Coding then progressively organises the metric entity on the basis of transcendence, the excluded middle, closure to the outside, and differentiated identity over time. The operation of the molar fold is to submit something to the expressionist coding of the molar fold. This folding necessarily constitutes something as coded and closed, whilst also constituting the outside as the uncoded of chaos and undifferentiation. The virtual and intensive is already occluded in molar fold hylomorphism, but is now further negatively coded as undifferentiated chaos. The virtual outside becomes the molar inside. The molar fold in itself absorbs the virtual problematic of organisation, the plane of immanence, and the virtual multiplicities. The continuous multiplicities are subjugated, the plane of immanence shut off, and the continuous exploration of the ever-respecifying problematic of the organisation of dynamic multiplicities in the virtual and the eternal return blocked.

The molar fold, having fallen back on the virtual multiplicities and plane of immanence, now bears down on creation. God has emerged from the plane of immanence and the organisation and development of creation is now unifying, hierarchical and binary. All the intensive assemblages of creation in the morphogenetic field are converted to molar assemblages, '... producing upon the body of the earth molecules large and small and organising them into molar aggregates ... giving form to matters, of imprisoning intensities or locking singularities into systems of resonance and redundancy' (D&G (1988) 40 (45)).

The development of expressionism is then the progressive development of the molar fold operation answer to the question of what it is that holds things together: 'If we ask the general question "What holds things together?", the clearest, easiest answer seems to be provided by a formalising, linear, hierarchised, centralised arborescent model' (D&G (1988) 327 (361)).

The progressive development of the molar fold abstract machine of expression is the answer to the question of organisation, and the answer to the closed down molar problematic and molar social field. The molar abstract machines build the actual earth through operations of 'coding and overcoding, phenomena of centring, unification, totalisation, integration, hierarchisation, and finalisation' (D&G (1988) 41 (46)). These coding and overcodings are the organisation of matter through the submission of all matter to transcendent unities, essences and laws. The abstract machine of molar organisation is to unify and organise hierarchically from the folded up dimension of transcendence on the binary of whole dimensionality attractors. This is to impose a model of expression on subjugated passive matter in which the expression is the unification of that matter into a closed content organised hierarchically on binaries and the excluded middle. This operation is the molar fold abstract machine drawing a plane of organisation over all of creation: 'The strata "take" on the plane of consistency itself, forming areas of thickenings, coagulations, and belts organised and developing along the axes of another plane (substance-form, content-expression)' (D&G (1988) 513 (565)).

The organisation of the earth as ecumenon is the expressionism of the judgements of God in coding that lays down stratification and establishes territories. This molar organisation of creation is the double articulation of a molecular coding and a molar overcoding in a first molecular articulation of matter-energy in forms and substances, and a second molar enveloping articulation of formed-substances in expression and content. The first articulation is the selection and ordering of molecular elements. There is a selection of an homogenous material from the molecular flows in the milieus to assemble a substance of content (D&G (1988) 41 (45)). There is then imposed a statistical ordering of connections and successions on this substance of content and producing a form of content (D&G (1988) 40–1 (45–6)). A second articulation is the operation of the molar abstract machine organisation. This is the imposition of a transcendent form of expression and coding that unifies, centralises and hierarchically organises. This second operation is the molar organisation and molar emergence of a new unifying holding organisational form with emergent properties of molar organisation. This is to produce the imposition of expression on content and the production of a substance of expression as the new organisational form of content. These articulations between form and substance and between expression and content all operate in reciprocal presupposition. The reciprocal presupposition of the articulations of form and substance, and expression over content, are the operations that are the coding and overcoding of molar organisation and the operations that build up the arborescent linear and binary organisation of the plane of organisation and of creation.

The molar God, having shut down the forces of the cosmos and the virtual, thus emerges as the double articulation of repeated splicing and cutting of the ecumenical tree of life: 'To express is always to sing the glory of God' (D&G (1988) 43 (49)). The expressionism is about building up the actual world in hierarchical and increasingly internally complicated nested sets of molar folds of expression. The creation of the plane of organisation operates with these molar abstract machines of expressionism that are 'structure generating processes that give rise to more or less permanent forms but are not unique to those forms' (D&G (1988) 71 (79)). Expressionism operates by organising and building systems, structures and entities through operations of folding in a totalised unity and organising this on the basis of the hierarchical binary tree. Thus, the molar expressionism builds the 'ideally continuous belt or ring of the stratum – the Ecumenon defined by the identity of molecular materials, substantial elements, and formal relations' (D&G (1988) 52 (58)).

The molar fold thereby develops in molar assemblages. The molar abstract machines generate the structure for the molar assemblages that then lay down the developed coding, emergent territories and strata. Molar assemblages operate in the modality of the actual, operating near-to-equilibrium and with linear causation. There is the unification of the assemblage, with a distinct inside-outside boundary, and an organisational identity. Molar assemblages are closed, hierarchical, whole dimension attractors, linear, homeostatic, homogenous elements, relations of interiority, considerable internal complexity, and structural coupling with the environment. The molar assemblage develops along the organising lines of a regime of expression and a regime of content. The articulation of expression develops as coding of the strata and the overcoding stratification. The side of content in the assemblage develops by establishing a territory as strata as an emergent property of molar overcoding. It is by these two operations that the molar assemblages lay down the extensive and metric existence of the earth as ecumenon.

The molar abstract machine, the plane of organisation, and the molar assemblages operate in all aspects of the earth and life. There are molar operations and the laying down of strata that are energetic, physico-chemical, geological, organic, territorial and social organisation. With a given stratum there is a unity of molar composition in the stratum's substantial elements, formal relations, formed substances and homogenised components (D&G (1988) 52 (59)). Before the emergence of the strata of social organisation, the two principal strata of the earth are the geological strata and the organic strata. The geological stratum operates with resonance of expression operating on scales of magnitude. Rock is stratified by the selection of homogenous material from the molecular flows into the formed matters of sedimentary layers. Then there is the second articulation of cementing these sedimentary layers into functional structures of rock. There is a further double articulation of rock through plate tectonic movements to produce mountains and other features through a folding operation.

In organic strata expression is the transduction of the linearity of the genetic code. There are many different scales of stratification, and many complex operations; however, the core of organic stratification is a double articulation of a double articulation of genetic coding. In one operation amino acids are selected and formed matters of proteins. There is then a second articulation in the organisation of these proteins into nucleotide base sequences and the functional structure of genes. The second operation takes the organs of molecular life and flows and selects a regulated homogenisation of these organs and flows. There is then a second articulation of homeostatically organising these regulated flows into the emergence of unity of composition of the organism.

When viewed on the broad scale of continents, the rock strata are constantly churning, splitting up and crashing together. When viewed on the broad scale of evolution, the biological strata are constantly producing variations within genetic development of the epistrata and parastrata. Beneath the strata of essence is the parastrata of populations: coded and decoded populations. Beneath the strata of development is the epistrata of differential relations with the milieu: deterritori- alised and reterritorialised populations. Parastrata are not the strata of species but where variations of forms develop through populations as virtual multiplicities, and epistrata are not the degrees of perfection of essence but where degrees of development vary, understood as differential rates in morphogenesis (D&G (1988) 53 (60)). However, the actual earth, though necessarily centred on the molar abstract machine and the unity of composition of the strata, is subject to a very considerable range of variations and available alternative states of the actual. The ecumenon is the ideally continuous ring of the stratum, but it exists only as shattered and fragmented in the epistrata and parastrata. Below the strata there are intensive consistency molecular assemblages and the virtual abstract machine of creation. These together are the forces of decoding and deterritorialisation. There is an entire rumbling nonorganic life and plane of consistency. The earth as ecumenon breaks up into mechanosphere, and to the eternal return of the planomenon.

By way of conclusion on the ecumenon, Professor Challenger, with a view to the later consideration of the strata of social organisation, remarked that with the organisation of the ecumenon in the molar fold of coding and overcoding through the abstract machine of imposing a form on matter, a form on substance, and expression over content, the actualised earth falls ready made for the idea that it is law that assures organisational coherence (D&G (1988) 408 (450)). When the social strata are considered, the organisation of the ecumenon will assume a central role in how law assures organisational coherence. Desiring production and social organisation would fall back in the judgement of God.

Intensive molecular assemblages and the morphogenetic field earth

Between the planes, between the earth as planomenon and the earth as ecumenon, there is the earth as mechanosphere. This is the intensive earth of the morphoge- netic field of intensive problems and their playing out in intensive machinic assemblages. Between the planes the intensive morphogenetic field faces the plane of immanence and the molecular and supermolecular abstract machines, and on the other side it faces the plane of organisation and the molar abstract machines.

This position between the planes results in there being two tendencies with assemblages, which gives the impression of there being two types of assem- blages. There are, of course, the molar assemblages that effect molar abstract machines, and are coded and overcoded in the double articulation of form over substance and expression over content. These assemblages are closed, linear, and internally organised hierarchical tree overcoding. However, there is another tendency and type of assemblage, very different from molar assemblages. These are intensive machinic assemblages of matter and energy that are not organised by the expression of the molar fold and which are not fully actualised. There are assemblages of matter-energy that organise not through unification and coding, but through dynamic consistencies that remain intensive but are nonetheless sophisticated and very capable organisation with high capacities for storing, processing and transmitting organisation and creating emergent potentials. These assemblages have a relation not to molar abstract machines, but to molecular and supermolecular abstract machines that are organisation that is immanent to matter-energy. These abstract machines are dynamic virtual consistencies in continuous variation on fractal attractors and potentially very high dimensionality degrees of freedom and many dynamic thresholds.

These assemblages have a crucial genetic role in creation and they operate in an ontological modality of their own other than that of the virtual multiplicities and the plane of immanence and the actualised entities and the molar fold plane of organisation. The molecular and supermolecular assemblages operate in an intensive morphogenetic field of intensive problems and forces where their organisation is immanent intensive consistencies in continuous variation with emergent capacities. Intensive machinic assemblages operate in an intensive field that on one side connects to the actualised plane of organisation and the strata, but on another side connects to the virtual plane of immanence. The intensive machinic assemblages are the intensive earth field between the two planes of immanence and of transcendence. The organising molar fold of expression on matter and the associated hylomorphism separate the plane of organisation from its connection to the intensive morphogenetic field. However, in facing the plane of organisation the intensive machinic assemblages break the ecumenon earth up into epistrata and the parastrata and make the ecumenon holey.

It is thus from the virtual and the connection with the plane of immanence that the intensive morphogenetic field draws its resources, but also the field from which the virtual plane of immanence sections new events. It is this intensive morphogenetic problem field drawing on the plane of immanence creating the actual strata and facing the plane of organisation where intensive machinic assemblages develop, in which virtual abstract machines enter into matter in intensive processes. In the intensive morphogenetic field the discovery is of a nonorganic life to matter under conditions of intensity whereby matter possesses immanent forces of self-organisation and emergence as the virtual enters into matter. With the morphogenetic field, as opposed to the plane of organisation, it is precisely not an operation of imposing a set form on matter and imposing a unifying expression over content, but of rather connecting materiality to imma- nent forces of intensive organisation and machining. When matter is taken up in an intensive assemblage connecting it to the forces of the virtual and machining, and then elaborates its own intensive processes of self-organisation and emergence. With the molecular and supermolecular assemblages of the intensive morphogenetic field: '...what one addresses is less a matter submitted to laws than a materiality possessing a nomos' (D&G (1988) 408 (451)).

The intensive morphogenetic field is a 'following where it leads by connecting operations to a materiality instead of imposing a form upon a matter' (D&G (1988) 408 (451)). In the morphogenetic field 'it is no longer a question of imposing form upon matter but of elaborating an increasingly rich and consistent material, the better to tap increasingly intense forces' (D&G (1988) 329 (363)).

This nonorganic life that is discovered to operate as the organisational forces of the virtual enter matter in intensive assemblages is demonstrated in metal and the processes metallurgy has discovered and operates in metal. It is metal that best demonstrates the intensive nonorganic life of matter (D&G (1988) 411 (454)). Metals are intensive matter flows that are laden with singularities. Metal attests to the potentials of intensive materiality over prepared matter, and of the potentials of intensive transformations over the form that is incarnated. Metals have immanent points and thresholds of transformations when it is pushed into the intensive morphogenetic field by heating. Metal operates in the gap between matter and form, in which 'operations are astride the thresholds, so that an energetic materiality overspills the prepared matter, and a qualitative deformation or transformation overspills the form' (D&G (1988) 410 (453)). Through processes such as tempering there is self-organisation in the metal as it repeatedly crosses thresholds and discovers attractors, with emergent capabilities of significantly increased hardness and strength. Metal introduces the nonorganic life of matter of the intensive assemblages and the intensive morphogenetic field because what 'metal and metallurgy bring to light is a life proper to matter, a vital state of matter as such, a material vitalism that doubtless exists everywhere but is ordinarily hidden or covered, rendered unrecognisable, dissociated by the hylomorphic model' (D&G (1988) 411 (454)). The abstract machine is metal and organises the transversal consistencies (D&G (1988) 499 (550)):

> If everything is alive, it is not because everything is organic or organised but, on the contrary, because the organism is a diversion of life. In short, the life in question is inorganic, germinal, intensive, a powerful life without organs, a Body that is all the more alive for having no organs, everything that passes between organisms ("once the natural barriers of organic movement have been overthrown, there are no more limits").
>
> (D&G (1988) 499 (550))

The intensive machinic assemblages, instead of organising through unification and imposing a form of expression on content, organise matter-energy in open immanent consistencies of heterogeneous materials in continuous variation without these heterogeneous materials ceasing to remain open and heterogeneous. From this self-organisation what emerges are not a unified property as with molar assemblages but rather emergent potentials and capabilities of dynamic organisation. The intensive assemblages establish a consistent dynamic organisation by forging aggregates of heterogeneous materials in inclusive disjunctive syntheses drawing upon singularity attractors of the virtual that the assemblages senses and operates with in the far-from-equilibrium intensive conditions. It is in intensive assemblages that the problem field of the earth is explored, and that nonorganic life forces are tapped and that the machinic phylum is taken up in self-organisation and emergence. These intensive consistency aggregates are matters that are only traits of expression and traits of content. These traits of expression and content are intensities, affects, events and sensations. There is a field of speeds and slownesses, ways of affecting and being affected, singularities and becomings. These intensive traits have only traces of codings and broken lines of territorialisation, remaining intensively decoded and deterritorialised.

Indeed, not only are intensive machinic assemblages made up of consistencies of decoded and deterritorialised intensive traits, the dynamic consistency of the aggregate of heterogeneous materials is in precisely the most decoded and deterritorialised aspect of the intensive assemblage, holding the assemblage together on a line of continuous variation. The immanent self-organisation and emergence in intensely assembled consistencies occurs by virtue of the ontological modality of the virtual abstract machines and plane of immanence presenting matter in intensive conditions with the machinic phylum.

The machinic phylum is the ideally continuous phylum of matter-movement of the plane of consistency and all the abstract machines as they are available and enter into matter in intensive conditions. The machinic phylum includes all the abstract machines of consistencies and the singularities of the virtual multiplicities, and makes available to matter in intensive conditions dynamic consistency resources for self-organisation and emergence of new capacities and potentials, including the fractal abstract machine that draws the plane of consistencies itself. The machinic phylum is 'an entire energetic materiality in movement, carrying singularities or haecceities that are already like implicit forms that are topological, rather than geometrical, and that combine with processes of deformation' (D&G (1988) 408 (450)). The machinic phylum is 'metallurgical, or at least has a metallic head, as its itinerant probe-head or guidance device' (D&G (1988) 411 (454)). The machinic phylum consists of traits of expression, operations that converge on those traits of expression, and array of singularities that are tapped by the operations (D&G (1988) 406 (448)). The machinic phylum is a vectorial field, which is scattered with singularities, accidents, and complex intensive and dynamic problems to be explored and cases of solutions devised and triggered (D&G (1988) 372 (410)). It is the machinic phylum in variation that creates the intensive assemblages, and assemblages invent the various phyla (D&G (1988) 407 (449)).

The morphogenetic field between the two planes is a field of forces and materials, with vectors of becomings. The intensive field consists of intensities, waves, vibrations, axes and vectors, migrations, gradients and thresholds, and energetic transformations (D&G (1988) 153 (169)). In addition to these intensive forces and materials, the morphogenetic field is made up of differential relations of speeds and slownesses of flow, intensities, affects, bifurcation points, events and distribution of singularities.

The intensive morphogenetic field is where the intensive machinic assemblages self-organise and emerge. The assemblages self-organise and emerge precisely in relation to matter confronting the battle of intensive forces and events in the morphogenetic field. The morphogenetic field is therefore the intensive problem field made up of problems of the battle of forces, problems of competing and diverging attractors, problems of intensities, problems of affects and being affected, and problems of differential relations and thresholds.

These intensive problems are the corollary of virtual problematics. The virtual poses the problematics of organisation and creation, and the abstract machines emerge in relation to virtual problems and events, and operate only with the dimensions of a problem and the distribution of singularities. However, in the morphogenetic problem field, the problem is precisely how these problem dimensions and distribution of singularities play out in material forces of intensive assemblaging. Intensive problems are problems of forces, attractors, intensities, affects, sensations, traits of expression, traits of content, traits of territory, event-affect consistencies, lines of becomings and incorporeal transformations.

The intensive assemblages of consistencies of matter operate in an intensive morphogenetic field and an intensive problem field, and they operate with intensive morphogenetic problems. In the morphogenetic field, matter is not only intensive in sensations and affects but it is also problematical and taken up in problems. Intensive assemblages of consistency in continuous variation take up a position in morphogenetic problem field space, and take up selected consistencies from the machinic phylum. The intensive morphogenetic assemblages occupy the morphogenetic field to the degree of its dimensions and its continuous variation. Thus, intensive assemblages emerge immanently in relation to intensive problems and assemble a consistency in continuous variation and operate in a morphogenetic field and problem space with a number of dimensions and a distribution of singularities.

The problem-solving abilities of intensive assemblages are very different from the problem-resolving operations of the molar abstract machines and assemblages. The intensive conditions high energy-matter flow, far-from-equilibrium, at a phase transition allows the tapping of the virtual forces of abstract machines and multiplicities in order to steer intensive consistencies of affect-events as draft answers to the problem.

There are many intensive assemblages. There are intensive assemblages that effectuate an abstract machine in reciprocal relay to create a finally actualised system or entity. There are intensive assemblages that explore processes of self-organisation and emergence and explore the problem field, moving on attractors and creating new attractors and consistencies. For both intensive assemblages, ideas from maths and physics enable an understanding of these non-representational operations. Intensive assemblages are not representational, but instead really are the unfolding or exploring of a manifold of dimensions of degrees of freedom and distribution of singularities. These processes of unfolding and exploring are the differential relations and differential geometry of the assemblage's relation between various degrees of freedom. The degrees of freedom are related together through differential calculus with the assemblage as a single point in phase space by taking an instantaneous reading of all its degrees of freedom. Phase space models processes as they intensively individuate an actualised entity or as they continuously vary and explore their problem space. Intensive assemblages, either by virtue of their abstract machine or simply by the intensive problems they explore, have a number of dimensions to their problem field and a distribution of singularities. The dimensions of the problem field are the number of ways in which the intensive assemblage can change, and so the process can be modelled to a single point in the problem field manifold varying in time as the process unfolds or explores. In phase space actualised assemblages are integrated trajectories. In intensive assemblages the assemblage can be thought of as a point being a co-ordinate in the manifold from moment to moment in its progressive actualisation or continuous variation. In intensive assemblages of continuous variation the line is the vectors that repeatedly draw out all the distributions of singularities in the manifold. The line will move through the problem space manifold constrained or attracted by the distribution of singularities in the problem field. Although every point in a problem manifold could be traversed by the phase space line, the existence of attractors will squeeze the line into particular regions of the problem space. The movement of the line in phase space gives the intensive assemblage its phase space portrait. The phase space portrait maps the intensive assemblage's speeds and slownesses, its attractors, bifurcation thresholds, its ability to affect and be affected.

The intensive morphogenetic field is where the progressive specification of virtual multiplicities as the virtual problematic is explored as an intensive problem in relation to material processes of creation. An intensive assemblage may have a nested set of attractors that progressively differentiate and specify the process of creating an actual product, and the process may stay in the morphogenetic field for quite some time. These intensive assemblages do effectively resolve problems by producing extensive solutions, but they leave the problem open and do not close it. Always, though, the progressive differentiation of an intensive assemblage is a unique individuation of an abstract machine, with intensive processes of creation that are non-linear, time irreversible, with sensitivity to initial conditions, varying effects on attractors, varying events at thresholds, whereby the final product is a unique individuation of a population and rates of change.

Intensive assemblages may also explore problem space where they are organised as dynamic consistencies in continuous variation (at least as long as they survive). Rather than as a process that operates between the abstract machine and actual entities, the intensive assemblages in continuous variation remain intensive and in the problem field. The intensive assemblage can sense new attractors in its problem space, can machine new consistencies between new attractors, moving between topologically invariant dynamic organisations, and can move in or out of different dimensional problem spaces. Just as abstract machines can explore the virtual problem space and machine new consistencies, intensive assemblages can also explore intensive problem space, undertake transformations, and create the new in intensive materials. This intensive assemblage of continuous variation and intensive creation are, thus, very close to the fractal abstract machine of the eternal return.

All the intensive assemblages mesh together to become the rhizomatic evolution of life that creates and undercuts the whole molar evolution of the ecumenon. Evolution in the intensive morphogenetic field is itself a rhizome, organised without restrictions to species and degrees of perfection but rather in populations of forms, combinations and relays between heterogeneities, and differential relations. Evolution is an intensive rhizome of animals, viruses and humans (D&G (1988) 10 (11)). The rhizome is intensive, and operates intensively with population multiplicities and differential rates of speeds and slownesses: 'Darwinism's two fundamental contributions move in the direction of a science of multiplicities: the substitution of populations for types, and the substitution of rates or differential relations for degrees' (D&G (1988) 48 (54)).

Thus, with intensive assemblages, the abstract machine is the number of dimensions of the manifold and a distribution of singularities, and the intensive assemblage in continuous variation is the movement of that assemblage through the dimensionality of the problem field and around the distribution of singularities. The intensive assemblage cuts up and selects from the machinic phylum, though the machinic phylum is transversal to all the assemblages. Thus, the intensive assemblages effect and individuate an abstract machine, entering into matter, in a reciprocal presupposition of the intensive and the virtual, selecting a phyla machine. The intensive assemblages operate event-affect intensive consistencies and with dynamic thresholds of bifurcations in the problem space dimensionality of the assemblage and its distribution of singularities. In these intensive processes of the assemblages, the assemblages operate to extract intensive events from states of affairs and making them available to the virtual for the sampling of new virtual events, singularities and multiplicities. The intensive assemblages thus operate towards the ever respecification of the virtual. Intensive assemblages occupy a morphogenetic problem field in which intensive assemblages tap the machinic phylum exploring the problem field on lines of becoming, decoded, deterritorialisation, to find new attractors, and to potentially shift to topologically invariant virtual multiplicity distributions and to transformed dimensional problem spaces. In this way intensive assemblages can become probe head intensive assemblages effectuating the fractal abstract machine of becoming, continuous experimentation and creation.

Thus, the earth is, as well as the planomenon and the ecumenon, the mechanosphere and the intensive rhizome of evolution. The earth is the exploration of an intensive problem space of life, where the earth is the following of intensive flows in matter-movement, prospecting for new ways of organising things and creating things, detecting the genesis of events, tapping the resources of the virtual and the machinic phylum, triggering intensive and virtual incorporeal transformations and becomings, and establishing ever newer intensities and consistencies of event-affects.

Ecology of the eternal return: the infinite superfold

The relationship between the plane of immanence, plane of organisation and the intensive morphogenetic field is the relation between the virtual, the intensive and the actual, and the two-way relay from the virtual to the actual, and from the actual to the virtual through the intensive. In this, it is difference and the new that is selected and which returns. What is selected and returns is the infinite superfold, the cosmic machinic opera, and the ecology of the eternal return.

In this, the abstract machine exists in two states.

There is the abstract machine enveloped within the stratum (D&G (1988) 56 (62)). The abstract machine molar folds and is stratified, captured by the strata and the plane of organisation it imposes. The abstract machine is the ecumenon of unifying and totalising abstract machines. This abstract machine lays down the strata of the actualised world in codes and territory.

There is the abstract machine that develops on the plane of consistency and that fractal abstract machine that draws the plane of immanence and operates the superfold of the infinite speeds of coming and going of the virtual. The abstract machine operates the earth as planomenon and enters into matter in the intensive assemblages and machinic phylum.

However, there is no equivalence between the two states of the abstract machine. The molar fold establishes an earth as ecumenon and tree of life, coded, territorialised and stratified. The molar fold abstract machine is, of course, inseparable from life on earth. But, life on earth is in many respects redundancy. The stratified earth is 'girded, encompassed, overcoded, conjugated as object of a mortuary and suicidal organisation surrounding it on all sides' (D&G (1988) 510 (562)). In the actual world the strata reproduce and pile up. It is the strata that rigidify on the plane of consistency: 'system of strata that rigidify and are organised on the plane of consistency, and that the plane of consistency is at work and is constructed in the strata, in both cases piece by piece, blow by blow, operation by operation' (D&G (1988) 337 (372)). Yet, the plane of consistency is always working the strata with processes of deterritorialisation (D&G (1988) 144–5 (159–60)), and the strata are continuously broken up by the forces of the virtual and intensive into the epistrata and parastrata. The epistrata and parastrata are continually 'moving, sliding, shifting and changing on the Ecumenon, some are swept away by lines of flight and movements of deterritorialisation, others by processes of decoding or drift' (D&G (1988) 55 (62)).

This is because what is primary is the earth as absolute deterritorialisation, the plane of consistency, and an absolute line of flight (D&G (1988) 56 (63)). This is the ecology of the eternal return. The earth as absolute deterritorialisation is the plane of immanence and the fractal abstract machine. The plane of consistency is everywhere, always primary and always an immanent cosmic line of flight (D&G (1988) 70 (78)):

> Yet we have seen that the earth constantly carries out a movement of deterritorialisation on the spot, by which it goes beyond any territory; it is deterritorialising and deterritorialised.
>
> (D&G (1994) 85)

> In fact, what is primary is an absolute deterritorialisation an absolute line of flight, however complex or multiple – that of the plane of consistency or body without organs [or desiring production] (the Earth, the absolutely deterritorialised).
>
> (D&G (1988) 56 (63))

This exploration of the problematic of creation and the problem field of creation is properly cosmic. It is then an earth 'consolidated, connected with the Cosmos, brought into the Cosmos following lines of creation that cut across it as so many becomings' (D&G (1988) 510 (562)). The earth is connected to the cosmos and belongs to the cosmos: 'These are no longer territorialised forces of the earth; they are the liberated or regained forces of a deterritorialised Cosmos' (D&G (1988) 326 (359)). It is the abstract machine as plane of consistency and absolute deterritorialisation that enters into matter-movement and produces the new. It is the virtual and intensive abstract machine that creates the new and selects on the basis of increasing the connectivity of the plane of consistency and the increasing of intensity of the morphogenetic problem field and the organisation of the earth on a fractal line of becoming, connecting the earth and the cosmos. Such is the cosmic ecology of the eternal return.

The lecture was over. Professor Challenger had left some time ago. The lecture theatre had long since been cleared. All that remained were the odd wide-eyed loners scattered around the theatre, and a back row of people with big hair, smoking cigarettes, and chatting amongst themselves.

Chapter 2

To Engender Thinking Within Thought

(Dr Nome Has the Brain Problem)

> The conditions of true critique and a true creation are the same: the destruction of an image of thought which presupposes itself and the genesis of the act of thinking in thought itself.
>
> Deleuze ((1994) 139)

> Many people have a tree growing in their heads, but the brain is much more a grass than a tree.
>
> (D&G (1988) 15 (17))

Introduction

It was the second lecture from the conceptual personae of the Transfaculty of Deleuze & Guattari Studies, and it was billed as being a lecture on the brain and thinking. The lecturer today was Dr Brian Nome, an obscure noologist. Noology, he explained, is the study of the brain, thinking and images of thought.

The starting point for noology is that it is the brain that thinks, and that the understanding of all thought must always be related to the operation and organisation of the brain: 'It is the brain that thinks and not man – the latter being only a cerebral crystallisation' (D&G (1994) 210). The brain is understood to operate in three registers, and to be organised in a number of different images of thought. There is the register of the actualised brain as the cerebral nervous system, but there are also registers of a virtual brain operating with the forces of the virtual and of an intensive brain operating with intensive processes. Like Professor Challenger's earths, there are a virtual brain, an intensive brain and an actual brain: Planobrain, Mechanobrain, Ecubrain. Thinking ranges across these three brains, with a prevalent operation of the virtual brain taking thinking down one line of organisation, a prevalent operation of the actual brain taking thinking another line of organisation, and the prevalence of the operation intensive brain infusing thinking with organisational intensive consistencies and lines of becomings.

The organisation of the brain is an image of thought. Noology is the study of the brain in all its registers of operation and also all of the brain's images of thought. Images of thought are what happens on the brain to organise thinking. An image of thought is a virtual multiplicity, and the image is a high dimensional manifold with a distribution of singularities and thresholds.

The task of noology is to think all images of thought and all intensive consistencies of thought. Noology does this by drawing a plane of immanence for all thinking. Once the plane of immanence has been drawn for all thinking, noology can think the three registers of the brain and think all the images of thought including its own. Precisely how noology does this is the central theme of this lecture.

Noology, in particular, focuses upon two images of thought. It focuses upon an image of thought that presupposes itself and which thinks with the plane of transcendence, and upon an image of thought that engenders thinking in thought and which thinks with the plane of immanence. The organisation of the plane of transcendence corresponds to the actual register of the brain, and the organisation of the plane of immanence corresponds to the virtual register of the brain. These two different registers of the brain and the different modes of organisation of the plane of transcendence and the plane of immanence in thinking largely determine the concerns of noology. In addition to these two different registers of the brain and modes of organisation in thinking, noology explores the intensive vagabond thinking that takes place between these two images of thought and between these two planes. Thus, noology's task to think all thought draws a plane of immanence for thinking and focuses upon three images of thought as three registers of the brain and modes of organisation of thinking that map out the key registers and organisation of all thought. In doing so, noology characterises the immanent image of thought as philosophy, the transcendent image of thought as legislation, and the vagabond image of thought as the thinking of the case.

Noology's central concern is the brain, thinking and images of thought. However, noology necessarily opens up into the thinking of social machines and social assemblages. It was an issue that would be taken up in the workshop that follows this lecture, but the problem is that the earth, the brain and social organisation, all are taken up and inter-related in reciprocal relay of forces and becomings. Noology discovers that 'thinking takes place between territory and earth' (D&G (1994) 85), and the noology of images of thought develops into a noology of social machines and social assemblages.

In thinking all of thought noology is not equivocal when it comes to images of thought. Noology is the study of the brain and images of thought on the basis of the superiority and practice of the immanent image of thinking and the plane of immanence. The superiority of the immanent image of thinking in noology is because it is only immanent thinking that thinks the image of thought that thinking immanently gives of itself in self-organisation and emergence and the engendering of thinking within thought.

In order to think this immanent image of thought, noology first turns to the emergence of thinking in the brain. Noology must then turn to the elaboration of the immanent image of thinking and of its own practice in schizo immanent thinking, before returning again to noology and its tasks. With this in place, consideration can then turn to the noological theorisation of transcendent image of thought and the vagabond practice of thought.

The brain problem: noogenesis

The brain problem is how thinking presents itself on its own immanent terms. The brain problem is the problematic of what it is to think, and what this problematic calls forth from the forces of the virtual is an immanent thinking of noogenesis.

The problematic can be formulated in a number of different ways (D&G (1984); D&G (1988); D&G (1994)): 'What is it to think?'; 'What is the image that thinking gives itself of what it is to think?'; 'How does one find one's bearings in thought?'; 'How does one orientate oneself in thought?'. The problematic of thinking is a problematic of the brain in that the image that thinking gives itself is an image machined solely by the brain and the forces of thinking that the brain can self-organise in emergent thinking. There are three inter-related aspects to the brain problem.

First, thinking is the operation of differential relations, continuums of differences, ordinary and singular points, and continuous multiplicities. Thinking involves making conjunctions of the flows and meshing consistencies amongst the differential relations, continuums of differences, ordinary and singular points, and continuous multiplicities. The brain is itself a virtual multiplicity (D&G (1988) 15 (17)). These consistency multiplicities of thinking are also in continuous variation, and the brain problem is of machining consistent multiplicities in continuous variation.

Second, the brain problem is a self-posing of the problematic of what it is to think. Thinking is inseparable from problematics and problems, and these are self-posed to thinking from the forces of the virtual. These problems are real, and have an autonomy from any thinking that strives to address the problematic or problem. The problems also re-specify themselves in relation to events, such that problems are also continually self-posed anew in different complexes of forces and singular points. The image that thinking gives of itself is that of a thinking that is engendered in relation to a problematic or problem.

Third, thinking is an operation of self-organisation and emergence. Thinking is engendered in response to the problematic when there arises immanently in the differential relations, singular points and conjunctions of flows a machining of self-organising processes that assemble dissipative consistencies amongst the multiplicities with emergent capacities for an engendered thinking. Just as the earth draws upon the immanent virtual and intensive forces to create and organise itself, thinking also taps those immanent virtual and intensive forces to create complex and sophisticated information processing dynamic structures.

Thus the brain problem presents itself of the self-posing of the problematic of 'what it is to think?' in the movements of the differential relations of thinking and draws upon the forces of self-organisation and emergence that are immanent to the differences and repetitions of thinking. This immanent self-organisation and emergence of the engendering of thinking in relation to the problematic of thinking is noogenesis.

Noogenesis in relation to the brain problem self-organises and emerges in two operations: confronting mental chaos, and laying a plane of immanence over the mental chaosmos (D&G (1994) 197). The brain problem and noogenesis present themselves under the condition of the confrontation with mental chaos. In the brain problem thought confronts chaos and plunges into chaos (D&G (1994) 218). The mental chaos is all the virtual differential relations and elements churning at infinite speeds. In the mental chaos there is simultaneous creation and destruction of relations and elements of thinking, in which the very moment a thought begins to assume an emergent consistency it is overwhelmed and plunged back into chaos. In this chaos of thinking the appearance and disappearance of thoughts coincide, and thinking takes shapes and vanishes at an infinite speed. Without bearings or orientation thinking flip-flops through so many variations of provisional holding ideas to bring some consistency to the maelstrom of thought, drowning in the sensations and intensities of the chaos of thought as equally as in the intellectual strivings and convulsions as thinking tries to tie together some order in the mental chaos.

Noogenesis renders chaos consistent by the meshing of consistencies in the movements of the chaosmos. In the difference in itself, and the flows of differential relations between the differences, and in the forces of these flows, there are continuums of differences, multiplicities, a distribution of singular and ordinary points as attractors, and thresholds for bifurcations. Thinking is these differentials and multiplicities. There are also forces of affect and being affected in sensations, intensities, and the emergence of traits of expression and traits of material in thinking. Noogenesis through the machining of consistencies draws a plane across chaos, throwing a plane of immanence across chaos (D&G (1994) 197). Noogenesis sections chaos (D&G (1994) 42), and the plane of immanence is drawn with no higher transcendent dimension (D&G (1988) 17 (19)) and as a meshing of a line drawing a fractal dimensionality for the plane (D&G (1994) 38). The plane of immanence is 'the image thought gives itself of what it means to think, to make use of thought, to find one's bearings in thought' (D&G (1994) 37).

The confrontation of thinking with chaos and the drawing of the plane of immanence are the machining of consistencies in noogenesis, and are the corollary of these multiplicities presenting themselves as a virtual problematic. The movements of the chaosmos of the plane of immanence are the self-posing of the problematic of thinking and the self-posing of new problems for thinking to tackle (D&G (1994) 27). Noogenesis and the engendering of thinking in thought are inseparable from the self-positing virtual problematic of the brain problem, and imply each other (D&G (1994) 11). It is the problematic of thinking itself, where the image of thought sets problems as the conditions for the noogenesis of thought, and does so without any recourse to law statements in the development of thought. The brain problem presents itself as a self-positing problematic such that noogenesis, all thinking, and the creation of concepts, on the plane of immanence image of thought is inseparable from the driving force of the problematic and of virtual problems.

In its self-positing problematic the brain problem, further, presents itself in the individual thinker with compelling force, where the problematic of orientating oneself in thought is sensed as the chaos of thinking and as an insistent posing of the problematic that needs to be solved. The resources that thinking has available for orientating oneself in thought are the immanent ones of noogenesis of rendering chaos consistent and of the abstract machine that sections chaos and draws a plane of immanence for thinking.

Thus, from the operation of the brain problematic, the two key features of thinking immanently emerge as the plane of consistency and the multiplicity abstract machine that simultaneously draws itself and the plane of immanence: 'the brain is a multiplicity immersed in its plane of consistency...' (D&G (1988) 15 (17)).

The noogenesis of the brain problem is the emergence in relation to the problematic of what it is to think of a virtual multiplicity that meshes together itself and the neighbouring multiplicities of thinking. This multiplicity is the abstract machine of thinking that machines consistencies amongst all the multiplicities of thinking on a fractal line of continuous variation. It is the abstract machine of thinking that thinking claims for itself immanently, and it is the fractal line that draws the plane of immanence for all thinking.

The brain problem and noogenesis provides a thinking that engenders thinking in thought, an image of thought rendering chaos consistent, an image of thought that selects what thinking can claim of right, and a thinking of 'that which must be thought but cannot be thought' (D&G (1994) 59), since it is a thinking of all that cannot be thought in the stratified organisation of thought. Noogenesis lays down the plane of immanence across the brain problem, and it is the brain problem itself that engenders thinking in thought. The virtual brain problem and noogenesis produce the image of thought of what thinking can claim by right (D&G (1994) 37).

The plane of immanence and the fractal abstract machine of this image of thought are taken up and developed in a schizo thinking, with a specific operation of continuously exploring the problematic of thinking, exploring problems, and creating new concepts. This image of thinking and practice of schizo thinking is further the basis for the development of a practice of noology to think all thought.

This brain problem of how thinking presents itself on its own terms is not everyone's problem. People who are taken up in social machines and assemblages that impose and teach a stratified organisation of thought think in perfectly reasonable ways without any need to directly encounter the brain problem. For some people, however, the brain problem is something they have, often with terrible outcomes. Maybe the operation of social machines and assemblages to impose stratified organisation just didn't take, or maybe one day the stratified organisation just cracked up and fell away, or maybe the forces of the brain problem are just too strong and overrun all defences. However, whatever the case, it is certainly the problem of all noologists to have the brain problem. For a noologist to be able to engender thinking in thought, and to think all thought, it is necessary always to start with the brain problem of difference and repetition and philosophy.

Schizo thinking (philosophy)

This image of thought is the thought of the brain problem, the virtual brain, and of the brain as absolute deterritorialisation. Schizo thinking operates with virtual differences and problems, the plane of immanence for thinking, the fractal abstract machine of thinking, and the creation of concepts and invention of conceptual personae (D&G (1994)). It is the thinking that confronts chaos and thinks for forces of an outside and exteriority. Schizo thinking is to confront mental chaos and render chaosmos consistent in thinking the exterior, the outside, the unthinkable, unsayable, unseeable. Schizo thinking works by adopting the plane of immanence and fractal abstract machine of the noogenesis of the brain problem, thinking of problematics and problems, creating concepts and inventing conceptual personae in relation to the planes that are constructed and the problems that are continually posed. Noogenesis drew a plane of immanence across chaos for thinking and created a first concept of a dynamic consistency multiplicity, and schizo thought develops on from this. The abstract machine that develops in noogenesis in the brain problem is the machining of a consistent distribution across singular and ordinary points in thinking, and keeping this consistency in continuous variation on the open plane of immanence of thinking. It is an abstract machine that 'involves a throwing of the dice' (Deleuze (1988) 87) and the eternal return.

The development of schizo thought constructs a problem space for thought of a problematic plane of thinking and a problem space for thinking from the transcendental field of the chaosmos of thinking. A problematic and problems connect actual things and states of affairs to their virtual and intensive conditions. At the heart of every problematic and problem there is always the self-posing compulsion to the engendering of thinking in thought. Problematics and problems are not logical, cognitive, linguistic or propositional, but are complex virtual and intensive multiplicities, where a problem is good by virtue of it being neither overdetermined not underdetermined. Constructing a problematic plane and problem space is a matter of grasping both the degrees of freedom in the problem and the objective distribution of singular and ordinary points in the problematic and problem. The problematic and problems are consistent multiplicities that operate an autonomy from any actual solution implemented in relation to the problematic and problem.

The plane of immanence that is drawn in schizo thinking from the noogenesis is the consistency that connects up all the multiplicities of the virtual. The plane of immanence for thinking is diagrammatic, with the machining together of all the virtual abstract machines in a transversal consistency, and so also the plane of all immanent virtual concepts. The plane of immanence is the consistency that rolls up all concepts, unrolls all concepts, and it is the plane of immanence on which new immanent consistency concepts self-organise and emerge.

The fractal abstract machine of schizo thinking operates in several key ways. The fractal abstract machine meshes the plane of consistency as a point of infinite survey, creating new concepts, and extracting new events from strata states of affairs and intensive processes. The abstract machine meshes the multiplicities of thinking into a plane of immanence of thought by setting forth a point of infinite survey at infinite speed amongst the multiplicities drawing the plane of immanence on a fractal line, and always machining consistencies of new concepts, to increase the number of connections across the plane of immanence. The abstract machine of schizo thought creates new connections, and only new difference in itself and new consistencies are selected by the abstract machine. The abstract machine creates consistencies through machining inclusive disjunctive syntheses of the multiplicity of elements, without reducing their heterogeneity or exteriority of relations, nor reducing the potentials for each of the elements to enter into new relationships and arrangements.

The activity of the abstract machine in meshing the plane of immanence and machining consistencies in schizo thinking is the creation of new concepts as new multiplicities with flat high dimensional manifolds and transversal consistency on continuous variation. In schizo thinking brain is the faculty for the creation of concepts:

> The problem of philosophy is to acquire a consistency without losing the infinite into which thought plunges…To give consistency without losing any of the infinite… By making a section of chaos, the plane of immanence requires a creation of concepts.
>
> (D&G (1994) 42)

Concepts in schizo philosophy are differentials and consistent multiplicities in continuous variation. The concept is defined by 'the inseparability of a finite number of heterogeneous components traversed by a point of absolute survey at infinite speed' (D&G (1994) 21). It is the creation of a multiplicity that is organised by an immanent consistency that is transversal to the multiplicity and in continuous variation. The schizo concept is a problematic, chaos rendered consistent, a multiplicity transversal consistency, a state of survey in relation to its components, an affective theme, and also an experimental throw of the dice (D&G (1994) 208). Concepts are machined in connections, linkages and consistencies (D&G (1994) 91). Concepts have relations to other concepts, particularly in their zones of neighbourhoods. This entails concepts not only having components and threshold, but also bridges and passages, shared with neighbouring concepts all in continuous variation.

The abstract machine of schizo thinking creates concepts through extracting events from changes in actual states of affairs, from emergence events in intensive processes, and from law-expressing statements. It does so by extracting from them the degrees of freedom in dimensions of their manifold and their distribution of singularities, and it does so as the event of the problem that calls for the creation of a concept. What schizo concepts are not are projective, hierarchical or referential, and they are not created representationally or discursively (D&G (1994) 22).

These multiplicity concepts emerge from problematics and problems that bring sensations, intensities and affects in the machining of the concept. Problematics, problems and concepts always have an emotional, physical and environmental background to their emergence. As such, a schizo concept works best when the formulation of the concept is dramatised, such that some of the intensities and sensations that went into the thinking of the concept are transmitted.

The practice of schizo thought and the creation of concepts operates with conceptual personae as the particular abstract machine that operates a particular concept or particular set of concepts. Whilst the plane of immanence is entirely diagrammatic, concepts do have intensive ordinates of virtual movements. It is because of the interface between the virtual and the intensive in a concept that concepts need conceptual personae (D&G (1994) 2). Conceptual personae are the abstract machines operating in the intensive field of thought. In the creation of a concept there is always the individual who senses it, and schizo thought is not a universal faculty and only ever occurs in relation to unique individuals. Similarly, the grasping of a problematic or a problem space and surveying set of virtual concepts is a unique individuation, portraying the plane, degrees of freedom and distribution of singularities of the individual. The conceptual persona provides a unique consistency to the individual point of survey that draws a plane, machines consistencies and creates concepts. Conceptual personae further convey that for schizo thought thinking is sensations, intensities, speeds and slowness, affect and being affected, the creation of concepts carrying consistencies and intensities that should directly touch the mind outside representation (Deleuze (1994) 16).

Schizo thinking is marked by the conditions of thinking the plane of immanence and of the noogenesis of the brain problem. Schizo thought is celerity, immobility and speeds, catatonia and rush. It is bathed in sensations and intensities, and movements of affect and being affected: 'Thought is, rather, one of those terrible movements which can be sustained only under conditions of a larval subject' (Deleuze (1994) 118). It is to think the outside, exteriority, thinking that is absolutely decoded and deterritorialised, non-stratifed, non-formal, and outside representation (D&G (1988) 376–7 (415–16)). It is not the operation of a universal faculty but rather an abstract storm of all the faculties in discord going beyond their limits (Deleuze (1988) 117). As with the noogenesis of thinking in chaosmos, schizo thinking is engendered by encounter, shock, sensations and intensities when they force thought to take place. In schizo thought: 'thought is born from the violent shock of an encounter with pure intensive differences (being of the sensible)' (Deleuze (1994) 140). Schizo thinking only ever arises as a unique event of an individual's apprenticeship of the problematic and problems of thinking. For the schizo thinker it is a matter of becoming obscure and imperceptible as the point of infinite survey at infinite speed, the absolute fractal line of flight.

Thus, the schizo image of thought is the plane of immanence that holds all the concepts together (D&G (1994) 36), and 'concepts are like multiple waves, rising and falling, but the plane of immanence is the single wave that rolls them up and unrolls them' (D&G (1994) 36). On this plane of immanence the noogenesis abstract machine of thinking and conceptual personae operates as a point of absolute survey at infinite speed drawing a fractal line of machining consistencies and creating concepts (D&G (1994) 210). In this, schizo thinking involves a thinking that works 'to bring something incomprehensible into the world' (D&G (1988) 378 (417)).

Such thinking that strives to 'bring something incomprehensible into the world', is also to align thinking with a time to come and to the problematic of social organisation. The schizo image of thought is taken up in some social machines as the image of organisation and thought, such as the nomad war social machine (D&G (1988) 351 (387)). However, the social machine that schizo thinking really belongs to is the new earth and the social machine yet to come. Schizo thinking is a desiring investment of a social machine yet to come, an abstract machine of thought to think theory for a new society. It is thought for the social machine yet to come and for the people yet to come, an appeal to a people yet to come (Deleuze (1998) 378), and a thinking and desiring practice beyond the absolute limit of social organisation. With this social machine in mind, schizo thinking thinks 'in order to free itself from what it thinks (the present) and be able to finally "think otherwise" (the future)' (Deleuze (1988) 119):

> We will then think the past against the present and resist the latter, not in favour of a return but 'in favour, I hope, of a time to come' (Nietzsche), that is, by making the past active and present to the outside so that something new will finally come about, so that thinking, always, may reach thought.
>
> (Deleuze (1988) 119)

Noology: to think all thought

Noology is the study and practice of the brain, the exploration of the problematic of finding one's bearings in thought, schizo thinking, and the exploration of images of thought (D&G (1994) 37). Noology is the practice of thinking that arises in relation to the problematic of what it is to think (the brain problem, the virtual) and the problems that thinking confronts (brain problems, the intensive problem field of thinking) (Deleuze (1988) 378). Noology is itself the practice of engendering thinking in thought. Noology is to think the plane of immanence for thinking and draw up a topology of abstract machines of thinking and images of thought.

Noology starts with the brain problem and the drawing of the plane of immanence. This sets out the image of thought for noology and schizo thinking in the immanent image of thought that thinking immanently can give of itself. The drawing of the plane of immanence is for all thought in noology, not just for the schizo philosophical practice of thought. Noology thinks all thought but it does so from the image of thought of the plane of immanence, the abstract machine of thinking of an absolute fractal line of flight, and a thinking that thinks all thought at the risk of itself becoming unthinkable. It is the practice of thinking all the images of thought that can arise on the brain and organise the brain, and of diagrammatising all the images of thought on the plane of immanence brain in a topology of images of thought.

Because the plane of immanence image of thinking renders chaos consistent then the plane of immanence image of thinking 'is the base of all planes, imma-nent to every thinkable plane that does not succeed in thinking it. It is the most intimate inside within thought and yet the absolute outside' (D&G (1994) 59). To think the brain as the plane of immanence is to absorb all of thought. Thus, the plane of immanence image of thought has the potential to think all thought from its own image of thought, and, thus, the potential to think and study all images of thought, whether immanent, transcendent or intensive.

In studying images of thought there are two images that noology draws out and studies as the stakes of the problematic of thinking and to the problems thinking encounters. These two images of thought are the noology and schizo philosophy image of thought with the plane of immanence, and the legislating State image of thought with the transcendent plane of organisation.

Noology explores and practises the schizo philosophy image of thought, and creates new concepts. As a result, in exploring the State image of thought, nool-ogy is critical of the dominance of the State image of thought, and criticises State thought for the imposition upon thinking of a transcendent plane of organisation, a molar abstract machine of overcoding, and its insistence upon unities, identities, recognition, signification, representation, interiority and stratifications in thinking.

In addition to pursuing the creation of concepts in schizo thinking, and the analysis and critique of State thought, noology also thinks the thinking that wanders between the two planes, and which is the vagabond thought of the inten-sive problem field of thinking. This is the intensive problem field of assemblages of thinking. In the intensive field of ideas, events and concepts, vagabond think-ing forms intensive consistencies of sensation-intensity-affect-events that are both the problem and draft solution of a case. This vagabond thought is between schizo thinking and State thought, and it is an interesting alloy of schizo and State thought that allows noology to consider thinking on a continuum rather than on two poles, and in terms of intensive assemblages of thought.

In this, noology is to think all thought in terms of planes, abstract machines, multiplicity concepts, conceptual personae, fields of intensity and machinic assemblages of sensation and affect (a topology of images of thought and a gene-alogy of images of thought). Noology is the study of the relationships between abstract machines of thought and intensive assemblages of thought, their mixtures, their hybridities and their transformations.

Noology in thinking images of thought at its full depth of exploration proceeds to connect the images of thought with the social machines and social assemblages that each image of thought is related by way of genesis. The image of thought of the plane of immanence is the image of thought effectuated in the nomad war social machine and social machine yet to come through its connection of the earth and brain and the drawing of a plane of immanence for thought. The image of thought of the plane of organisation is the image of thought created in the State social machine through its connection of earth and brain and the drawing of a plane of transcendent organisation for thought. The vagabond practice of thought is related to the social assemblages of smiths and artisan metal workers (D&G (1988) 404 (445)). Vagabond social assemblages connect on the one side to the nomad war social machine and plane of immanence, and on the other side conjugate with the State social machine and the plane of transcendent organisation. This vagabond image of thought is the image for all social assemblages that wander between the planes.

It is in this move to connect schizo philosophy to social machines and social assemblages that noology finds its highest calling: to think the abstract machine of a new earth and society yet to come, and create transformations in the intensive problem fields of both thinking and social assemblaging.

State thought (legislation)

With the State image of thought there is another fate for the virtual brain than that of schizo thought and the plane of immanence. There is a turning away from the noogenesis of thinking, with the coding and striation of the brain and thinking, and an actualisation operation for the brain and thinking. A social machine of the State emerges, and in that social machine the abstract machine of legality is an idea of organising, an image of organisation. The State social machine brought with it an image and a model for thought – the State image of thought (D&G (1988) 24 (25)). The State image of thought is the idea of how to organise things into unities and identities under one transcendent centre of organisation and control. It is a model of thought as universal legislation, which operates a molar fold, draws and imposes a transcendent plane of organisation for thinking, organises with a logos abstract machine, and establishes systems of recognition, signification, representation, judgements and opinions.

The State image of thought, even in its modern forms, has inherited specific characteristics by virtue of its circumstances of emergence. The State image of thought emerged against the background of an emulation on earth with God and its development in the machinery of Imperial bureaucracy (D&G (1988) 424 (468)). In the emulation with God, there is the operation of the molar fold expressionism that bestows a working unity and identity on things on earth, such as with organisms. In addition, from astronomy early social groups had a good grasp of celestial order, and this celestial order was linked to their gods. In the Imperial States where the State image of thought was developed there was the despot's claim to direct divinity, and the imposing of the celestial order as a plane of organisation on thought and social production. This was an emulation with the

God of the ecumenon, and the State image of thought subsequently always carries with it a theological and priestly aura. This puts the State image of thought in a lasting relation to the celestial order, the organic as a model of order, and to transcendence as divinity. The centrality of the State image of thought to the bureaucracy of the Imperial States also has lasting consequences on the character of the State image of thought. The State social machine gives the State image of thought an immense institutional embeddedness and the constant administration and development by the diverse officers of the State. However, in this institutional embeddedness and development, the State image of thought does not leave behind its origins in the despot emitting signifying orders from the apex of a vast bureaucracy, the structure of despotic pyramids, and the vast systems of Imperial writing, even in contemporary State images of thought. It was the despots and the bureaucrats that made the Imperial State itself the model for thought:

> The State as model...for thought has a long history: logos, the philosopher-king, the transcendence of the Idea, the interiority of the concept, the republic of minds, the court of reason, the functionaries of thought, man as legislator and subject.
>
> (D&G (1988) 24 (27))

The State image of thought draws on two key operations in relation to an immersion in the brain problem. These two operations are of a molar fold abstract machine operation upon thinking and a second operation of drawing and imposing upon thinking a transcendent plane of organisation. These two operations shut down the problematic of the brain problem and block the creative churning of the brain problem.

The molar fold operation is that of a molar abstract machine overcoding all of thinking. There is in the abstract machine a transcendent five-dimensional folding over of the flat multidimensional manifolds of consistencies with an overcoding operation. The molar overcoding is in an exclusive disjunctive synthesis of recording that organises thought into a closed totality (D&G (1984) 75 (83)). It is the embedding of thinking in a transcendent higher dimensionality space, and it moves the multiplicities of thinking from being continuous multiplicities to being discontinuous multiplicities.

The operation of the molar fold abstract machine closing thinking into a unity and embedding thought in a transcendent higher organising dimension draws for thought and imposes upon thinking a plane of organisation. From the transcendent embedding dimension, a plane or organisation based upon the structure of the molar fold and the exclusive disjunctive synthesis is projected on to all of thinking. The plane of organisation, in addition to establishing a unity for thought, establishes a structure and order for thought based on the organising principle of identity as essence that would determine the recognition of the same. The plane of organisation is a geometric grid imposed upon thinking, and ordering thought arborescently and hierarchically from a transcendent point or centre.

With the operation of the molar fold abstract machine and the drawing and projecting of the plane of organisation, State thought is organised through the double articulation process of molar expressionism in the manner of the articulation of form and substance and the articulation of expression and content. In the molar fold, all of thinking is submitted to the fold of expression of the despotic signifier of the One, with the unity and identity of thought as the emergent property of the operation. The molar fold overcodes thinking, and thought becomes integrating, centralised, arborescent, hierarchical, countable and representational.

The molar fold has two immediate consequences for thought: the cancelling of all intensities in thinking, and the establishment of a hylomorphism in the State image of thought. As the multiplicities of thinking are converted from continuous to discontinuous, from ordinal to metric, all intensity in thinking is cancelled out, heterogeneities become homogenous, and thought becomes a closed system where thought operates near-to-equilibrium and a homeostatic regulation. In addition, with the closing off of the virtual and intensive modalities, State thought is caught in a hylomorphism in which the virtual and intensive matters of thinking are considered passive, and the State image of thought cannot think immanence, intensities, difference in itself, or continuous multiplicities, and can only think transcendence, unities and identity as the same. The further consequence of cancelling intensities and hylomorphism in the State image of thought is that both the virtual and intensive problem fields are closed to State thought, with the only way of working with a problem being the analytical imposition of the plane of organisation to the problem as the application of the grid to a set of facts.

In the State image of thought the molar fold in the organisation of thinking is achieved by the molar abstract machine raising up in the transcendent molar fold and inserting a despotic master signifier in that molar fold. The despotic master signifier operates as the new molar fold of expressionism for the new social machine, and also as the new form of expression for thought. The operation of raising up of the despotic master signifier is accompanied by the detachment of the partial object as the repressed, and the consequent institution of a representational symbolic order of signifiers in relation to signifiers in a circulating chain, where the signified is always for another signifier. There is a S1 master signifier that organises all the other signifiers as S2, giving a structure to State thought and signification of S1–S2. It is then on this signifying representational symbolic order that all the organisation of State thinking depends as thought itself becomes aligned with thinking in words. State thought becomes organised by the master signifier, but only to ever think on the basis of a central paradox because the master signifier totalised the symbolic order only in the name of its own absence and withdrawal, which leaves an empty locus for the master signifier.

The form of expression for the State image of thought is the master signifier word of God/the despot, dispatched from a transcendent point which is simultaneously both power and absence into the circular signifying chain and symbolic order, which itself is organised as a closed homeostatic representational system of thought. The plane of organisation is, thus, lain out as the platform on which the State abstract machine deploys the despotic logos master signifier over all organisation of thought. The legislative image of thought had arrived.

The image of thought works through the consequences of the molar fold and the drawing of the plane of organisation through a central principle of recognition and a system of representation (Deleuze (1994) 129). It is a system of thought based on identities and unities, with the central operation of thought recognising identities, a unity of a signifying representational system, working with representational concepts of identities. It is the identity and essence found in representational concepts that constitutes the form of the same for recognition. The faculty of recognition unites all of the faculties in thought that recognises or fails to recognise a concept or a thing. If the concept or thing is recognised as same to an existing concept or category then it is admitted into thought, otherwise the concept or thing will be excluded from State thought. What is important in the State image of thought is clear and distinct knowledge about what are the properties of a concept or thing, not of its genesis, capacities or transformations. Further, State thought is initiated by the recognition of the same in harmony, precisely not by the encounter with shock that compels schizo thinking. It is a reproductive thought of what has already been thought.

The system of representation is based on four principles in the State image of thought. There is identity in the understanding of the concept and the subject, there is resemblance in objects in perception, there is opposition in determining concepts in the imagination, and there is analogy between concepts, propositions and things in hierarchical judgements (Deleuze (1994) 137). This system of representation is thought operating through recognition of identity, resemblance, reproduction and analogical judgements (Deleuze (1994) 138). Representational concepts are the identities, universal and eternal in form, based in abstraction and generalisations, extracting variables from states of affairs, whilst denoting states of affairs and truths.

The image of State thought in addition to the exclusive disjunctive synthesis of the molar fold, the master signifier, the signifying order, underlying principle of recognition in the same and order of representation, relies upon a number of other assumptions and principles. There is presupposed the amity of truth and thinking, that the only negative of thought is error, the importance of propositions, the centrality to State thought of solutions and integrations, the aim of arranging the S2 knowledge of the social machine, all underpinned by the blessing of common sense and good sense behind the State image of thought (Deleuze (1994) 129). It is this assumption of common sense and good sense, together with the organising principles of recognition and representation, which account for how State thought may often fail to produce thought that is much beyond opinions and the exchange of inter-subjective communication.

The State image of thought develops as laws and the interpretation of laws, an arborescent analytical method and hierarchical ranking, and an interiority of sovereignty and the subject. The State image of thought is organised on a molar fold of a transcendent legislating repressing interdiction. Further, it is this law that establishes the organising principles of totality and essence of State thought, these principles in turn driving the thinking of more laws that relate the operations of totalities and essences, unities and identities. Both considerations result in the State image of thought thinking in exclusive disjunctive syntheses and laws, and in a compulsion to interpret what language-text-discourse-speech means. The State image of thought develops as inescapably legalistic, dogmatic, centred on the question 'what does it mean?' and thought as exegesis, hermeneutics and a generalised interpretation (D&G (1984) 206 (224)). State thought also develops as an arborescent analytical method, which operates on the basis of making distinctions and of using that basis to order into hierarchical rankings. The exclusive disjunctive synthesis, together with the commitment to unities and essences, is the very model for an analytical image of thought where what is important is the clear and distinct, and the organisation always focused on assigning things their correct place in the arborescent schema and hierarchical rankings of categories. The thought tends towards a method of abstraction and generalisation, closing totalities, making distinctions, applying a plane of organisation to states of affairs, and through analysis producing law-like statements. The organising principles of unity and identity also lead State thought to proceed on the basis of the strong identity of the thinker. The thinker of State thought is closed with a strong identity, with thought given an interiority in which to operate (D&G (1984) 213 (232)). In State thought, the assured thinker operates State thought in the certain knowledge that this is the correct way to think, with the harmony of his faculties, his analytical skill, and determination in others of error.

In the State image of thought the State thinker as a corollary of the image of thought, stakes thought on the basis of beliefs and fidelities to the transcendent operation of the State social machine and to the transcendent image of thought. These beliefs and fidelities are, of course, given the centrality of recognition to the image of thought, conservative, and invest the social field in terms of established values of power, wealth and honours. However, despite a placid appearance of those possessed of the State image of thought and a State investment of the social field, there are for these people very considerable, even tremendous, cerebral erotic investments of aspects of the social machine and image of thought, which are not without consequences for the thinker and the nature of State thought. There is a massive cerebral erotic investment in law and transcendence, but not without the submission of thought to repression, to Oedipus, and to desire as lack (D&G (1984) 296 (326)). There is massive cerebral erotic investment of the S1–S2 chain, the co-extension of thought with this chain, and the model of thinking as interpretation, but not without the constant paranoia of the 'what does it mean?' and the anxiety of interpreting the S1 and chain. There is, also, a massive cerebral erotic investment of the State image of thought in itself, but not without the State thinker turning thought into the interminable operation of obsessional neurosis as an organisationally closed system that thinks interminably precisely so as never really to think (D&G (1988) 114 (126)).

Vagabond thought (cases)

Schizo thinking and State thought draw planes. There is the plane of immanence of schizo thinking, and there is the plane or organisation of State thought. There is, however, a thinking that takes place between the two planes and which forms a twin formation and hybrid image of thought. This is vagabond thought that does not commit to either the plane of immanence of thinking or the plane of organisation of thought, but rather moves in an intensive field of thought between immanence and transcendence and between the virtual and actual of thought. Vagabond thought sets out and moves in ambivalence, connecting to the plane of immanence of schizo thought and conjugating with the plane of organisation of State thought, taking from each, occasionally making a communication between the two images of thought (D&G (1988) 415 (458)). Sometimes vagabond thinking will move close to the plane of immanence and schizo thought, and sometimes it will move close to the plane of organisation and State space, becoming more or less intensive and less or more actual. Its hybridity, however, means that vagabond thought is in principle always framed by State thought. The plane of organisation image of thought (and the social machine behind it) imposes a unity on its thinkers and codes the outside on the plane of organisation as undifferentiated. Vagabond thought takes the plane of organisation and the State image of thought, but it knows something of the plane of immanence and of the schizo image of thought, and it moves into a zone of indistinction where the State image of thought buckles and gives way to a logic of sense and the thinking of many strange incorporeal transformations triggerable in bodies and states of affairs.

What vagabond thought discovers and moves to think in is the intensive morphogenetic field of thought. This is the field where noogenesis and schizo thought enter into intensive morphogenetic processes whereby the abstract machine diagrams take on intensive features, and where the State thought of recognition and representation break up into pathos, drama and crisis. The intensive morphogenetic field of thinking is a field of the forces of thinking and the entanglements of the forces of thinking in thinking. It is a field in which thinking is sensations, intensities, affecting and being affected, distributions of strange attractors for thinking, thresholds, bifurcation points, transformations and becomings. This field of sensations, intensities and affects is pulled from the one side by forces of immanence, and from another side by the forces of transcendence, such that vagabond thought is always an intensive thinking aside sensational thresholds of immanence and transcendence.

The result of thinking this intensive 'in between the planes' field of thinking is that vagabond thought is characterised by a wandering, a mercurial combination of gravitas and speeds, and the making of a holey space for thought. Vagabond ambivalence is also ambulant, whereby vagabond thinking has an internal itinerancy (D&G (1988) 413 (456)), wandering around the intensive field, wandering on and off the plane of organisation, wandering on and off the plane of immanence. Vagabond thought can go where it wants to go, because in the intensive field of thought thinking is both virtual and actual. This intensive field is also a field of matter-movement where always new flows will be encountered to convey thought along some line, where new attractors will continuously emerge to draw the intensive lines of continuous variation in thought into new intensive fields, and where wandering vagabond thought will always evade the police and border controls of State thought. Vagabond thinking, thus, carries off the achievement of simultaneously thinking of some aspects of the schizo image of thought and some aspects of the State image of thought. It is not that the vagabond thought thinks both the plane of immanence and the plane of organisation, but that speeds of thinking and a gravitas of thinking are combined when, in principle, they should not be. From the point of view of State thought, the vagabond thinker thinks State thought, but with added not understood elements and strange outcomes. This is the mercurial character of vagabond thought, and the maverick character of its thinkers. Vagabond's relation to the State image of thought also accounts for its characteristic of always making holey spaces for thought. Vagabond thinking makes holes in State thought, working on the stratification of State thought to break it towards becoming epistratic and parastratic through introducing bursts of the machinic phylum of thinking, and of mining tunnels and passages in State thought so as to introduce the machinic phylum across State thought, allowing strange new connections and bridgings in thinking. Vagabond thought makes these subterranean passages and stems in State thought so as to better think the plane of organisation and the State image of thought than the State thinkers themselves, and it is down these holes that the vagabond thought can disappear when it needs to.

What is crucial to vagabond thought is that though it will always in principle be framed in a State image of thought of recognition and representation, it does not hold to the hylomorphism of the State image of thought nor to a non-porous conception of the fold of expression over content. It is the non-porous concept of the molar fold and the resulting hylomorphism that stops the State image of thought sensing the intensive morphogenetic field of thinking. However, vagabond thought is precisely ambivalent to the exclusive operation of the molar fold (which is why it is ambivalent between the plane of organisation and plane of immanence), and although orientated in thought by the State image of thought, the vagabond thinker also senses the intensive field of thinking and knows that there is a lot more to thinking than the imposition of a plane of organisation on thought and the use of representational concepts. Vagabond thinking is ambivalent to being submitted to laws or bound to the molar double articulation, and is ambivalent on the expression-content organisation of thought, and works also with intensive forces and materials of thinking, and putting variables into variation rather than routinely extracting them. Through becoming ambivalent to hylomorphism (not rejecting it – sometimes it is the case, sometimes it is not) the intensive materials of thinking become available for thinking and thought is scattered with singularities and thresholds. What is discovered are the traces and traits of the noogenesis in thinking, and thinking is moved by forces of intensive self-organisation and emergence. In the intensive field of the sensations, intensities, affects and vague essences of forces of thinking there is discovered the machinic phylum of thinking, and the conditions explored and found of the battle of intensive forces that makes an intensive thought and explains the genesis of an actual thought.

In all this, vagabond thought is the corollary of the vagabondage of metallurgy, and vagabond thought is a smithy thought:

> Smiths are not nomadic among the nomads and sedentary among the sedentaries, nor half-nomadic among the nomads, half-sedentary among sedentaries. Their relationship to others results from their internal itinerancy, from their vague essence, and not the reverse. It is in their specificity, it is by virtue of their itinerancy, by virtue of their inventing a holey space, that they communicate with the sedentaries and with the nomads... They are themselves double: a hybrid, an alloy, a twin formation... Holey space itself communicates with smooth space and striated space. In effect, the machinic phylum or the metallic line passes through all of the assemblages.
>
> (D&G (1988) 414–15 (457–8))

What vagabond thinking discovers in the intensive morphogenetic field of thinking is the intensive problem field of thinking and the intensive problems of thinking. What is definitional about vagabond thought is that it thinks problems intensively and intensively assembles unique cases of solution. Beyond the State image of thought and recognition and representation there is an intensive problem field of thinking. Intensive problems of thought are relations of forces, intensities, sensations, affects, thresholds and transformations, and these intensive problems of thinking are self-posing and continuously becoming respecified and re-posed. Vagabond thought does not want to think the virtual brain problem but it does sense that thinking is a shock encounter and compelling. For vagabond thinking problems are intensively expressed in sensations and signs, and these intensive problems have a sensed high dimensionality manifold and a distribution of sensed singular and ordinary points. Vagabond thought supplements the State image of thought conception of a problem with an intensive problem field concept of a problem that it intuitively operates in sensation as a consequence of its thinking being in connection with the schizo image of thought and the plane of immanence. In this vagabond thinking is the simultaneous co-existence in thought of two images of thought. Vagabond thinking can conceptualise a problem in the State image of thought but also simultaneously conceptualise that problem in the schizo image of thought in terms of sensation and intensive forces. The vagabond thinker, as such, has available two co-existing contrast spaces for thinking about problems. In many cases a problem may be so actualised that the State image of thought is perfectly adequate to thinking the problem through to solution. However, even with a simple problem, vagabond thought may find a superior way to solve the problem, and there are many problems that are not amenable to

State image of thought and then vagabond thought may be the only way to proceed with the problem.

Vagabond thought intensively thinks problems and thinks their corollary cases of solution without precedent. For vagabond thought it is problems that have to be thought, explored and explained. Even when a case of solution is thought through, the understanding of intensive problems is that they always demonstrate autonomy with respect to the case of solution and always exceed the case of solution. Vagabond thought thinks the problem by tapping the self-organising and emergent forces of thinking that are available in the intensive field. The problems pose themselves, but there are also in the machinic phylum of the intensive social field the machinic operations that can operate on the problem that engender a case of solution without precedent just as they engender the problem in itself.

In exploring the conditions of a problem and tapping the intensive forces of thinking vagabond thought is a prospecting, a detection and a diagnosis. The prospecting is the following of the flows in the intensive problem space, looking for the singularities, affects and events that are scattered in that problem space, looking for those significant intensive points in a problem by which connections can be made to trigger cases of solution. Vagabond thought is a detective, counter-actualising a state of affairs, exploring the conditions of an event as an intensive problem field, intensively thinking through the problem of 'what has happened here?', locating the singularities of the problem, and tapping intensive forces to allow the denouement of the 'what happened here?' to unfold (D&G (1988) 192 (212)). It is diagnosis through specifying the dimensions of the problem field manifold and determining the distribution of singular and ordinary points and diagnosing points of the ability to affect and be affected. For vagabond thinking it is always a matter of 'symptoms and evaluations, and not measures or properties' (D&G (1988) 479 (528)). Vagabond thought goes further, though, than detection and diagnosis. Vagabond thought can find the points, signs and statements in the intensive problem field and trigger their triggering of incorporeal transformations. By entering into the intensive problem field of forces that arrange a given state of affairs, vagabond thought can enter into this problem field and by connecting significant points, signs and statements together can effect intensive transformations that produce cascade transformations in actual bodies and states of affairs.

Vagabond thinking emerges and operates in intensive machinic assemblages of thinking. These machinic assemblages do not produce representational ideas, but produce more or less obscure or distant connections in the forces and materials of thinking, the contraction of dissipating matters, sensations of significant points and affects, and transversal consistencies of matters of thought. The problem and cases of solution without precedent are taken up in a heterogeneous consistency of the forces and materials of thought that are blocks of sensation-intensity-affect-event in continuous variation, with the cases of solution as emergent capacities of the intensive machinic assemblage. For each problem, vagabond thought machines a unique topical plane of composition and an intensive machinic assemblage of sensation-intensity-affect-event laid out on that unique plane of composition. The intensive problem field, between the plane of immanence and the plane of organisation, becomes so many thousand fleeting planes of composition and intensive flat assemblages of thought. It is an intensive brain thinking an intensive mechanosphere. From this vagabond thought and the intensive field the cases of solution to problems emerge, at the juncture of the virtual as events to be sectioned, and at the juncture of the actual as new signs and new statements to effect transformations in bodies and states of affairs.

Indeed, with its consistencies of sensation-intensity-affect-events and its operation of intensive transformations, vagabond thought is the most gregarious of thinking. The schizo image is solitary, and the State image is segregative. However, it is vagabond thought that not only talks to the schizo image of thought, and talks to the State image of thought, vagabond thought finds its calling in the social machines and social assemblages. The line of vagabond thought may pass through metallurgy, and indeed through so much minor science, but it is in the intensive material social field of the earth and social organisation that vagabond thought is most creatively deployed: 'thinking takes place in the relationship of territory and the earth' (D&G (1994) 85). Vagabond thought enters into the world, a flow of thinking inseparable from flows of intensive sensation and affect materials, spreading transformations into the social field, creating new intensive sensation-affect assemblages of social desiring production. Vagabond thought is ambivalent and ambulant in its investments of the social field, but it is a fully worked-out position on social desire and in the exploration of the intensive social field of desiring and social production. Indeed, vagabond thought works the fractal line that operates in the central non-relation of all intensive social assemblages: the line between what is sayable and what is seeable in any social assemblage, the line between what can be said and cannot, the line between what can be seen and what cannot. The central non-relation of an intensive social assemblage is, of course, the intensive problem field of the social assemblage, and it is this intensive social field that vagabond thought excels at thinking. It is vagabond thought that connects with the philosophy of the outside and the virtual, but also conjugates with the power and knowledge of social assemblages, in its unique sensibility with respect to signs and statements. However, in working this line between the powers of social organisation and the forces of the outside and of desiring production, it is the forces of the outside and of desiring production that can prevail in vagabond thought. Vagabond thought tends to make State thought holey and it also tends to make coded and territorialised social organisation holey, and to make the social machines and social assemblages into an intensive rhizome of passages and bridges of desiring production.

The brain between the cosmos and the refrain

Thus, there is noology, which is to think the brain, to draw a plane of immanence for all thought, and so be able to think all thought as the schizo image of thought

of the plane of immanence, the State image of thought of the plane of organisation, and the vagabond thought of the intensive problem field of thought between
the planes. It is the brain as planomenon, ecumenon and mechanosphere.

For noology, the State image of thought is the abstract machine of the molar
fold and the master signifier, and the drawing of a plane of organisation. It is an
image of thought on the model of transcendence and legislation. It is a stupendous
capture of the forces of thinking. Noology would take State thought as its enemy,
its nemesis, precisely because of the intellectual robustness of its operations, and
power the image of thought garners. However, the State image of thought rose up
on the plane of immanence of thought, and despite its success in occupying its
plane of organisation on the plane of immanence, the State image of thought and
plane of organisation is continually being broken up, holed out by vagabond
thinkers, prone to mental pathologies, and always haunted by a collapse of all the
walls from which it protects itself from chaos.

Vagabond thought is one of the discoveries of noology. There are not just two
planes for thought, but there is also a morphogenetic intensive problem field of
thinking. This intensive field is between the two planes and facing both, and is
crucially an intensive problem field. Whilst schizo thinking continually addresses
the virtual problematic of what it is to think, and the State thought has integrated
the problematic of what it is to think in the solution of the molar fold, there is also
an intensive problem field of thinking where thought struggles with problems and
drafting cases of solution to those problems without precedent. This vagabond
thinking is the forming of intensive machinic assemblages of thought in emergent
consistency blocks of sensation-intensity-affect-events. It is a thinking of a problem and the thinking of a case. For noology, this intensive morphogenetic field of
thinking is an important zone for thinking assemblages of thought and desire.
Noology thereby, further, studies and explores complexes of vagabond thought:
vagabond thought and State thought; vagabond thought and schizo thinking; and
complexes that select from all three organisations of thinking.

Above all, noology is the practice and study of schizo thinking and the schizo
image of thought, the name and image of thought that Deleuze (Deleuze (1994)
148) and Deleuze & Guattari (D&G (1984); D&G (1988); D&G (1994)) call
philosophy. Schizo image of thought is the image of thought that thinking can
claim for itself, and it is to draw the plane of immanence for thinking, invent
conceptual personae, create new concepts, and to draw close to the eternal return
in thinking.

In this activity, schizo thinking's fate is to approach absolute decoding and
deterritorialisation. Schizo thinking is to break through any of the stratifications
of the State thought that constrain thinking and the engendering of thinking in
thought, but, further, to then move to the creation of concepts absolutely decoded
and deterritorialised on the plane of immanence, drawing the fractal line itself of
the continuous creation of the plane of immanence. At this point of schizo thinking, whereas it is most often the case that it is a social machine that connects the
earth and the brain, when the eternal return enters thinking, the brain moves

between cosmos and refrain. Here thinking calls forth a new social machine, a new people and a new earth. Thinking and existence blur, become indistinguishable, and absolutely decoded and deterritorialised thinking becomes creation capable of calling forth a new people and a new earth.

The lecture on the brain was over. The same motley crew were left in the lecture theatre as there was at the end of Professor Challenger's lecture. The two groups could now be named. The wide-eyed loners scattered around the theatre were the schizo thinkers, the rather louche back row talking amongst themselves were the vagabond thinkers. The few State thinkers that had been in the theatre had left long ago.

Chapter 3

Workshop on Social Machines and Social Assemblages with Caprica Six

(Eternal Return)

> We define social formations by machinic processes and not by modes of production (these on the contrary depend on the processes).
>
> (D&G (1988) 435 (480))

> There is only machining and the social, and nothing else.
>
> ('Cylon Social Theory')

Introduction

The workshop was on social organisation and legality. Social organisation was a major theme in Deleuze & Guattari's work. For Caprica, this theme encompassed many things but centred upon desiring, machining and the assemblaging of an epic machinic opera. More precisely, that in this theme social organisation is the connecting of the earth and the brain, with this connection connecting social organisation to the forces of the cosmos, culminating in social organisation taking a cosmic line of flight to a new earth.

Following this perspective on social organisation depended, though, upon the initial step of grasping social organisation and legality as the virtual problematic of social organisation. Social organisation and legality are first of all a virtual problematic before they are instances of particular cases of solution. The starting point of the workshop was, therefore, that when considering social organisation and legality it is not adequate to consider only the extensive realm of social organisation and actualised legal systems. What needs to be explored, and indeed accounts for and operates the extensive and actualised social organisation and law, are the virtual and intensive modalities of social organisation and legality. This conceptualisation of social organisation and legality as a virtual problematic involves the drawing of the plane of immanence for social organisation and legality and upon opening up the intensive morphogenetic problem field of social organisation and legality.

Social organisation and legality are made up of the virtual problematic of social organisation, virtual machinic processes of social organisation, intensive machinic processes of social organisation, and the laying down of the social strata in extensive and actualised social systems. Social organisation and legality are multiplicities, abstract machines of legality, self-organisation and emergence, desire and the direct libidinal investment of the intensive social morphogenetic field, social assemblaging, and systems of stratifications.

Caprica introduced the three key topics to be covered in the workshop: virtual social organisation, intensive social organisation and actual social organisation.

The virtual modality of social organisation and legality concerns a cerebral machining and investment of the problematic of social organisation and the operation of drawing a plane for social organisation. This involves conceptualising legality on a virtual problem plane in terms of continuums of virtual multiplicities and of a topology of abstract machines of legality. In the topology there are the abstract machine concept-diagrams for various social machines and diverse diagrams for social assemblages. It further involves connecting social organisation and legality to cosmic forces and a necessary relation to a line of absolute social flight. The desiring investment of the virtual plane is of a people and social organisation yet to come, to desiringly invest in thinking about social organisation and legality absolutely deterritorialised, and to think of new concepts of legality and of social transformations.

The intensive modality of social organisation and legality involves the machinic desiring production and desiring investment of the intensive social problem field and of the intensive machinic social assemblages that self-organise and emerge in that intensive problem field. The intensive social field concerns the operation of social assemblages and their morphogenetic self-organisation and emergence from the intensive machinic phylum, and is a field of forces, intensities, sensations and affects. The intensive problem field of social assemblages concerns social power, the battles of social forces, and issues of what can be said, seen and lived in a social machine and social assemblage.

The extensive and actualised social organisation and legality are the existent discourses and institutions of a society's legal system and other diverse orders and systems of power and social control. These are the codings, territories and general stratifications of a social machine and other diverse social assemblages. These extensive stratifications are often the product of transcendent molar operations that organise social assemblages into unified homeostatic systems. There is the coding of regimes of discourse and regimes of bodies, and the laying down of extensive social territories. Such social systems involve systems of representation, belief in existing social values, normative social production and desire as lack.

This framework for theorisation of social organisation and legality in terms of images of social organisation, abstract machines, and intensive and extensive assemblages is, of course, a development of noology. The noology of images of thought casts thinking as a virtual problematic of what it is to think, drawing a plane of immanence for thinking so as to think all thought in terms of abstract machines of thinking, intensive assemblages of thinking and molar assemblages of thinking. Caprica's workshop would do the same for social organisation: cast social organisation and legality as the virtual problematic of social organisation; drawing a plane of immanence for social organisation and legality so as to think all social organisation and legality; and, to do so in terms of abstract machines of legality, intensive assemblages of legality, and molar assemblages of legality. In this noology the terms social organisation and legality are the concepts of the problematic of social organisation, and interchangeable as the virtual problematic, but with legalities emerging as social machines as draft solutions to the virtual problematic of social organisation, with these solutions operating across the virtual, intensive and actual modalities.

However, Caprica pointed out that in this noology of social organisation and legality much is pinned on social organisation and legality as the operator of something over and above what has previously been considered as the ontology of the earth and the noology of the brain. The claim is, as was made in the opening address of the workshop, that it is social organisation and legality that connects the earth and the brain and relates them and itself to the forces of the cosmos. Hints of this operation of social organisation and legality in connecting the earth and the brain were present in Dr Nome's lecture: the State image of thought was developed in and from the abstract machine of organisation of the State social machine; vagabond thought was inseparable from intensive social assemblages; and, schizo thinking that drives the whole of the noology is inseparable from a social machine of a new earth and a people yet to come. All these images of thought also come with constitutional relations to the earth, and with a particular relation to the forces of the cosmos, but they do so in relation to social machines and social assemblages that inform the image of thought. It would appear that in the virtual problematic of social organisation and legality that a large part of the problematic itself involves producing a solution of social organisation and legality directly addressing the problematic of how to connect the earth and the brain, and of the question how to relate this relation to the forces of the cosmos.

Of course, the claim for the operation of connecting earth and brain was tentative. Our machinic opera, our mechanosphere, is a relay of earth, brain and social organisation, all in a reciprocal presupposition in transversal consistency, all relating to the forces of the cosmos. However, from Caprica's perspective, transversal consistencies operate with an abstract machine, and if social organisation is a transversal consistency of earth, brain and social organisation, then the abstract machine of social organisation and legality would indeed be the abstract machine of our social mechanosphere.

This is why the workshop, whilst exploring social assemblages, would place at the centre of Deleuze & Guattari's social theory their concept of social machines. A social machine directly addresses the virtual problematic of social organisation, it machines an abstract machine of legality, it draws a plane and intensive body for social organisation, machining an intensive social assemblage, and laying down an actualised social assemblage of code, territory and strata. Social machines are necessary for a noology of social organisation and legality because the opening principle of this noology is to cast social organisation and legality as a virtual problematic and to draw the plane of immanence for social organisation and legality. It is the social machines that address this problematic, draw planes for social organisation and legality, and issue forth abstract machines of legality. Along the way through there would be full discussion of intensive and actualised assemblages of legality not in a direct relation to a social machine, but the noology of social organisation and legality would take Deleuze & Guattari's theory of social machines as the focus of discussions.

The noology of legality: the virtual problematic of social organisation and intensive problem field of social organisation

Thus, the noology of legality is drawing the plane of immanence for all legality theorising law as a virtual problematic, and opening up the intensive morphogenetic field of legality. The noological approach establishes two tasks for the noology of legality: to explore social machines; and, the consideration of diverse social assemblages as assemblages of legality. The noological conceptualisation of legality and social organisation are of a virtual irresolvable continually respecifying problematic of social organisation and legality. This involves an absolute counter-actualisation of all existing legalities and social organisation. The conceptualisation of legality moves from any existent legal system to the conceptualisation of an immanent problematic plane and the arising of abstract machine of legality on the plane as draft answers to the problematic without ever extinguishing or freezing the continual respecification of that problem plane. Legality and social organisation become a virtual machining in relation to the irresolvable problematic of social organisation. Thus, social organisation and legality have a problematic manifold, a plane of multiplicities, and the operation of machining consistencies amongst the multiplicities. Social organisation and legality become the virtual plane of abstract machines that self-organise and emerge in relation to both the ever respecifying problematic of social organisation, as well in relation to self-organisation and emergence in matter-energy flows in intensive and extensive social assemblages that present events into the social plane. Given the drawing of the plane of immanence to legality, the problematic of social organisation is to think about social organisation and to form new concepts of legality. This is also to hold open that existent social organisation and legality are always in a relation to transformation, to lines of flight, and to the creation of new societies and new earths.

The drawing of the plane of immanence to legality and social organisation is also to open up the intensive morphogenetic problem field for legality and social organisation. There is thus exploration beyond the extensive stratifications of legality and social organisation, connecting with the plane of immanence of social organisation and legality, an intensive social problem field. This intensive social field is a field of processes of becomings, of intensive forces and affects, in which there is the machinic phylum of legality and social organisation that is tapped to enable immanent processes of self-organisation and emergence in legality and social organisation. This intensive field is where desire directly invests the social field in desiring productions of intensities and affects, and where immanent desiring assemblages of bodies and words emerge and are occupied. It is in this intensive field that the real battles of legality and social organisation are fought, and where there are many intensive assemblages of legality, with the strata merely the record of which forces prevailed in the conflict.

In exploring social organisation and legality in its virtual register of an immanent problematic and of abstract machine multiplicities, and in its intensive register of machinic assemblages in a morphogenetic problem field, there are two different but related tasks. One is to explore the social machines that arise in relation to the virtual problematic of social organisation and which draw a plane of inscription for social organisation. This is to draw the problem plane for social organisation and the plane-body of the socius, and to machine the abstract machine of social organisation. These social machines have abstract machines of legality, their intensive machinic social assemblages, together with the code and territory they deposit as extensive stratifications. These social machines play a profound role in social organisation, and their tendencies and strategies for social organisation, together with the relations between different social machines, can be studied in the noology of social organisation in terms of a topology of abstract machines of legality. The two tendencies within social organisation are towards an immanent organisation of transversal consistency or towards a transcendent organisation of the molar fold. There are, thus, immanent abstract machines of legality and intensive social assemblages, and transcendent abstract machines of legality and molar social assemblages.

In addition, however, in exploring the virtual and intensive registers of social organisation and legality, the intensive social field opened up by a social machine drawing a plane of immanence, there are many social machinic assemblages that make up social organisation. These are intensive assemblages that perform many social functions. These include social assemblages such as market places and cities, and institutions such as hospitals and prisons. These machinic social assemblages may operate intensively or extensively, operate with virtual diagram abstract machines, and occupy large regions of the social field and lay down massive stratifications. These assemblages may be organised either intensively or molarly. All social assemblages, however, have a virtual diagram, operate a regime of signs and a regime of bodies, lay down a territory, and deal with the forces of deterritorialisation inherent in social organisation. The study of social organisation and legality, thus, also involves the extensive consideration of diverse social assemblages.

However, in noology and answering the problematic of social organisation and in laying down a plane for social organisation, and opening up the intensive problem field of social organisation and social functions, social machines have an operation that set them apart from many social assemblages, and brings directly into their operation a concept of legality.

This noology of social machines, abstract machines of legality, and intensive and molar social assemblages develops into an ecology of social organisation and into a four-stage pragmatics of social assemblages that is noological, machinic, generative and transformative. The transformative pragmatics of social organisation looks towards the absolute limit of social organisation and the emergence into social organisation of the eternal return.

Social machines

A social machine is a 'non-unifying immanent cause that is co-existent with the whole social field' (Deleuze (1988) 37), which draws a plane for addressing the problematic of social organisation and for the inscription of the socius. In this drawing of the plane for inscription of the socius, social machines have two tendencies in drawing planes, and four strategies in organising the social flows. Further, in traversing the problem field of social organisation, social machines must come to terms with the three thresholds that the problematic of social organisation presents to social organisation.

Social machines address the virtual problematic of social organisation, and they are a virtual abstract machine of legality, an intensive social assemblage, and an extensive social assemblage of code, territory and strata (D&G (1984) 139 (153)). Social machines are responses to the problematic of the plane of immanence of social organisation, and they develop and operate in the intensive problem field of social organisation, and lay down the extensive strata of their social organisation. This social machine idea connects the two modalities of becoming of earth and brain into an emergent new ethos.

The problematic of social organisation is self-posing, and the social is a virtual problematic rather than an actual entity. Social machines directly address the problematic of social organisation. Social machines are set apart from many social assemblages because social machines emerge in relation to the virtual problematic of social organisation, and it is the social machine that draws the plane of recording for all social organisation of both not only the social machine itself but also the very many diverse social assemblages that arise in the social field.

Each social machine produces a draft solution to the problematic that is flawed. The problematic of social organisation always persists beyond any draft answer by a social machine, and the problematic itself is always continuously respecifying itself, and every social assemblage has a fractal line running between its two multiplicities. The result of this is that all social machines are necessarily flawed.

The social machine is the multiplicity connecting the multiplicities of earth and brain. The social machine, through the creation and organisation of social arrangements, relates the organisation of thinking to the organisation of the earth as home. The social machine connects social organisation to the machinic multiplicities of the virtual earth and to the multiplicities of virtual thought. In organising social arrangements and in organising thought, the social machine selects the modality of the earth that is to be the ethos and connects the earth and the brain through the abstract machine of legality in a direct relation to the forces of the cosmos. Transversal to the social machine are its lines of flight that are always cosmic. The organisation a social machine operates, thus, has profound effects upon the earth selected as ethos, the organisation of thought, the connection of earth and brain, and the relation of social organisation to the cosmos.

The social machine draws a plane for addressing the problematic of social organisation and as the plane for the inscription of the socius. The social machine abstract machine draws a plane for the new socius as a recording surface for inscription, and it organises according to the multiplicity of this abstract machine that simultaneously draws the plane and organises all around it. On this plane, the social machine organises desiring production and social production. Social machines operate on the flows of social matter-energy and desiring production, blocking some flows, connecting some flows, coding these flows, and detaching elements from the coded chain (D&G (1984) 141 (155)). These operations are processes of an inscription on the recording plane-surface of the socius. The inscription allows a debtor-creditor relationship, rather than exchange, to under-pin the system of coding and inscription, and this provides for the dynamic operation of the social machine as the circulation of blocks of debts and credits. The social machine further operates to extract a surplus value from these flows of social production through the organisation of processes of anti-production, and attributes and directs this flow of surplus value to the plane-body of the socius. The social assemblages extract this surplus value from social production and attribute it to the social plane-body that is drawn by the social machine's abstract machine of legality (D&G (1984) 10 (11)). The plane-surface of inscription of the socius is:

> ...a full body that functions as the socius. It falls back upon all production constituting a surface over which the forces and agents of production are distributed, thereby appropriating for itself all surplus production and arro-gating to itself both the whole and the parts of the process, which now seem to emanate from it as a quasi-cause.
>
> (D&G (1984) 10 (11))

Social machines in drawing a plane for organisation and abstract machine of legality demonstrate two tendencies in addressing the virtual problematic of social organisation. In drawing the plane-recording surface of the socius, social machines draw recording surfaces that, whilst on a continuum, tend to approach either a plane of immanence for social organisation or alternatively a transcendent plane of organisation for social organisation.

Every social machine has an abstract machine of legality. It is the abstract machine of legality in the social machine that connects the two multiplicities of the earth and brain. The abstract machine of legality is a cerebral idea for organ-isation. It is in social machines that thinking emerges and develops. What thinks in me is the social machine in which I am taken up in, desire in and invest in.

This idea of social organisation operates as both the abstract machine of legality of the social machine and also as the abstract machine of thought. In a social machine this idea of organisation is also the image of organisation and also the image of thought of that social machine.

The social machines are effectuated in intensive and extensive social assemblages. These assemblages operate on the flows of social matter-energy, and social machines operate four strategies for organising these flows. Social machines in organising the intensive and extensive social assemblages of social organisation operate by: coding flows; decoding flows; territorialising flows; and deterritorialising flows. As the plane of the social machine draws or tends towards a transcendent plane of organisation the social machine strategies selected are those of coding and territorialising, whilst as the plane drawn or tending towards is the plane of immanence the strategies selected are those of decoding and deterritorialisation (although some social machines can combine complex combinations of all the strategies).

There is a territorial social machine defined by the organisational strategy of tightly coding and territorialising the social flows, accompanied by a mechanism of anticipation-prevention in relation to other social machines (D&G (1984) 145 (159)). There is a State social machine defined by the organisational strategy of both overcoding the territorial coding of the flows and an instant absolute deterritorialising-reterritorialisation of the territory, held together in a mechanism of apparatus of capture (D&G (1984) 192 (210); D&G (1988) 424 (468)). The territorial social machine and the State social machine tend towards drawing a plane of transcendent organisation, although with the territorial social machine doing so loosely and the State machine tending to absolutely. There is the nomad war social machine defined by the organisational strategy of decoding the coded flows and of deterritorialising all territories, without recoding or reterritorialisation, in an open distribution of a line of flight (D&G (1988) 351 (387)). There is the capitalist social machine defined by the hybrid organisational strategy of a thorough-going decoding, deterritorialisation and generalised arbitraging of economic flows, together with a substantive recoding and reterritorialisation of all the social flows in an axiomatic of social production and desiring production (D&G (1984) 222 (242)). The nomad war social machine and the capitalist social machine tend towards drawing a plane of immanence for social organisation, although the capitalist social machine requires its plane of immanence for capital to be continually supported by a plane of organisation for social production (the immense importance of nation State social machines for the capitalist social axiomatic). The nomad war social machine and the social machine of the new earth draws the plane of immanence for social organisation, and keeps thinking, desiring and social organisation on that fractal line of flight, continuously experimenting and transforming.

In a social machine its social assemblage develops two regimes in reciprocal presupposition, one which is a semiotic regime of expression, and another which is a bodily regime of material social flows and the adoption of technologies in social production. These social assemblages effectuating the social machine lay down a territory for the social machine and make stratifications for the social machine.

Social machines also have in their intensive morphogenetic problem fields three limits to strategies of social organisation: a real limit; a relative limit; and an absolute limit. These limits are thresholds when particular tendencies of drawing the plane for social organisation, and particular strategies of organising the intensive flows, fail and give way to the forces of the future to come. The real limit is the presence in the socius of decoded and deterritorialised flows. The real limit inhabits the territorial social machine as its compulsion to code and territorialise, and to block all social flows that would destroy codes and territorial stratification. Of course, the territorial social machine constantly struggles on this real limit, cruelly enforcing the codes and territories and punishing uncoded and deterritorialised flows of desiring production. The State social machine also works on this real limit, set upon ensuring that all social flows are State overcoded, and all territories are State reterritorialised, in its apparatus of capture. However, many individuations of the State social machine have become very adept at tolerating decoded and deterritorialised flows. With the emergence of the capitalist social machine, however, social organisation now surpassed this real limit and moves to occupy the relative limit of social organisation. The strategy is of social organisation and legality through the generalised decoding and deterritorialisation of all the economic flows, only limited by the retention of a relative limit of this generalised decoding and deterritorialisation in the axiomatic of social productions. This limit to social organisation is always relative, however, and the fits and starts of capitalism must be accompanied by the surpassing and repositioning of this relative limit: 'the movement by which it [capital] counteracts its own tendency – continually drawing near the wall, while at the same time pushing the wall away' (D&G (1984) 176 (192)). This arrangement, however, means that the capitalist social machine also struggles with the absolute limit of social organisation. An absolute decoding and deterritorialisation of all the flows would be the collapse and immolation of the capitalist social machine. This absolute limit of social organisation is the tendency and strategy of social organisation and legality that nomad social war machines explore, and it is this limit that is explored in the lonely creative lines of flight of schizo thinking and creation (D&G (1984) 176 (192)). At the end of the strategies of code and territory in territorial social machines, State social machines, and at the end of capitalist social machines that can no longer restrain the absolute limit of social organisation as a relative limit to its machine, the absolute limit of the plane of organisation opens up and the occupation and exploration of this absolute decoding and deterritorialisation calls forth the thinking and creation of the abstract machine of legality and assemblage of legality of the nomad social war machine and the legality of a new earth and people yet to come. Social organisation reaches the eternal return.

Social machines can co-exist with other social machines in a given social problematic plane and intensive social field, and social machines may be taken up by a power and absorbed whole by competing social machines (D&G (1988) 437 (483)). In this, a social machine may operate on prior instances of social machines to reorganise them according to the new image of organisation.

Social machines can and will form complex multiplicities with many diverse social assemblages, the social machine bending the diverse social assemblages to its image of organisation and thought, but also the greatest of the diagrams of diverse social assemblages bending the social machine's image of legality into new arrangements of fundamental ideas. The operation of the monotheistic social assemblages in relation to the State social machine is a prominent example of the complex inter-relations between social assemblages and social machines.

Social machines and diverse social assemblages can form historical forma-tions. In the intensive problem field of social organisation where relations of force, power, sensations and affects direct the morphogenesis and intensive operation of individuations and social machines and diverse social assemblages alike, relative stabilities in these relations of force and power lead to the establish-ment of social formations. This is an alliance formed between the individuation of the social machine and the individuations of diverse social assemblages in a common field of individuation of sensations, forces and affects.

In short, in the social machines there is direct investment of the problematic of social organisation in the abstract machine of legality, and in the social assem-blages there is direct investment of the intensive problem field of social organisation. Social machines are planes and fields of forces and power, where it is a matter of knowing, believing, desiring, seeing, speaking and thinking.

Abstract machines of legality

The social machine is, thus, in large part the operation of its abstract machine of legality. The abstract machine of legality has a number of features and operations, and in the noology of legality they are taken up in a topology of abstract machines of legality that allows all abstract machines of legality to be mapped into a common virtual problem space.

The abstract machine of legality addresses the problematic of social organisation. The drawing of the plane for social organisation is the operation of the social machine's abstract machine of legality. The abstract machine of legality simulta-neously composes itself and also draws the plane of consistency for social organisation (D&G (1988) 511 (562)). In doing so, the abstract machine of legal-ity connects the earth and the brain, and in this connection connects social organisation to the forces of the cosmos.

The abstract machine of legality is a machinic multiplicity. Abstract machines of legality, just as any abstract machine, are virtual, and operate with differential relations, manifolds, attractors, multiplicities and events. The theory of multi-plicities and abstract machines entails the avoidance of any thinking of the abstract machine operation in terms of totalities and essences. The abstract machine works with unformed matters of the phylum of social organisation and tensors of nonformal functions of social organisation. The abstract machine works with the variables of traits of content and traits of expression in continuous variation in virtual multiplicities meshed in the plane of immanence. The abstract machine produces consistencies in the matters of expression of social organisation and produces continuums of intensities (D&G (1988) 142 (157)). The abstract machines of legality are virtual multiplicities self-organising and emerging in relation to the problematic of social organisation. The abstract machine has the dimensions of its problem space, the distribution of singularities, and thresholds of bifurcations. The dimensions of the problem space of the abstract machine are the degrees of freedom of the problem space in which the problem requires abilities to affect or be affected.

In establishing the states and strategies of the abstract machine of legality it becomes crucial to understand the different range of singularities that can be taken up in the multiplicity of the abstract machine of legality. It is the range and balance of singularities taken up in the abstract machine and multiplicities that give differing abstract machines of legality their mode of organisation. Singularities can be point singularities, cycle singularities and fractal chaotic singularities. Highly complex abstract machines, such as all the social machines of legality, will be made up from not only an extremely high dimensionality manifold but also a distribution of very many singularities.

If the abstract machine and multiplicities are made up from a predominance of point and cycle attractors, the machine will promote a limited range of states and preponderance to produce unchanging stratic residues. In such an abstract machine of legality there may, consequently, come to develop an organisational tendency and strategies to align all singularities on the model of whole dimensionality point and cycle attractors and to close the open dimensionality of the manifold. This abstract machine of legality will tend towards the central operation of a molar fold social organisation. Social organisation becomes extensive and actual, with organisation through unities and identities, and social systems of homeostatic social organisation near-to-equilibrium. Legality and social organisation are highly coded, overcoded, territorialised and stratified.

Alternatively, the abstract machine of legality multiplicity may be made up from an abundance of fractal chaotic singularities with only a few point and cycle singularities in the abstract machines and multiplicities. Social organisation in such an abstract machine is of the transversal consistency across all the singularities in a dynamic holding together, which is precisely the fractal line of flight and instantaneous point of survey that draws the consistency of the multiplicity in continuous variation. These consistencies are in the distributions of singular and ordinary points in the multiplicity, and are precisely what machining is. In these abstract machines of legality multiplicities, social organisation is virtual and intensive, and organisation is through dynamic consistencies in flux, bent towards exploring the problematic and problem field of social organisation, ever experimenting with new arrangements of legality and social organisation.

The abstract machine of legality pilots and drives the development of the social assemblage of the social machine. The abstract machine organises social production, and appropriates all of production and the forces and agents of production (D&G (1984) 10 (11)). It organises the flows, and sets some apart as surplus value attributable to the body of the socius of the social machine. The abstract machine in organising social production also organises and structures desiring production, and organises what can be thought, what can be seen and what can be said in the social assemblage.

The abstract machine also operates to extract social events to respecify the virtual problematic plane and problems space of the social machine. The abstract machine of legality extracts and relays social events in states of affairs and intensive social becomings back onto the problematic plane of social organisation (D&G (1988) 142 (157)). The abstract machines of legality tend to select all those social events that change everything both past and future for the problematic of social organisation.

It is the abstract machine of legality that, in connecting earth and brain, also opens up social organisation to the forces of the cosmos. The earth is selected as variations of planomenon, ecumenon and mechanosphere, and the cosmic forces that forge across all of these modalities of the earth are then directly injected into social organisation and the connection between earth and brain. However, the abstract machines of legality connect the social to the cosmos in differing ways depending upon their organisational multiplicity. The abstract machines of legality of mainly point and cycle singularities that draw the transcendent plane of organisation, or at least draw close to this plane, connect to the forces of the cosmos by way of the ecumenon, despot gods and theology. The abstract machines of legality of mainly chaotic fractal singularities that draw a plane of immanence for social organisation (leaving aside capitalism at this point) directly connect to the forces of the cosmos since the organisation of social arrangements is by way of immanent transversal consistencies.

This abstract machine of legality is the image of organisation of the social machine. This image of organisation in all circumstances is a virtual diagram multiplicity, and this abstract machine of legality will orientate how things are organised and work in the social machine, as well as orientating what it is to think in the social machine. In the abstract machine of legality the image of organisation is also the image of thought. The abstract machine of legality is the relation of the social organisation to thinking about the social, and also orientates the investment of thought and desiring production in the problematic of social organisation and of the social machine that has emerged from this problematic.

With abstract machines of legality understood in this way there can be established a topology of abstract machines of legality. With the abstract machine of legality there is, therefore, the noology of abstract machines of legality. In the virtual problematic plane there is a common problematic immanent plane where all the abstract machines of legality can be topologically diagrammed. Thus, the topological manifold of the problematic of social organisation is populated by the abstract machines of legality of the territorial, State, nomad social war, and the capitalist social machines. Each abstract machine of legality multiplicity occupies its own dimensionality, its own distribution of singularities, and its own abstract machine operation. However, the problem space of the problematic can be mapped and explored, the relation between different abstract machines of legality explored, relations of virtual transformations between social machines investigated, and, most importantly, the creation of new abstract machines of legality thought, and relations of transformations from existing social machines explored.

Thus, the noology and topology of abstract machines of legality develops on the following basis. The starting point is that social organisation needs to be understood in its virtual operation. Second, all social machines, even those that draw a plane of organisation, operate a virtual abstract machine of legality. Third, at the level of the virtual social organisation is the problematic of social organisation, and is thought in terms of a plane of immanence as a very high dimensionality manifold. Fourth, that this manifold is populated by abstract machines of legality as consistent distributions of singularities. Thus, different abstract machines of legality can be thought in the same problem space of social organisation. Further, from this the virtual relations between different abstract machines of legality can be thought, and thresholds of transformations explored. Finally, thus the problematic of social organisation is opened up to the future, to experimentation, and to the creation of new abstract machines of legality.

Introduction to social assemblages

> Assemblages swing between a territorial closure that tends to restratify them and a deterritorialising movement that on the contrary connects them with the Cosmos.
>
> (D&G (1988) 337 (371))

Social assemblages are about problems of what can be desired, of what can be believed in, of what can be said, and of what can be seen, and of social forces and social power. The operation of all social assemblages is 'the micropolitics of the social field' (Deleuze (1988b) 7), and assemblages operate in a social problem field of forces, power and knowledge. A social assemblage encompasses a regime of signs, a regime of bodies and technology, a territory and a relation to the forces of deterritorialisation. Social assemblages tend towards either a molar extensive organisation or an intensive immanent organisation.

Social assemblages both effectuate abstract machines of legality in social machines, and are social assemblages that self-organise and emerge without direct reference to any social machine. There are some social assemblages that effectuate and individuate social machines and which self-organise and emerge on the recording surface of the socius and establish the organisation of social production and desiring production. However, the social field is additionally constituted and organised by machinic social assemblages that are integrations of social functions, and form agencies and power institutions. These assemblages of agencies and institutions include the family, villages, market places, case law jurisdictions, cities, hospitals, prisons and religions. These assemblages of social functions attach to the recording surface of the social machine, tending to be isomorphic to the organisational tendencies and strategies of the social machine they arise within. This isomorphism though regular is not necessary, and there frequently arise organisational innovation in social assemblages as against that of the social machine. These diverse social assemblages have virtual abstract machine diagrams (Deleuze (1988b) 35). Indeed, there can be substantial supplementation and blending of the social machine with social function assemblages.

Social assemblages are dynamic and not fixed in their operation. Social assemblages may swing between territorial closure and open deterritorialisation, between the plane of transcendence and the plane of immanence, between being organised as a molar social assemblage and becoming organised as an intensive social assemblage. The intensive social assemblages operate in the intensive morphogenetic social problem field, and the extensive molar social assemblages operate in actualised molar coding, territorialisation and general stratifications. In the continuum between immanence and transcendence, every social assemblage will have a virtual diagram and intensive morphogenetic field, even if these are obscured by the assemblage.

However, despite the very wide range of social assemblages and different ways to organise social assemblages, there are a number of common features to all social assemblages: they all owe their genesis to processes of self-organisation and emergence; their assemblage is always of two multiplicities (expression and materiality); they produce a regime of signs as jurisdiction, and a material regime of bodies and technology; they operate machinic statements and order-words, with associated incorporeal transformations; they have a particular relation between the multiplicity of signs and the multiplicity of bodies; they have a virtual diagram; they lay down a territory; and they all maintain a relation to deterritorialisation and the forces of the cosmos.

Social assemblages all have a relation to self-organisation and emergence in the intensive outside space of the intensive morphogenetic field, although the way a social assemblage is organised will be the result of whether these immanent outside forces are used to organise intensively or molarly. In every social assemblage there is, or has been, the battle of the intensive forces of self-organisation and emergence. All social assemblages self-organise and emerge on the place of an outside where the forces of their genesis emerged. Self-organisation and emergence occur in composing forces operating 'in a different space to that of forms, the space of the Outside, where the relation is precisely a "non-relation", the place a "non-place"' (Deleuze (1988b) 87). This outside is where social assemblages organise social forces, social power and social knowledge, and carry out this organising in the intensive morphogenetic field of social organisation that is the social problem field where the assemblages tap forces of self-organisation and emergence that develop the assemblage in relation to these problems. The assemblages organise matter-energy flows at the level of the socius, connecting materiality to the intense forces of organisation.

Social assemblages are made up of two intersecting multiplicities. In the manner that social machines and abstract machines of legality connect up two multiplicities of the earth and the brain, social assemblages connect up intensively or extensively a multiplicity of expression and signs and a multiplicity of bodies and materials. The social assemblage's regime of signs and a regime of bodies constitute the knowledge of the assemblage. There is a multiplicity of the said, of discourse, language elements, expression and statements. The other multiplicity is that of the seen, of bodies, content, actions and passion, and technology. In connecting the multiplicities organising expression and the multiplicities organising bodies and technology social assemblages arrange a semiotic regime of expression and a material regime of bodies and technology. Social assemblages, whether effectuating a social machine or effectuating a social function, and whether intensively or extensively molar organised, develop as the morphogenesis of two multiplicities, a multiplicity of enunciative and language forces and elements and a multiplicity of body and technology forces and elements. There develops a regime of what is sayable in a regime of signs and a regime of what is visible in a regime of content, both in dynamic reciprocal presupposition, even when the assemblage heralds their separation.

In social assemblages it is a regime of signs and the multiplicity of expression that sets the pragmatic, performative, illocutionary and semantic context for the operation of signs, language and the language-face conjunction. The multiplicity of expression works on the semiotic flows across the social field. The multiplicity of expression develops as a semiotic regime that is a social collective assemblage of enunciation where speech and discourse are free indirect speech and discourse that comes from the social machine: 'My direct discourse is still the free indirect discourse running through me, coming from other worlds or planets' (D&G (1988) 84 (94)). This collective assemblage of enunciation is organised on the virtual and intensive implicit presuppositions that are the result of the ordering of forces and powers in the social field and which articulate what can be said and what cannot be said. In collective assemblages of enunciation the agents of enunciation are virtual and intensive multiplicities rather than actualised societies or individuals (D&G (1988) 37 (42)). The social assemblages attach statements to the socius in a collective assemblage of enunciation. The collective assemblage of enunciation is always much more than language and words (D&G (1988) 90 (100)). It is the collective assemblage of enunciation that is determinative and selective in the constitution and functioning of a particular language (D&G (1988) 63 (70)).

The social assemblages attach bodies to the socius in a machinic assemblage of bodies. The machinic assemblage of bodies is always much more than tools, techniques and goods (D&G (1988) 90 (100)). It is the machinic assemblage of bodies that is determinative and selective of what technologies are employed in social production (D&G (1988) 63 (70)). Social assemblages' multiplicities of materiality seek to organise diverse material flows of desire and of machinic vitalism. The multiplicity of content does so by diversely blocking off, cutting up, dividing, setting aside, the material flows of the intensive social field, selecting some flows and machinic vitality, and adopting from the machinic phylum only approved technological lineages to be taken up in the social assemblage (D&G (1988) 398 (439)). In the multiplicity of materiality it is the abstract machine of legality that selects and determines what flows and intermingling of social bodies will enter into social organisation and of how desiring production will become social production, and selects and determines what technologies will be employed in social production and the distribution and take up of tools, techniques and goods in the social assemblage (D&G (1988) 63 (70)). The multiplicity of materiality is primary in relation to the technical machines, inventing technical phyla (D&G (1988) 407 (449)), and selects the technical elements and usages (D&G (1988) 397–8 (437–8)). Desiring production and the continuous evolution of the machinic phylum are what the multiplicities of materiality take up in a regime of the materiality of social production, but they tend to do so in a way that blocks the immanent materiality of desiring production and of the machining of the material flows (D&G (1984) 116 (127)). Social production is always machining and desiring production but under the determinative conditions of the social assemblages' multiplicity of materiality (D&G (1984) 29 (31)).

Through the collective assemblage of enunciation the abstract machine of legality enters into the matters of expression and into the socius in the constitution and transmission of order-words and statements (D&G (1988) 333 (367) and 79 (87)). Statements and order-words appear in the social field as products of collective assemblages of enunciation. The statements and order-words of a collective assemblage of enunciation appear in the language discourse of the collective assemblage of enunciation as so many varying instances of how things are and what must be done. In this, the statements and order-words operate immanently and internally in enunciation but whilst remaining external to the constants of language (D&G (1988) 83 (92)). Statements and order-words are variables of expression of the collective assemblage of enunciation, and operate in the assemblage as integrations of the abstract machine of legality into actualised social organisation. In this respect, statements are the simultaneous expression of the social forces and powers of a problem and the intensive and actualising answer to that problem of social organisation. In their operation, statements and order-words establish the relationship between the pragmatic context of forces and powers of the social machine and the specifics of language, speech and discourse (D&G (1988) 82 (91)). The statements and order-words enter into the socius and organise it on the basis that the collective assemblage of enunciation attributes social bodies with incorporeal states and qualities. The operation of statements and order-words in a collective assemblage of enunciation is that they effect incorporeal transformations of social bodies, instantaneously and immanently, and the incorporeal attributes of that social body are changed in new configurations of social bodies (D&G (1988) 80 (89)). These statements and order-words effect incorporeal transformations that are veritable deterritorialisations and reterritorialisations of the body involved.

In a collective regime of enunciation a connected family of statements is a set that constitutes a discursive formation that is accompanied by its corollary set of incorporeal transformations. The set of all statements arising in a social field of a collective assemblage of enunciation constitutes the knowledge of social organisation produced and operative in that social assemblage.

In a social assemblage the multiplicity of expression and the multiplicity of materiality will have a particular relation to each other. This relationship crosses the fractal line that runs between these multiplicities, operating either a transversal consistency of intensively interweaving them, or of establishing a double articulation that always folds materiality into molar expression.

In the intensive self-organisation and emergence of the social assemblage each multiplicity provides an exterior for the other, and their warp and woof reciprocal presupposition is a non-relation, and a fractal line runs through the relation of what can be said and what can be seen. In this respect, intensive social assemblages are heterogeneous and flat, with the assemblage speaking on the same level as bodies and content (D&G (1988) 87 (96)). Indeed, it is in this feature of intensive social assemblages of speaking on the same level as bodies that the operation of the machinic statement and order-word are to be found. The social assemblage is the intensive interweaving and reciprocal presupposition of the regime of signs and the regime of bodies, the incorporeal transformations as the expressed of statements (events), and the passions of bodies as formed contents (intermingling of bodies). In this interweaving of the semiotic traits of expression and the material traits of content in the constant intersection of their multiplicities that are immanent to each other: 'The form of expression is constituted by the warp of expressed, and the form of content by the woof of bodies... The warp of the instantaneous transformations is always inserted into the woof of continuous modifications' (D&G (1988) 86 (95)).

All social assemblages have a virtual abstract machine diagram of the interweaving of their two multiplicities (Deleuze (1988b) 35). These diagrams of social organisation operate in 'a cartography coextensive with the whole social field' (Deleuze (1988b) 34), and there have been 'as many diagrams as there are social fields in history' (Deleuze (1988b) 34) in the virtual plane of social assemblages.

Social assemblages lay down a territory. The territories may be intensive territories as well as extensive territories. Social territories distribute people and regulate access to resources. They are an autonomous zone amongst the milieus, and have an interior region, an exterior region, some boundary or threshold between the two, and a region of resources. They are defined by the emergence of matters of expression (D&G (1988) 315 (348)). A territory emerges in the self-movement of expressive qualities and the self-movement of the material flows, and the relations between the two: 'What defines the territory is the emergence of matters of expression (qualities)...The T factor...in the emergence of proper qualities (colour, odor, sound, silhouette...)' (D&G (1988) 315–16 (348)).

The territory is the expression of the assemblage's diagram of the interweaving of the multiplicity of expression and materiality. In this, the nature of the available milieus for territorialisation will have, of course, a very significant impact upon how the social assemblage organises itself and its territory. Further, the territories are always laid in relation to the earth (actual earth, intensive earth, cosmic virtual earth) and so, depending upon the type of earth the social assemblage connects to, there will be scope there to change and transformation to the territory.

Social assemblages are also characterised, finally, by their relation to forces of decoding and deterritorialisation, and to the cosmic forces of the earth and brain that are injected into all social assemblages. It is in this relation that the most profound differences between intensive and molar social assemblages are found.

Indeed, beyond a certain common ground on operating two multiplicities, the operation of the social assemblage crucially turns on whether it is organised intensively between the two planes of immanence and transcendence or whether it is organised by the molar fold. In the case of extensive molar social assemblages, the operation of the molar expressionist fold organises the social assemblage in the model of self-contained unity, truth, knowledge, and desire as lack, largely blocking the relation to decoding and deterritorialisation. However, nonetheless, the molar social assemblages are burdened with the breaking up of their strata into epistrata and parastrata, as the cosmic creative forces mutate and put in variation their stratifications. In the case of intensive social assemblages the molar fold is not organisational, and rather it is precisely the forces of decoding and deterritorialisation, and all the forces of self-organisation and emergence that decoding and deterritorialisation tap, that provide the social assemblage with its dynamic and transversal consistency organisation. The social assemblage is organised on the multiplicity consistencies of its abstract machine, and upon intensive consistencies of intensities-affects-events that deploy blocks of sensation-affects-forces, extensively laying down only traces of code and broken lines of territory.

Molar social assemblages

Molar social assemblages are those assemblages that operate on or at least face a plane of organisation, and which organise social assemblages through strategies of coding, overcoding, territory and reterritorialisation. There are molar social assemblages effectuating molar social machines, but there are very many molar social assemblages providing diverse functions. The clear characteristic of molar social assemblages, in addition to this mode of organisation, is their extensive actualisation and ostensive closure to virtual and intensive processes of organisation.

This characteristic of molar social assemblages is the propensity for coding everything, territorialising everything and generally stratifying the socius, and goes some way to explain why so much of social organisation and law appears to be organised in molar social assemblages. Molar social assemblages have been successful in occupying the social field and in spreading molar understandings and practices of thinking and desiring, with the result that the vast majority of human beings are caught up and individuated within molar assemblages, with the consequent impact upon how they think and desire. From the perspective of molar social organisation there is only molar social assemblages and the social, and nothing else.

The success of molar social organisation is grounded in the fact that there is on the earth a molar expressionism in creation and in nature, and in the arrival of the God with the molar fold and the double articulation so necessary to the development of organic life. In the discussion of the social machines it was seen that social machines can take molar abstract machines of legality as their mode of organisation. So also, some social machines develop a molar social assemblage for the social machine, and there can be many other social functions and problems that are taken up in social assemblages that are organised on the model of molar organisation and ideas originating in the molar social machine. In a social space in which a molar social machine is dominant in the form of a State, that social space would also be occupied by many social assemblages organised molarly.

However, before proceeding to set out an account of molar social assemblages, it is important to note that this account is of an ideally molar social assemblage. Some molar social assemblages may only just face the transcendent plane of organisation coding and territorialising their flows without a full implementation of a molar fold organisation to their social machine and social assemblages. Thus, with the territorial organisation of a social machine the goal is to tightly organise all the flows in code and territory whilst warding off the molar fold (D&G (1984) 151 (166)). In this situation, molar social assemblages may be organised in code and territory. Also to be noted is that social assemblages are rarely ideally molar (or, for that matter, ideally intensive), rather than pursuing a social existence that is one of a becoming more or less molar or of becoming more or less intensive. A molar social assemblage may, further, be constituted in large aspects of what must be considered an immanent intensive operation of power, but which could nonetheless be organised as a molar social assemblage (an assemblage of surveillance, but which is organised by a line of command hierarchy, for example). In practice, however, the operation of molar organisation in a social assemblage will be clear to identify.

Molar social assemblages deal with the same problems that intensive social assemblages deal with. The molar social assemblage is concerned with issues of what can be said, by whom, and when, issues of arranging material social flows, of what can be seen, and the organisation of bodies. It is concerned with statements and order-words and incorporeal transformations. The molar social assemblages also lay down complex territories, and must deal with issues of forces of deterritorialisation. However, the organisation of the social assemblages as molar leads to a very different operation than that of intensive social assemblages.

Molar organisation of social assemblages pulls the molar God and the molar fold of expressionism into diverse social assemblages. This is the operation of a transcendent idea of organisation through a unity, the operation as against the plane of immanence of a despotic signifier that draws a transcendent plane of organisation and effects a totalising overcoding. This involves the operation of the translation of social multiplicities into a four-whole dimension abstract machine for organisation together with a closure to an outside with a strong inside-outside boundary. Thus, molar social assemblages differ in very significant respects to the intensive social assemblages.

Molar social assemblages are organisationally closed, tend towards clear inside-outside/member-non-member group segregation, with group membership to be largely homogenous. Molar social assemblages are organised in a hierarchy or arborescent tree structure, organisationally arranged as a system that is internally regulatory and homeostatic. The assemblages tend towards being organisationally reflexive to concerns of essence and identity of the assemblage, with high levels of built-in redundancies and bureaucracies. Such molar social assemblages demonstrate an ability to only interact with other molar social assemblages, and then only in a structural coupling that does not compromise their organisational closure.

In relation to the semiotic social flows and the material flows of bodies the molar assemblage, following on from the molar fold, operates the double articulation of substance and form, and expression and content. In place of a multiplicity of expression and a multiplicity of materiality interweaving on a reciprocal fractal line, the molar double articulation operation separates out a distinct formed plane of expression and a distinct formed plane of content. This produces a unity of composition of the molar stratum in formal traits and substantial elements (D&G (1988) 513 (565)). The molar social assemblage develops from the formed plane of expression a regime of signs and expression and from the formed plane of matters of content a regime of bodies and content. In the operation of the double articulation it is content that is submitted to the fold of expression. The reciprocal presupposition of expression and materiality is settled by the imposition of molar organisation on matter. The substances and forms of material are organised into the formed substances that expression fold into content, with the emergent property of unified organisation and homeostatic internal regulation. The molar social assemblage has a regime of signs consisting of a form of expression and a substance of expression, and a regime of bodies consisting of a form of content and a substance of content.

The molar regime of signs is transcendently structured by the master signifier in the molar social fold, and expression is now overcoded by the signifying order. In the molar regime of signs the set of statements firmly become order-words demanding compliance and shaping bodies through discourse, and it is this set of order-words that is the form of expression of the molar social assemblage, with the substance of expression being the language that the set of order-words are deployed in. The scope and the range of the operation of the set of statements of a molar social assemblage is its jurisdiction.

The molar regime of bodies is now cut off from virtual and intensive processes, and structured as passive matter by the overcoding of expression. The regime of bodies becomes the submission of all matter to imposed forms and the exercise of an overpowering ability to affect bodies. The substance of content makes up all the bodies and raw materials taken up in the molar social assemblage's regime of content, and the form of content being the complex inter-operation of power in the social field.

The upshot of the double articulation operation in molar social assemblages is that these assemblages are further characterised by a pervasive hylomorphism. Hylomorphism is to see matter as necessarily passive, and that the only way it is possible to organise anything in nature or social organisation is the imposition of the transcendent organising imposition of expression and form. Molar social assemblages, thus, operate with an overcoding in both expression and materiality that closes down the intensive problem field and the virtual problematic of social organisation, and denying anything other than actualised and extensive organisation. Molar social assemblages, further, code the intensive and virtual modalities of organisation as chaos and undifferentiation. The composed forces are cut off from the composing forces.

Just as with intensive social assemblages, molar social assemblages develop a territory and engage with forces of deterritorialisation, though in a very different way to intensive social assemblages. The organisational principle of the molar fold and the absolute centrality to organisation of coding and territory means that molar social assemblages are clearly characterised by the extent of their territories and the unity of their coding with the territory. Molar social assemblages will always have an actualised, fixed, bounded, developed, built on, invested in, extensive territory. The passion for closure of the molar fold is physically played out in a passion for the enclosure of the territory and for the territory of the assemblage as patrimony. The unity of the molar social assemblage's regime of signs and regime of bodies will coincide with the unity of the territory, with the territory being the physical unity and operation of the two regimes. It is the molar territory that doubles the jurisdiction of the molar assemblage's regime of order-words, as it is the territory that grounds and encloses the assemblage's regime of bodies: the molar social assemblage's unity of jurisdiction and territory.

Indeed, molar social assemblages do not merely lay down a territory. Rather, molar social assemblages are intrinsically territorial. The point of social organisation is precisely to occupy territory, and to expand that territory if possible. The social field is carved up in the territories of so many molar social machines. This territory is built in stone and steel as the materials of the greatest durability and strength, and the occupation of the territory involves a great counting and record keeping of the territory.

However, with molar social assemblages much more is organised than territories and the administration of those territories. The stratification of the social field extends into the organisation of the bodies and brains of those that are caught within the territory of the molar social assemblage. Molar social assemblages are responsible for the great stratifications of organism, subjectification, signification and interpretation (D&G (1988) 134 (148)). It is these stratifications that produce the subject within molar social machines as a subject of desire as lack, and an Oedipal and paranoic investment of the social field and of all the molar social machines. Through molar social machines the strata pile up: archaeological and historical compositions, a stratified socius, and the archive of knowledge of all these molar social assemblage residues.

Yet, the molar social assemblages are never free from forces of deterritorialisation. The earth is absolute deterritorialisation and the strata merely transiently occupy that plane of consistency, taking on the plane of consistency 'forming areas of thickenings, coagulations, and belts' (D&G (1988) 513 (565)). Molar social assemblages are inseparable from processes of decoding and deterritorialisation (D&G (1988) 336 (370)). The molar social assemblages do substantial work to try and resist and contain deterritorialisation and lines of flight from their territories and strata. There are three key strategies deployed by molar social assemblages. A first approach is to reterritorialise the deterritorialising line of flight, whether by order-word, power over bodies, or institutions of territoriality. Second, the deterritorialising line of flight can be assigned a wholly negative value, and so segmented and broken. Third, the line of flight can be seized upon by a molar social machine and that line plunged into black holes of abolition (D&G (1988) 143 (158)). However, the lines of flight continue and the molar social assemblages' stratifications are continually broken up in social epistrata and parastrata, where desiring machines and intensive social assemblages can self-organise and emerge and deterritorialise the molar social assemblages in some ways.

Intensive social machinic assemblages

The vagabond intensive social assemblages operate in the intensive morphogenetic problem field of social organisation. This field is immanent (Deleuze (1988b) 27), and a field of immersion in sensations, affects and becomings. It is an intensive field of self-posing social problems and of corollary immanent processes of machinic desiring production and of self-organisation and emergence in the social flows. The self-posing social problems of the intensive morphogenetic field are the issues of organising expressive and semiotic flows and of organising the passions of bodies and the material social flows. These intensive problems present themselves as sensations, intensities, affects, events, desire, and the social battles of forces and powers. This intensive social field is immediately invested and produced by desire as an issue of flows, intensities, affects and becomings. This desiring investment of the intensive social field is of the whole intensive social field, and is a direct investment of the intensive field without any need of metaphor, mediation or sublimation (D&G (1984) 29 (31)).

This desiring production and investment of the intensive social field is an intensive machining. From the perspective of the intensive social field 'there is only desire and the social, and nothing else' (D&G (1984) 29 (31)). This intensive desiring production operates in sensation, intensity and affects, and so does intensive machining. Virtual machining operates in the virtual multiplicities in the manner of mathematics or music. Intensive machining operates in the intensive morphogenetic field in the manner of sensing singularities and thresholds, of being run through with intensities, of machinic processes affecting other machinic processes, and, in turn, being affected by machinic processes that possess them. Intensive desiring is intensive machining, such that from the perspective of the intensive social field there is intensive machining and nothing else. Indeed, it is the virtual and intensive machinic processes that account for desiring production (D&G (1984) 42 (45)), and 'desire is a machine, and the object of desire is another machine connected to it' (D&G (1984) 27 (29)). The intensive social field is inseparable from the engendering of desiring machines.

The intensive forces of machining and assembling are to make connections in the social flows and to work with sensations, intensities, affects and events. It is to pursue a following, prospecting, and detecting of the flows and the events in the morphogenetic problem field of social organisation, so as to tap and trigger immanent forces of self-organisation and emergence of the intensive field. These processes are of increasing intensities, composing plateaus of intensities, and creating transversal consistencies of sensation-intensity-affect-event. It is the work of desiring production that moves in an intensive field of vibrations, waves, speeds and slowness, sensations, intensities, affects and being affected, and the crossing of thresholds.

What emerges in the intensive morphogenetic field are intensive social assemblages (an intensive social assemblage is a desiring machine). These assemblages concern the social problems all assemblages confront, and intensive social assemblages develop regimes of signs, regimes of content, intensive territories, and establish a relation to forces of deterritorialisation. However, by virtue of their involvement with intensive forces, and by virtue of their mode of organisation that remains intensive, these assemblages operate very differently from molar assemblages.

Intensive social assemblages organise themselves through the organisational strategies of decoding and deterritorialistion. Whilst for molar assemblages the issue was to maximise the formalisation and separation of expression and content, the issue with intensive assemblages is to attain a consistency of expression-materiality in continuous variation. Whilst for molar assemblages the issue was to maximise the operation of territoriality and minimise deterritorialisation, the issue with intensive assemblages is to ever increase the operation of deterritorialisation and to create a dynamic intensive territory. For intensive assemblages the issue is not that of organising so as to obtain an emergent property of unity and homeostatic regulation of a social assemblage, but an issue of attaining an emergent capacity for intense becomings and transformations. For an intensive social assemblage it is a matter of how a material vitalism of social organisation is followed and tapped, and of how a nomos enters into social materiality. The relations and elements of an intensive social assemblage are decoded and deterritorialised intensities, and it is in the emergence of a transversal consistency of transformation across these intensive relations and elements that the social assemblage finds its immanent organisation. It is the decoding of the relations and elements of expression and content, and deterritorialisation, which define the organisational modality of intensive social assemblages. Decoding and deterritorialisation are the cutting edges of intensive social assemblages (D&G (1988) 141 (155)): 'In effect, what holds an assemblage together is not the play of framing forms or linear causalities, but, actually and potentially, its most deterritorialised component, a cutting edge of deterritorialisation' (D&G (1988) 336 (371)).

The intensive social assemblages are assemblages of the exterior forces of composing, and not the assemblages of the composed stratifications. This organising consistency of decoding and deterritorialisation in intensive social assemblages puts these assemblages in a direct and continuing relation to deterritorialisation and the forces of the cosmos. Whilst molar social assemblages subject the forces of the cosmic to transcendence, intensive social assemblages are constitutionally connected to cosmic lines of flight and to the tapping of cosmic forces.

The intensive social assemblage emerges as the intersection of the multiplicity of expression and the multiplicity of bodies-technologies. The multiplicity of expression is an intensive consistency of heterogeneous traits of expression and traits of language that itself has emerged from immanent processes of matters becoming expressive and becoming semiotic in social organisation. The multiplicity of bodies-technologies is also an intensive consistency of traits of content and traits of technology that has emerged from immanent processes of matter-movement and the material vitalism of the machinic phylum of social organisation. The intensive social assemblage is the interweaving of these two multiplicities in a new multiplicity consistency that draws upon the high levels of decoding and deterritorialisation in the consistencies of expression and content to transversally organise the consistency of the social assemblage. There is no hylomorphism in these arrangements, and expression and content are not separated out in a double articulation of the imposition of expression on content. Rather, the intensive social assemblage interweaves a highly heterogeneous consistency across all the relations and elements of expression and materiality. In this consistency the two multiplicities operate as the outside for the other, and their non-relation in the consistency becomes the fractal line that draws the plane of composition for their transversal consistency. The matters of expression and the matters of content speak on the same level as each other in the consistency.

This consistency that the intensive social machine composes is a consistency of sensation-intensity-affect-event. The traits of expression and the traits of content that the multiplicities presented to the intensive social assemblage in the intensive morphogenetic problem field are precisely the sensations and intensities, and relations of affect and being affected, which make up this intensive field. What intensive social assemblages do is to compose blocks of consistent sensation-intensity-affect-events, and compose consistent planes of intensive social forces in plateaus of intensities. The intensive assemblage may compose many new consistencies of sensation-intensity-affect-events, and an intensive social assemblage may be a rich and complex knowledge and operation of intensive consistencies.

For intensive social assemblages these blocks of intensive consistencies are not just triumphs of composing with the immanent forces of the intensive morphogenetic field. These block consistencies are precisely intensive cases of solution without precedent to intensively posed social problems. Intensive social assemblages are assemblages of problem solving. Their intensive field presents to the assemblage social problems as problems of forces, intensities, affects and power that may befall a body or social circumstance. An intensive social assemblage does not simply impose a plane of transcendence on the social problem and apply an already formulated universal rule. Intensive assemblages are assemblages of the social problem field, and each problem is a unique problem set, and worked with as a problem of desire, affects, force and power. The composed consistency is the creation of a case of solution to the problem without precedent.

Indeed, in intensive social assemblages these consistencies of sensation-intensity-affect-event that the assemblage composes and which the assemblage generates as intensive problems and cases of solution without precedent are precisely the machinic statements of the assemblage. The machinic statements of an assemblage are those key pragmatically set statements whereby the assemblage diagram abstract machine enters into the arrangements of the social affairs to effect incorporeal transformations and attribute these to bodies. In intensive social assemblages the operation of the machinic statements and the incorporeal transformations are, of course, all interweaved in intensity. However, the consistencies that the assemblage creates are what operates in the assemblage as that machinic intervention that enters into bodies' circumstances in the social field and transforms them in relation to social problems that confront them.

Thus, intensive social assemblages are the social assemblages of social transformations. It is the social formation that deals with the battles of immanent forces, warding off the establishment of power that for the most part dominate the organisation of social assemblages, and strive to press forward with difficult problems, to create new consistencies, and to trigger becomings and transformations.

The territory that an intensive assemblage creates is intensive itself, and is a consistency in its movements and wanderings. This intensive territory is the intensive connection multiplicity between the multiplicity of expression and the multiplicity of content. The minimal arrangements for the establishment of an intensive territory would be an expression of the connection multiplicity in an autonomous zone of expression (a refrain) (D&G (1988) 310 (342)). Intensive territories draw very close to the intensive earth, and they exist only in traits of code and broken lines of territorialisation. Some intensive social assemblages do develop complex intensive territories of expressive matters and song lines. However, the territorial principle of intensive social assemblages is that desiring machines are rolling stones.

Yet, intensive assemblages claim for themselves an intensive territory undreamed of in molar assemblages. Their territory is the intensive morphogenetic problem field itself. This can be in an extensive territory of the holey space of the intensive assemblage's own operation between desert and the State walls. There are the holey spaces of mines that the social assemblages of miners and metallurgists intensively hold (D&G (1988) 414 (456)). However, for intensive social assemblages it is the intensive problem field itself that is the territory as ethos. The territory is the belonging to the ethos of an intensive problem field, and where ever the intensive problem field leads the assemblage in its following and prospecting is the intensive and actual territory of the assemblage.

Thus, in intensive social assemblages there is always a following of the intensive social flows and intensities, and of a prospecting of the problem field and the intensive social flows. Intensive social assemblages are accordingly inherently experimental in exploring the problem field and in creating unique morphogenetic individuations of cases of solution to the intensive traits of the problem.

Thus, a full list of the features of intensive social assemblages can now be drawn up. There is: an intensive morphogenetic problem field of sensation, affect and desiring production; the organisational operation is in processes of decoding and deterritorialisation and connects the assemblage directly to cosmic forces; this organisation is of decoded and deterritorialised consistencies of the multiplicities of expression and materiality; these consistencies of traits of expression and traits of content are consistencies of sensation-intensity-affect-event as a composed plane of intensive forces; these consistencies of sensation-intensity-affect-event are the cases of solution without precedent to intensive social problems; that these consistencies of sensation-intensity-affect-event as cases of solution without precedent to social problems are the social assemblage's machinic statements, and, hence, also its incorporeal transformations; and, the intensive territory is the assemblage's wanderings and followings, but it is primarily the intensive problem field itself. Intensive social assemblages are: desiring machines; assemblages of deterritorialised consistency; assemblages of composition; assemblages of transformations; assemblages of following, prospecting, looking for intensive problems and the generation of intensive cases of solution; and assemblages, in all this, of experimentation.

A conclusion can then be advanced on intensive social assemblages. An intensive social assemblage, just as with a molar social assemblage, has a jurisdiction and a territory. The jurisdiction of an intensive social assemblage is its intensive problems, its cases of solution without precedent, and its machinic statements of transformation. The territory of an intensive social assemblage is its intensive problem field and its wanderings and prospecting. It is vagabond.

A diverse ecology of social machines and social assemblages

The social theory of the virtual and intensive machining and the theory of molar social assemblages would have to come together in a larger account of a diverse ecology of social machines and social assemblages, comprising, minimally, a social plane of immanence, a plane of transcendent organisation, an intensive social problem field, and actualised social stratifications, with many different social machines and social assemblages arising and moving across this space. In this it would be agreed that the molar social assemblages are extremely successful in occupying social space and stratifying it, but that this molar occupation and stratification is very far from the full story of social organisation and legality.

Thus, there are social machines, consisting of abstract machines of legality, social assemblages effectuating an abstract machine of legality, and the social strata laid down. There are also diverse social assemblages meeting diverse social problems, and the diverse strata that the social assemblages lay down. Some of these social machines and social assemblages have a tendency to operate organisational strategies related to a social plane of immanence, some other social machines and social assemblages have a tendency to operate organisational strategies related to a social plane of transcendent organisation. What all social machines and social assemblages share and participate in is an intensive morphogenetic social problem field. This intensive field is the field of self-organisation and emergence in social organisation and legality where machining creates social assemblages as relays between diagrams and the strata as social organisation. A pragmatics of social organisation and legality takes all social machines and social assemblages as connected as a rhizome in this intensive social problem field between the social plane of immanence and the social plane of organisation, and pursues a number of lines of thought in relation to these social machines and social assemblages (this is schizoanalysis (D&G (1984) 340 (373))). These lines of thought are: a noological pragmatics of abstract machines of legality; a machinic pragmatics of effectuation of a social machine in a particular social assemblage; a generative pragmatics of diverse social assemblages tracing their self-organisation and emergence; and, a transformative pragmatics of the inter-connectedness of all social machines and social assemblages and of the emergence of new social machines and social assemblages. This four-fold pragmatics maps the intensive rhizome of social organisation and legality in terms of the relation between the form of expression and form of content of the social assemblage as two multiplicities exploring and occupying the intensive social field, in relation also to neighbouring and overlapping forms of expression and forms of content of other social assemblages. There is an intensive ecology of this virtual plane and intensive social field of the relations between all the social machines and social assemblages. A given historical formation will contract and add to different social machines and social assemblages from this intensive field of social organisation.

The first aspect of the pragmatics of social organisation and legality is the problematic itself of social organisation and legality and of the abstract machines that arise in relation to this problematic. This is to address the abstract machines of legality that arise in social machines, and it is a noology of abstract machines of legality and a topology of the diagrams of social machines, considering the relationship and transformations between abstract machines of legality, and considering the creation of new concepts of legality as new abstract machines of legality. The diagrammatic pragmatics distinguishes abstract machines of legality from more common abstract machine assemblages accompanying social assemblages on the basis that abstract machines of legality perform specific tasks characteristic to them. Abstract machines of legality arise in relation to the virtual problematic of social organisation, they draw a plane or a body of the socius for social organisation, and they are an abstract machine idea for social organisation. This diagrammatic pragmatics is concerned with concepts of legality and the creation of new concepts of legality, and hence an activity of noology.

On the basis that there are social assemblages that are piloted by abstract machines of legality as social machines, the second aspect of the schizoanalytical study of social organisation and legality is the machinic pragmatics of considering the particular social assemblages that develop out social machines and abstract machines of legality. Every social assemblage that individuates out a social machine and produces variations in that social machine is a unique intensive and actualised social assemblage, and the task is to trace the abstract machine of legality and social machine in the social assemblage. Thus, there is the examination of territorial social machine assemblages, State social machine assemblages, capitalist social machine assemblages, and nomad war social machine assemblages, and the genealogy of the abstract machine in the social assemblages. This machinic pragmatics would include the examination of when diverse social assemblages merge with a social machine, as in the merging of monotheisms with State social machines.

The third aspect is a generative pragmatics of diverse social assemblages and the genealogical study of individual social assemblages. There are many social assemblages that are not social machines, and the generative pragmatics takes a social assemblage and considers its self-organisation, emergence, relations to social machines, relation to the plane of immanence or plane of organisation (consistency or molar fold), the code-territory/decode-deterritorialise strategies of assemblage organisation, its virtual abstract machine diagram, whether it is an assemblage of forces or of power, its regime of signs (statements-incorporeal transformations-jurisdiction), its regime of bodies, its territories and its lines of flight. The generative pragmatics considers institutions as social assemblages:

> Take a thing like the prison: the prison is a form, the 'prison form'; it is a form of content on a stratum and is related to their forms of content (schools, barracks, hospitals, factories). This thing or form does not refer back to the word 'prison' but to entirely different words and concepts, such as 'delinquent' and 'delinquency', which express a new way of classifying, stating, translating, and even committing criminal acts. 'Delinquency' is the form of expression in reciprocal presupposition with the form of content 'prison'... Moreover, the form of expression is reducible not to words but to a set of statements arising in the social field considered as stratum (that is what a regime of signs is). The form of content is reducible not to a thing but to

a complex state of things as a formation of power (architecture, regimentation, etc.). We could say that there are two constantly intersecting multiplicities, 'discursive multiplicities' of expression and 'nondiscursive multiplicities' of content... Form of content and form of expression, prison and delinquency, each has its own history, microhistory, segments.

(D&G (1988) 66 (74))

Or, an historical formation facing a receded State social machine:

Taking the feudal assemblage as an example, we would have to consider the intermingling of bodies defining feudalism: the body of the earth and the social body; the body of the overlord, vassal, and serf; the body of the knight and the horse and their new relation to the stirrup; the weapons and tools ensuring a symbiosis of bodies – a whole machinic assemblage. We would also have to consider statements, expressions, the juridical regime of heraldry, all of the incorporeal transformations, in particular, oaths and their variables (the oath of obedience, but also the oath of love, etc.): the collective assemblage of enunciation. On the other axis, we would have to consider the feudal territorialities and reterritorialisations, and at the same time the line of deterritorialisation that carries away both the knight and the mount, statement and acts. We would have to consider how all of this combines in the Crusades.

(D&G (1988) 89 (98))

Particularly in common law traditions, a lot of legal decision making occurs outside social machines in social assemblages of the case (assemblages of legality). Thus, a generative pragmatics of legality would write, for example, a genealogy of Equity, with its recessed relation to a State social machine, its intensive assemblaging of the case in consistencies of equities of sensations and affect, its abstract machine diagram (T-B), its regime of signs (statements-incorporeal transformations-jurisdiction), its regime of Chancery bodies, its (many) territories, and its lines of flight of gender in patriarchy and of lines of flight of its reach in global capital.

The machinic and generative pragmatics of social organisation and legality are, however, absorbed by and assume the transformative pragmatics of social organisation and legality, where the diagrammatic pragmatics rejoins consideration of social assemblages. The transformative pragmatics of social organisation and legality considers abstract machines of legality, social machine assemblages, diverse social assemblages on the basis of an intensive inter-connectedness of an intensive nonorganic life of sociality and legality, with a view to understanding transformations in and between abstract machines of legality, social machines, diverse assemblages and of the emergence of new abstract machines, social machines, social assemblages. The transformative pragmatics considers how all the machines and assemblages of the intensive social field co-exist, interrelate, combine, come and go, change, transform, self-organise and emerge anew.

The intensive field of social problems, and the virtual plane of abstract machines of legality, becomes the rhizome of the inter-connectedness of all social machines and social assemblages in a univocal nonorganic vitality of social organisation and legality. The transformative pragmatics, therefore, understands an ecology of social machines and social assemblages, and that this ecology is dynamic with transformations and the emergence from this ecology of new social machines and social assemblages. For the transformative pragmatics of social organisation and legality it is a matter of understanding this ecology and how to understand and to tap the immanent forces of eternal return that ultimately drive this ecology of social machines and social assemblages that is so much more than a strata factory.

The cosmic line of flight of social organisation (eternal return)

> Let us recall Nietzsche's idea of the eternal return as a little ditty, a refrain, but which captures the mute and unthinkable forces of the Cosmos. We thus leave behind the assemblages to enter the age of the Machine, the immense mechanosphere, the plane of the cosmicisation of the forces to be harnessed.
>
> (D&G (1987) 343 (378))

The superfold of the plane of immanence, the plane of organisation and the intensive field, operates in social organisation and legality. The workshop had been through the theorisation of social organisation and legality in virtual abstract machines, intensive assemblages and molar assemblages. In the intensive ecology of these social machines and assemblages there are two key sets of forces at work in social organisation and legality. There are the forces of the molar fold, the plane of organisation, strategies of coding and territory, and systems of stratification. There are the forces of eternal return, the plane of immanence, strategies of decoded and deterritorialised consistencies, and intensive social assemblages.

It would be fair to say that the forces of the molar fold have been very successful at occupying the social field and recruiting and holding loyal subjects. The molar social machines have additionally been successful in limiting decoding and deterritorialising social machines.

However, of course, the plane of consistency and the eternal return have always been at work under the stratifications, and the ecology of social machines and social assemblages has always been principally organised by eternal return. The issue was that social organisation in the molar machines had set up an absolute limit to decoding and deterritorialisation in social organisation and legality.

The question must then be posed: what happens when the absolute limit of social organisation is crossed, and social organisation and legality turn away from the plane of organisation, and codes and territory? What happens when there is absolute deterritorialisation of social organisation and legality?

At the absolute limit of social organisation the eternal return directly enters social organisation, and becomes a cosmic line of flight, absolute deterritorialisation with no reterritorialisation, connecting social organisation to the forces of the cosmos (D&G (1988) 336 (371)), where the return is the return of that which differs, the returning of the returning and the return of the new (Deleuze (1983) 48).

> The assemblage no longer confronts the forces of chaos, it no longer uses the forces of the earth or of the people to deepen itself but instead opens onto the forces of the Cosmos... The essential relation is no longer matters-forms (or substances-attributes); neither is it the continuous development of form and the continuous variation of matter. It is now a direct relation material forces. A material is a molecularised matter, which must accordingly 'harness' forces; these forces are necessarily forces of the Cosmos.
>
> (D&G (1988) 342 (377))

There are two simultaneous aspects of eternal return in social organisation: one destructive, one creative.

The eternal return necessarily operates as the forces of forgetting, having done with, abolition, collapse and waste: 'the genius of the eternal return lies not in memory but in waste, in active forgetting' (Deleuze (1994) 77). The eternal return is forgetting and abolition: 'the machine, on the contrary, is shaped by a desire for abolition. Its emergence is doubled with a breakdown, a catastrophe – the menace of death' (Guattari (1995) 37). It is a 'question of a model [of social organisation] that is perpetually in construction or collapsing, and of a process that is perpetually prolonging itself, breaking off and starting up again' (D&G (1988) 20 (22)). When eternal return is connected to social organisation 'the ground has been superseded by groundlessness, a universal ungrounding which turns up on itself and causes only the yet to come to return' (Deleuze (1994) 122). The eternal return is the harbinger of death and the exterminating angel (D&G (1984) 35 (38)).

At the same time, eternal return entering social organisation is endlessly creative. Social organisation becomes a machinic opera (D&G (1988) 330 (364)), and the socius '...leave[s] behind the assemblages to enter the age of the Machine, the immense mechanosphere, the plane of the cosmicisation of the forces to be harnessed' (D&G (1988) 343 (373)). In the machinic opera 'forces are in a perpetual state of evolution: there is an emergence of forces which doubles history, or rather envelops it, according to the Nietzschean conception' (Deleuze (1988b) 85). Social organisation elaborates a memory and dream of an angel that doubles history and links the forces of social organisation to the cosmos: 'The memory of an angel, or rather the becoming of a cosmos' (D&G (1988) 350 (386)). The eternal return in social organisation is to develop an abstract machine of legality of a dark precursor of a society yet to come: 'there is an abstract machine of the field of immanence that only selects eternal return' (D&G (1988)

165 (183)). With the eternal return in social organisation there develops on the abstract machine a social assemblage as a cosmic fractal line of flight. This cosmic line of flight is the creation of a new earth:

> D is absolute when it conforms to the first case and brings about the creation of a new earth, in other words, when it connects lines of flight, raises them to the power of an abstract vital line, or draws a plane of consistency.
>
> (D&G (1988) 510 (561))

The absolute limit of social organisation in the eternal return extends '…the line of flight to the point where it becomes an abstract machine covering the entire plane of consistency' (D&G (1988) 11 (12)).

The workshop had reached its conclusion.

There had been the development of the concepts of the virtual problematic of social organisation, social machines, abstract machines of legality, intensive assemblages of legality and molar social assemblages. There were the earths of planomenon, ecumenon and mechanoshphere that legalities could connect with. In so far as abstract machines of thinking are also the basis for abstract machines of legality there had been the introduction of two abstract machines of legality and of the intensive problem field of legality and its machinic assemblages of legality. From all this there was, therefore, the scope to go further and draw a plane of immanence for all legality, so that a noology of legality can explore all the abstract machines of legality and all the intensive assemblages of legality by means of noology's image of thinking. Further, in all three sessions, the same conclusions had been drawn whether it had been the earth, socius or thinking. In the earth, socius and thinking there is an overriding tendency and fate to approach absolute decoding and deterritorialisation, for the eternal return to directly enter into their assemblages and become their abstract machines. Thus, from all the sessions, but particularly from Dr Nome's lecture, there had been developed a schizo image of thought that could think the absolute decoding and deterritorialisation of legality and think a legality for a new people and a new earth.

Four Laws
From the Ecumenon to the Planomenon

Introduction

The noology of legalities studies the plane of immanence that is drawn for all legalities. On this plane of immanence for all legalities social machines self-organise and emerge in relation to the problematic of social organisation of how to connect the earth and the brain in a consistent social organisation that connects to the forces of the cosmos. On this plane of immanence four social machines have emerged that have been recurrent and which mark out the stakes of the problematic of social organisation. Each of these social machines, in their own way, establishes a means to address the problematic of connecting the earth and the brain in social organisation that connects to the forces of the cosmos. The four social machines are the territorial social machine (D&G (1984) 145 (159)), the despotic State social machine (D&G (1984) 192 (217)); D&G (1988) 424 (468)), the capitalist social machine (D&G (1984) 222 (242)), and the nomad war social machine (D&G (1988) 351 (387)).

In marking out the stakes of the problematic of social organisation the four key social machines demonstrate four significantly different images of legality, abstract machines of legality and assemblages of legality. These significant differences in the social machines are the issue of the nature of the plane that the social machine draws for social organisation, and of the consequent issue of the nature of the strategies for organisation that the social machine operates on its own plane. The issue of the plane for legality that the social machine draws is the issue of whether it is a plane that is extensive and tends towards a transcendent plane of organisation, or whether it is intensive and tends towards a virtual plane of immanence. The consequent issue of strategies of organisation is the issue of whether the social machine proceeds through operations of coding, territorialisation and generalised stratifications, or whether it proceeds through operations of decoding, deterritorialisation and tapping immanent cosmic forces. Social machines that tend towards drawing a plane of organisation adopt organisational strategies that proceed through coding and territorialising, whereas those that tend towards drawing a plane of immanence adopt organisational strategies that proceed through decoding and deterritorialisation. The territorial kinship social machine and the State social machine tend towards drawing a plane of organisation and proceed through coding and territorialising. The capitalist social machine and the nomad war social machine tend towards drawing a plane of immanence and proceed through decoding and deterritorialising.

The territorial social machine emerged to address the fundamental social problematic of constituting an extensive kinship social organisation out of intensive germinal life. The social machine operated through coding of social flows and the coding of a kinship system, in which the image of legality is to block and to code.

The Urstaat State social machine addressed the problematic of the organisation of the parts and the flows of a loosely territorial social machine into conforming to a cerebral ideality of an organic unity. This State social machine proceeded by a capture of kinship systems, and the operation of a deterritorialisation followed by an immediate reterritorialisation overcoding of all the territories and signifying chains under a transcendent unity of the despot, in which the image of legality is to unify and overcode.

The capitalist social machine developed to address the economic (not primarily social) problematic of organising the social field through the connecting of decoded and deterritorialised flows and extracting surplus value from the flows. It does this with an abstract machine of an intensive and virtual arbitraging of the flows. However, this organisation of the flows cannot organise the social field without a compensating organisation. The capitalist social machine also develops a regime of legality of an axiomatic for the decoded and deterritorialised flows, together with a large-scale and far-reaching borrowing from and resuscitation of the two social machines of the territorial kinship regime of legality and the social machine of the Urstaat as legal neo-archaisms. The axiomatic is in place of an image of legality to the capitalist social machine, and which does not constitute an image of legality in the same manner in which the capitalist social machine cannot constitute an image of thought (the capitalist machine cannot create transversal consistencies).

The nomad war social machine adjusts to the problematic of social organisation through a dynamic consistency on a line of flight of decoded and deterritorialised flows. Organisation is here understood as not coding, not overcoding, and not as an axiomatic of flows. Rather, organisation is a matter of a consistency and distribution in smooth space in continuous variation. The nomads have effectuated the war machine in their social organisation of the nomad war social machine, and the war social machine calls forth social machines yet to come. The image of law is of decoded and deterritorialised lines of flight held together in dynamic transversal consistencies.

The fundamental differences between the social machines result in there being three very different adventures in legality and social organisation. With the territorial social machines and the Urstaat State social machines there is the adventure of the ecumenon, in which legality and social organisation is all a matter of the extensive organisation in terms of codes and territorialisation. For the capitalist social machine, with its mixed regime of intensive and virtual arbitraging of all the decoded and deterritorialised flows, together with the recoding and reterritorialising axiomatic, there is the singular adventure of capitalism with its occupation and organisational centre of the intensive mechanosphere. The nomad social machine, together with the social machines yet to come, operates with the plane of immanence and with organisational consistencies in flows that tend towards absolute decoding and deterritorialisation. The adventure here is open ended, venturing forth on lines of flight that are unimaginable, but which all refrain on an adventure of the planomenon as ethos.

These three adventures work the three topological thresholds that characterise the problematic plane and problem field of social organisation and legality: the real limit of social organisation; the relative limit of social organisation; and, the absolute limit of social organisation (D&G (1984) 336–8 (369–72)). The real limit of social organisation is that the social flows will not submit to coding and territorialisation, but instead run free, decoded and deterritorialised over the body of the socius. The real limit of social organisation is the real limit of the adventure of the ecumenon, of both the territorial social machine and the despotic State social machine. Instances of these social machines may tolerate some decoded and deterritorialised flows that they can topically recode or reterritorialise, but whilst the overall framework of legality and social organisation is coding and territorialising the real limit is not passed. Capitalism is marked as its own adventure as it is only with the capitalist social machine that the real limit of social organisation is surpassed, as the operation of social organisation is precisely in decoded and deterritorialised flows. Indeed, capitalism substitutes for the real limit its own internal relative limit: the limit across which the capitalist organisation would collapse in its inherent systemic crisis, were this relative limit not displaced by adjustments to the axiomatic and the nationalisation of losses. The absolute limit to the problematic of legality and social organisation is attained when social machines of the planomenon leave the ecumenon and capitalist intensive field and organise legality and social organisation as absolute decoding and deterritorialisation. At this absolute limit the adventure becomes that of the problematic of legality itself.

The social machines and the three adventures should not be thought of in terms of progressive stages. The social machines and the adventures are simultaneous to each other: their virtuality has meant that they have always been present to each other. It is not a matter of independence but of coexistence and competition in a field of interaction and a field of the problematic of social organisation (D&G (1988) 430 (475)). The social machines are in coexistence, of becomings and goings, and of metamorphoses from one to another in the social field. The problematic field of social organisation has many assemblages, and the field is always open to the creation and emergence of novel social machines. All the history of civilisation does is to translate the coexistence of becomings of social organisation into linear succession, missing the virtual problem field and the processes of self-organisation and emergence (D&G (1988) 430 (475)).

Adventure of the ecumenon: the territorial kinship social machine

The adventure of the ecumenon of legality and social organisation takes place in two social machines: the territorial social machine, and the despotic State social machine. They are very different, and have complex relations between them, but both address the problematic of social organisation with the one common operation of the ecumenon social machines. They both code and territorialise desiring production and the social flows: 'To code desire – and the fear, the anguish of decoded flows – is the business of the socius' (D&G (1984) 139 (154)).

The territorial machine does address the problematic of social organisation of connecting the earth and the brain in a consistent social organisation that connects to the forces of the cosmos, but it does so from one very precise concern. The territorial social machine does connect the brain as an ecumenon image of thought with the earth as an intensive earth made extensive in a social organisational image of legality of a coding, in relation to a mythical natal. However, for the territorial machine the problematic of social organisation was more specific than that. The problematic was how to breed an animal capable of a memory of social obligations, of precisely how to breed man and create the human race. This was a matter rendering man from a biological existence to a social existence of an embedded debtor-creditor register and an innate capability of entering into and remembering relations of alliance (D&G (1984) 190 (206)). This problematic requires two linked operations. First, a social organisation of alliance and memory of alliance would require a leaving of the intensive germinal field of existence. Second, a whole system in extension would need to be developed to articulate an organisation of alliance and the memory of alliance, together with a system of representation and a regime of the new social bodies.

The adventure of territorial social machines and their image of legality is inseparable from a starting point that social organisation is incompatible with the intensive germinal morphogenetic field. The intensive germinal field is the field of sensation, intensities, affects and becomings, where intensive desiring production machines intensive consistencies, and in which there is a unity of desire and production. All the social flows move across an intensive field in becomings that are flights in intensity, with no discernible individual persons, no unambiguous signs, no qualified filiation, and no extensive memory. The intensive germinal implex was the great nocturnal biocosmic life and memory of filiation, of intensive flows and intensive machinings, of twinness, bisexuality and becomings animal (D&G (1984) 155–9 (169–73)); D&G (1988) 232 (256)). For the territorial social machine the intensive germinal implex was a total threat to the viability of sustainable social collectives (D&G (1984) 190 (208)). What had to be done to establish a system and new memory of alliance was the closure and repression of the intensive germinal implex and biocosmic memory of filiation: 'Man must constitute himself through the repression of the intensive germinal implex, the great biocosmic memory that threatens to deluge every attempt at collectivity' (D&G (1984) 190 (208)).

Together with achieving the repression of the intensive germinal implex, the territorial social machine must establish its own extensive system for organising a social collective and constituting a new extensive memory to replace the intensive filiative memory. The territorial social machine represses the germinal implex, creates an extended social, establishes a new extensive memory, and succeeds in breeding man through processes of coding and territorialisation in operations of a kinship system of alliance and filiation (D&G (1984) 145 (159)). In the territorial social machine the organisation of alliance and filiation proceeds through processes of coding and territorialisation. The processes of coding and territorialisation operate through the establishment of an extensive system of representation founded upon the prohibition and repression of the intensive germinal flux.

The core operation of the territorial social machine is that the principle of exogenous alliance is the extensive form that supervenes on the filiative lineages and thereafter guides the circulations of social production. This supervening of the principle of exogenous alliance is an inscription of the territorial socius in an operation of coding and territorialising. Just as with the earth and the brain there is in social organisation a second self-organising and emergent second synthesis of disjunction and recording (there is never a flow without there also being a scribble). In social organisation there are connective syntheses of social production, disjunctive syntheses of recording and inscription of the organisation of social production, and there are conjunctive syntheses of the consumption of social production. The operation of the disjunctive synthesis of inscription and recording is one of the fundamental operations of the abstract machine of the social machine, involving the drawing of the body and plane of the socius and of the exact operation of the disjunctive synthesis in the social machine. In the territorial social machine the socius that is drawn is the earth rendered extensive and ecumenon, and the operation of the abstract machine and disjunctive synthesis of inscription is coding. Territorial machine coding is the double operation of the inscription of an extensive system of representation (both in depth and surface), and of a repression of the intensive germinal flux. This double operation of coding both organises the signifying chains and organises the social flows now coded as either blocked or passing into social circulation. The consequence of this operation for the territorial social machine is that social organisation appears as founded on an incest prohibition, the image of legality is that of coding the flows, the social field is co-existent with an extensive kinship system guided by the circulation of alliance debts, a tribal collective investment of all the organs and the coded flows, and a system of inscriptive representation that marks bodies and territories (the bodies with terrible cruelties), and thus constitutes the necessary socius and memory for breeding the human race.

The double operation of the inscription of a system of representation and the repression of the intensive germinal flux is crucial to the territorial social machine and its image of legality. Not surprisingly, it is the earth that is taken up in the territorial machine as the basis of all production, that to which social production can be attributed to, and the surface on which social organisation can be inscribed and recorded on (D&G (1984) 141 (156)). The earth that is drawn by the social machine is precisely that extensive earth as the ecumenon that the whole action of the social machine works at organising and emerging. The operation of the inscribing disjunctive syntheses, that inscribe this earth as the socius, both in the operation of the founding coding and in the whole system of representation, now come to operate as exclusive disjunctive syntheses. This inscription of the earth does certainly code and territorialise the earth in an extensive manner. However, the earth that is drawn as socius and plane in the territorial social machine is a plane of organisation that offers up a supple and flexible surface of inscription. Although the founding inscription is an exclusive disjunctive synthesis, the earth as socius of inscription allows for a system of representation and articulations of alliance and filiation that are polyvocal and flexible. The earth as socius is drawn by the social machine as a plane of organisation for the extensive organisational strategies of coding and territory, but the earth plane of inscription is an open and polyvocal surface of inscription (D&G (1984) 187 (204)).

The territorial inscription that founds the social machine and prohibits and represses the intensive germinal implex is the inscription of a representational metaphor. The inscription comprises three elements: the repressing representation; the repressed representative; and the displaced represented (D&G (1984) 184 (201)). The repressing representation operates on the repressed representative prohibiting and repressing that which cannot enter social organisation and representation because it is uncodable. This allows a system of coding as flows can be coded as extensive and passing into social production (coded as +), or coded as blocked and prohibited (coded as −). The field of intensive filiation can then be coded in this manner and rendered extensive and organised on the basis of an exogenous alliance and a representational system of unambiguous signs. However, within the newly established system of coding and representation that which is blocked and repressed cannot enter into representation (it is uncodable), but must itself be stood in for by a displaced represented that is conceptualised in terms that do not precede the operation of the territorial coding itself. Thus, in the territorial machine what must be prohibited and repressed are the intensive germinal implex, intensive filiation, and the unity of desiring production and the earth. What is desired, but which must be prohibited and repressed for the sake of the sustainable collective, is the intensive earth and intensive filiation. These intensities are uncodable and unrepresentable by the territorial inscription but they certainly are prohibited and repressed. What the territorial machine must block in order to pass from an intensive filiative ordering to an extensive filiative ordering organised through exogenous alliance is relations with the sister (thus sealing lateral alliance and producing relations of mobile debt) and relations with the mother (thus sealing extensive ascending filiative lineages and a new memory of lineages) (D&G (1984) 159 (174)). However, these discernable persons and categories did not exist prior to the territorial inscription, and are not relations that were previously desired but now are prohibited and repressed. In the territorial inscription the repressing representative comes to be reduced to what is blocked in the system (D&G (1984) 165 (181)). The prohibition on incest appears as the displaced represented and as a retroactive effect of the repressing representation on the repressed representative of desire. In the territorial inscription the displaced represented of incest passes into the interior of the socius, passing between the representation of desire and the representative of filiation. Oedipus appears in the territorial socius as a disfiguration of desiring production and the displaced limit of the socius as ecumenon, though in the territorial social machine Oedipus is structurally unoccupied and is neither repressing nor repressed.

The problem with coding in the wake of the founding representational repression is to ensure the reciprocal adaptation of the flows of production with the signifying chains. In the territorial social machine the abstract machine of coding takes advantage of the presence within the flows of production and within the signifying chains of surplus value of code. In the founding repression of the intensive flows not all of the flows are prohibited and repressed, and some of the intensive flows remain in the flows and some of the flows enter into the signifying chains in coded elements, both constituting a surplus value of code in the machine (D&G (1984) 203 (221)). Such surplus value of code within the territorial social machine includes privileged coded positions, possession of outstanding alliance debts, and the sanctioned enjoyment of coded flows. The articulation of this surplus value of code is the mainspring of the whole operation of the territorial social machine of alliance and filiation, and it organises all of production, recordings and consumptions of the territorial machine (D&G (1984) 142 (156)). It is the operation of the surplus value of code in the machine that ensures there is a dynamic circulation and consistency within the social machine. The coding abstract machine operates a double articulation of a reciprocal relation whereby the abstract machine makes deductions from the flows of production and makes detachments from the signifying chains. Deductions from the flows of production are surplus value of code and a filiative stock in the signifying chain. Detachments from the signifying chains are surplus value of code and mobile blocks of alliance debt in the flows of filiation. The detachments from the signifying chain are territorial signs of desire and power, and these signs effect the changes in the flows of production, guiding and directing these flows (D&G (1984) 150 (164)). The abstract machine operates with these primary detachments of alliance debt as that which guides the double articulation of surplus value of code (D&G (1984) 149 (163)). The detachments from the signifying chains organise the flows of production, organise deductions from the flows, connecting flows and breaking the flows of the alliance debt and filiative lineages, and allocating portions of the production to persons (D&G (1984) 150 (164)).

The inscribing action on the body of the socius and the double articulation of the abstract machine inform the surface representation of the territorial machine. Territorial representation is concerned with the inscribing and marking of bodies and the inscribing and marking of territories. It is articulated in a complex and supple extensive assemblage, where there is a mix and interweaving of a regime of signs, and regime of bodies, and the marking of the assemblage territory.

The territorial representation is a double articulation of chains of inscription and bodily flows in a collective enunciation that is open and conative, and where statements are polyvocal and the substances of expression multiple (D&G (1988) 117 (130)). In this territorial double articulation there is the operation of the 'magic triangle' of the territorial assemblage: the triangle of voice-graphism-eye (D&G (1984) 189 (206)). In the wake of the alliance coding of intensive filiation the voice becomes aligned with alliance, and with the words of alliance obligations and the operation of alliance coding. Graphism becomes aligned with the body and filiation, and particularly with the marking of extended filiation and alliance physically onto the bodies of the tribes and the clans. The voice aspect of the regime of signs and the graphism of the regime of bodies are operationally independent. There is, in line with the territorial assemblage as a whole, a heterogeneity and disequilibrium in the relations between the voice and graphism, connecting in a conative collective assemblage of enunciation as a complex network covering the entire social field. The voice of alliance is dominant in the collective assemblage in line with the key coding role of the words of alliance, but the assemblage is a continual jumping from voice-words to graphism-bodies, and from graphism-bodies to voice-words, acting on each other at different levels. Vocal signs designate bodies and things, but not without bodies and things being themselves signs, with the vocal signs and the body signs being taken up in heterogeneous conjunctions. To this, continual jumping from voice-words to body-inscriptions is added to in the territorial assemblage with the eye as the third element of the magic triangle of territorial representation. What holds the conjunctions of the voice and physical graphism together in the collective assemblage is the presence of the eye that sees all the suffering and traumas deployed by the territorial social machine in order to repress intensive filiation and inscribe an extended alliance and filiation and in order to enforce the social codes (D&G (1984) 203–4 (221)). The voice-graphism operation of the territorial social machine inscribes the territory of the social machine on the bodies of its members, to create for each body an obligation and participation to the territorial social machine, to create an extensive memory, to repress the intensive filiation and memory, and to ensure that the bonds of this coding be not breached without cruel punishment. The eye sees the pain and suffering of the initiation rite on the body, it sees the pain and suffering of the markings of alliance, and it sees the cruel punishments inflicted upon those bodies that have not fully taken the codes or who flout them. This eye connects the voice of alliance and the graphism system of the body of filiation in an appreciation of a surplus value of code that watching the rituals of physical inscription injects into the circulation of territorial surplus vale of code (D&G (1984) 191 (208)).

Beyond its coding and its systems of representation, the territorial machine and assemblage constitutes a new memory of alliance and a vast cycle of alliance and filiation:

> An extensive somatic memory is produced from the filiations that have been extended and the alliances that the filiations presuppose, and this extensive

somatic memory represses the great nocturnal memory of the intensive filiation that is repressed for the sake of an extensive somatic memory, created from filiations that have become extended (patrilineal or matrilineal) and from the alliances that they imply.

(D&G (1984) 160 (175))

The new extensive memory of alliance and filiation is opened up in the in-depth operation of the repressing representation of the alliance code, but it is in the mixed regime of signs, regime of bodies, and the marking of the territories that the mechanism for the creation and embedding of the new memory take place in the territorial social machine. The substance of the memory is the codes themselves as voice of alliance, but the instruments for the remembering the codes are the cruel initiation rites and the cruel punishments for infractions. It is so important to the adventure of the territorial social machine that the intensive germinal field be forever prohibited and that a new extensive memory of alliance with a collective pledge of all the bodies to the body of the socius that pain without stint is employed to burn and brand the capacity for a memory of obligations.

In all these operations of coding and territorial representation there is prepared the position for the drawn body of the socius to fall back on all social production and reproduction and to appropriate it all for itself (D&G (1984) 148 (162)). The earth as established as extensive and ecumenon becomes the plane and the body of the socius, and all social production is an engendering by the earth and thereby attributable to the earth as such. This earth that falls back is not the intensive earth, let alone the virtual and intensive earth of the planomenon. The planomenon earth and the intensive earth are precisely what the territorial machine represses in order to constitute itself and breed man. The ecumenon is forged as against the intensive and the virtual. However, even in a system centred upon an extensive alliance overcoding, the relation of social organisation to the virtual and intensive forces of the earth and the cosmos remain in the problematic and problem field of the territorial social machine. In its very problematic the relation to cosmic and intensive forces are there in the creation myths that territorial machines furnish for themselves, and the presence and practices of the shaman in the problem field of the socius attest to the role of an inherent relationship and role of intensive and cosmic forces in territorial social organisation.

The falling back of the earth on all production is accompanied in the territorial social machine by the pledging of all the bodies of the social group of all their organs and flows to the collective investment of the organs, their flows, the social field, and to the body of the earth. It is an issue both of the problems of coding and of the necessary attributes of the body of the earth in the territorial social machine. In order to code the flows all organs within the social field capable of producing or breaking these flows must be isolated and rendered as partial objects. The collective prohibition and repression of intensive filiation and the coding of all the flows requires that there be no instances of private possession or exercise of organs of the flows, because only an absolute and collective investment by the group of all the organs and all the flows can support the system of coding all the flows. In the territorial desiring regime there are only group identifications of collectively invested organs, and each member of the social group has their whole body marked under the regime that consigns their organs to the collective. It is to the body of the earth as socius that these collectively invested organs become attributed, attached and operate in relation to (D&G (1984) 142 (156)). Desiring production and social production are collective and directly plugged into the earth as the social field, and all the organs and all the flows cleave to the earth and to the socius. Man, thereby, completing the process of intensive repression and coding, ceases to be a biological organism to become, alongside the obligations of alliance, a body and organs wholly and collectively sewn into body of the territorial socius.

Beyond the code, representation and the new memory, the territorial social machine is, of course, a vast assemblage and cycle of kinship and collective sociality. It is a vast network of brain elements and earth elements, words and bodies, qualitative alliances and extended filiations, flows of production and chains of inscription, deductions from the flows and detachments from the signifying chains, mobile blocks of debt and filiative stock, and the movements of the surplus value of code. It is social organisation and social production through a praxis of alliance and filiation that is a strategy rather than a structure and that is co-existent with the entire social field (D&G (1984) 147 (161)). Though the social field is the field of flows, and though social machines operate through the inscription of the disjunctive syntheses of recording, social machines do indeed have a circulatory regime. In the territorial machine the system of alliance imposes debtor-creditor obligations upon every body on the basis of the inscribed prohibition of the enjoyment of some social production and reproduction. The vast cycle of alliance is animated by alliance debt that circulate as surplus value of code, so that mobile blocks of alliance debt can circulate so that everything can circulate in the territorial assemblages: 'It is in this sense that the economy goes by way of alliance' (D&G (1984) 147 (161)). This circulation of alliance debt in no way, however, brings the cycle and operation of the territorial social machine into equilibrium. The circulation of alliance debt is the surface phenomena of the machinic processes of a double articulation of heterogeneous flows of production and chains of inscription that maintain for the cycle of alliance and filiation a dynamic non-equilibrium consistency. The territorial assemblage is coded and it does circulate, but it does this in the setting of a social machine that operates with a dynamic and polyvocal consistency between two heterogeneous articulations, with an openness, flexibility, no unifications, and re-set functions when needed. This circulation of the mobile blocks of alliance debt do not cancel out, and the cycle also remains open and flexible.

The territorial social machine also makes use of practices of antiproduction. In the cycle of the circulation of the debts of alliance and the deductions of the flows, stages will be reached in which there is a build up in the system of a surfeit of surplus value of code and of production. In line with the machinic falling back of the body of the earth on all production and the attribution of all production to the body of the earth, the surfeit is expended in antiproduction practices of sacrifice, feasting and potlatch. Antiproduction, whilst at one level simply the destruction of so much hard-won social production, is for the territorial social machine not only the core of its relationship to the earth but also one of the conditions for its survival. It is antiproduction that serves to ensure that there be no build-up of wealth in the social field that could pose the potential emergence of a general equivalent of value, since this emergence of a general equivalent of value would prove fatal to the open and non-cancelling system of the circulation of alliance debt.

From the founding repressing representation coding image of legality, across all its social organisation and practices, the territorial social machine works with the horror of decoded flows. The threat of decoded flows and forces of deterritorialisation strike the territorial social machine from its beginning to its end. First, decoded and deterritorialised flows are the real limit of the social machine. Its founding operation of repressing the germinal implex of intensive filiation and its accompanying organisation all-or-nothing strategy of coding the flows results in the circumstances that no decoded flows can be tolerated. Hence the often perverse mania for coding and the unstinting system of cruelty for both marking the initiation of bodies into the collective and for the punishment of transgressors of the codes. At its end the territorial social machine lives in fear of the instantaneous wave of decoding and deterritorialisation that the State machine brings as the precursor for the subsumption of the territorial assemblages under the new monster social machine of the Imperial State. In line with the virtual, intensive and actual co-existence of the social machines, territorial social machines know of State social machines, and ward them off precisely in their constitution and operation. So many of the organisational features and practices operate to these ends: the open and heterogeneous double articulations; the circulation of non-cancelling but finite mobile blocks of debt; the assemblage operational disequilibrium; and the centrality of practices of antiproduction. All these features and practices of the territorial social machine operate to prevent the build-up of power centres amongst the chieftains, and to ward off a unifying and transcendent power takeover of the Imperial State social machine.

The outcome for the territorial social machine is, however, that when the State machine does arrive on its wave of instantaneous decoding and deterritorialisation, it does so to double the adventure of the ecumenon social organisation, to deepen it, to overcode it, and connect it to a unitary God of a transcendent ecumenon.

Adventure of the ecumenon: State social machine

The State social machine adds to the adventure of the ecumenon in the problematic of social organisation a new idea of legality and another organisation of social production. Whilst the territorial ecumenon social machine operated an image of legality of coding the flows and an alliance led flexible extended kinship social organisation, the State social machine adds to the ecumenon the State image of legality of transcendent overcoding and a transcendent overcoding social organisation of the State form.

The State social machine's idea and image of legality is the Urstaat abstract machine. The structure and operation of this Urstaat image of legality and abstract machine, the manner in which the abstract machine can be effected in the territorial milieus, and the structure of State representation that the abstract machine develops, will be considered in some depth.

The instantiation in social assemblages of the Urstaat abstract machine has proved extremely flexible, such that one can speak of at least three forms of the State and three ages of State law (D&G (1988) 448–53 (495–500)). The Urstaat abstract machine has been fully and extensively developed as the Imperial despotic State and its Imperial regime of legality. The genealogy of the State social machine puts the emergence of the State abstract machine and the social machine in the setting of the arrival of the Imperial States in the territorial milieus. These are the great social machines of a transcendent overcoding and overterritorialising Urstaat abstract machine and image of legality. However, the State abstract machine has been instantiated in many extremely diverse State social assemblages: evolved empires, autonomous cities, feudal systems, monarchisms, etc. (D&G (1988) 459 (507)). These diverse State social assemblages all in various ways retain the basic fundamentals of the State abstract machine, whilst combining it with many different strategies for organising social production and the integration of new tasks for the State social assemblage. The State social form takes upon itself a profound spiritualisation that sets State assemblages on great enterprises of subjectification of its citizens, and State form also is turned to the task of regulation of privatised decoded and deterritorialising flows in topically recoding and reterritorialising laws. The third form and age of the State, however, marks the transition of the State abstract machine and assemblage into a completely different adventure of civilisation. The third form and age of the State social machine and its legality is the capitalist modern State as the model of realisation of the capitalist axiomatic that participates in the intensive mechanosphere social organisation of the capitalist social machine. It is, indeed, in this third form and age of the State social machine that the Urstaat abstract machine will have a model contemporary realisation.

Imperial State social machine: the Urstaat abstract machine

The problematic for the State social machine is the connection of the earth and the brain in a consistent social organisation and image of legality that connects to the cosmos. The problematic is no longer that of the repression of the germinal implex and the breeding of man, since this problem is addressed in another social machine. The specific problem of the State social machines is to address the problematic of social organisation but to do so in a 'bigger and better' manner than the territorial social machines. The State social machine is first of all a new idea: a new idea to organise things on the basis of an imposition of a transcendent unity. It is on the basis of this new idea that the problematic of social organisation would have be to be reconsidered again, the new idea inserted into the problematic, a new abstract machine coalesce around the idea, and a new social machine be developed on the new abstract machine. From the start the State abstract machine is the cerebral ideality of a transcendent unity as the organisational principle for social organisation: the State social machine 'is perhaps the only one to appear fully armed in the brain of those who institute it' (D&G (1984) 219 (238)).

This idea was already an idea of the earth ecumenon. Just as the abstract machine of coding and flexible double articulation assemblage of the territorial social machine for social organisation has virtual links to the abstract machine and assemblages of genetic organisation, there are many operations of the molar fold abstract machine and assemblage in nature where a functional closed unity is established through an overcoding with emergent properties of that closure. The establishment of an organism is an operation of this molar fold abstract machine and assemblage. The idea of the State abstract machine is of a social body, and that this social body should be organised and ruled in the manner of a molar folded organism. However, in the idea of organising the social field by means of a transcendent unity there is more in the idea than an emulation of ecumenon organised nature. The idea is to organise the social field in an emulation with the God of the ecumenon. In the problematic of social organisation the idea of the brain links through social organisation to the forces of the cosmos, in this case linking a thought of the ecumenon brain to the God of the ecumenon. This linking of a new idea for social organisation with an idea of a transcendent unifying God would entail a different solution to connecting the ecumenon brain and the ecumenon earth than was achieved in the territorial social machine. There would need to be an overcoding of the territorial ecumenon in a manner that would take into account a transcendent unity and a new relation to cosmic forces. Indeed, the idea of social organisation as a transcendent unity is an idea of astronomy that looks to the celestial heavens for an astronomical pyramid that would serve as a plane of organisation to be folded down onto the social such that a transcendent unity could reign over that plane of social organisation.

The abstract machine for this new State, the abstract machine for the Urstaat, would need two key operations to institute a new State social machine. There would need to be an overcoding operation on the coding of the territorial social machines, and there would need to be drawn a transcendent plane of organisation for social organisation. The overcoding operation would require many steps and have many consequences for the operation of the social assemblage.

The abstract machine would need to establish a dimensionality of the social field that was accompanied by a higher transcendent dimension from which the social field was organised as a unity. In addition, for the plane of transcendent unity organisation to work, both the dimensionality of the social field would need to be aligned on whole dimensions and the nature of the attractors in the abstract machine multiplicity would also need to converge on a distribution of point and cycle attractors. In the territorial abstract machine these considerations did not bother the abstract machine because much was left open and heterogeneous in the organisation of the assemblage. However, with the State abstract machine there would need to be the operation of the molar fold, whereby the problematic of social organisation is collapsed from a very high dimensionality continuous multiplicity with an open distribution of fractal as well as point and cycle attractors to a whole dimensional manifold and distribution of point and cycle attractors. This molar fold operation also gives the idea of transcendent unity to social organisation the higher structuring dimensionality, although, of course, in the State social machine this higher dimension can only be constituted a paradoxical empty transcendent for the operation of overcoding.

The State abstract machine would then require a new image of legality and a new operation of the inscription of the State socius. Overcoding would require a double operation. First, there would need to be the displacement of any codings and territories that may pre-exist where the State machine was emerging. There would need to be an instantaneous operation of a massive decoding of all the codes and a massive deterritorialisation of all the territories. As an abstract machine of the ecumenon the State abstract machine would have to immediately then recode and reterritorialise all the flows it had just set loose, but in that instance it will have had to establish its own new inscription of the social field. The overcoding inscription would require a new repressing representation and organisation of the signifying chains.

The State abstract machine of overcoding draws a plane of transcendent organisation for social production because this is the plane that an overcoding inscription is capable of writing on. The plane of organisation is a flat extensive recording surface, the edges of which are the fixed closed boundaries to the social field inscribed on it. The plane of organisation has a transcendent point from which the whole of the plane is organised both as a closed flat plane and as the point from which the social field is actually inscribed. The plane, as such, takes of a triangular shape, with the acute angle corner inscribing the transcendent organisational point. The plane of organisation is then inscribed on the basis of the operation in the overcoding abstract machine of the recording disjunctive synthesis in an exclusive manner. Thus, social production can only be recorded on the plane in the manner of binary distinctions. The social field is thus sorted hierarchically on the plane of organisation on the basis of the requirements of the transcendent organising operation and on the basis of binary tree branching structures. Thus, social production and the social field are only inscribed on the plane of organisation to the extent they can be overcoded and to the extent they can be inscribed upon a plane of organisation. The territorial social machine operated an extensive coding operation that reduced the social field to an actual ecumenon social field, but the relative openness of the double articulation of the machine left the organisational plane of the earth relatively open and supple. In the State social machine the social field is reduced to an extensive social field capable of being inscribed on a strictly transcendently organised extensive flat surface.

Further, when the social field is capable of being overcoded and inscribed on the plane of organisation, it must be coded on the plane in terms of unities, identities and hierarchies on an exclusive binary basis.

This plane of transcendent organisation is the kernel operation of the Urstaat abstract machine. The self-organisation and emergence of this plane and abstract machine is associated clearly with the Imperial States, but it always needs to be noted that it is the one and same abstract machine and plane in all State social machines across the three ages of the State and the three orders of State legality. Not all State assemblages are in a position to effect a massive overcoding of all the flows or to be able still to control an overcoding of all the flows. Many State assemblages find their operation to be primarily the recoding and reterritorialising of decoded and deterritorialised flows. However, the idea of transcendent unity, the operation of a molar fold, an exclusive disjunctive synthesis of inscription (overcoding, recoding), and the transcendent plane of organisation are the Urstaat abstract machine and define all State social machines.

Imperial State social machine: abstract machine and machinic assemblage

The conditions and operation of the emergence of the instantiations of the Urstaat abstract machine were in the assemblages of archaic Imperial States. The State social machine emerges in the milieus of the territorial social machines, with the failure of the structures and processes of the territorial social machines that worked to avoid power centres and to ward off the formation of States. The archaic Imperial State emerges in a single stroke, fully formed:

> The State was not formed in progressive stages; it appears fully armed, a master stroke executed all at once; the primordial Urstaat, the eternal model of everything the State wants to be and desires. 'Asiatic' production, with the State that expresses or constitutes its objective movement, is not a distinct formation; it is the basic formation, on the horizon throughout history.
>
> (D&G (1984) 217 (237))

In this at-a-stroke emergence of the Imperial State the operative figure is the despot-emperor who institutes the Urstaat image of the State by capturing a people in new social knots and bonds of State desire (D&G (1988) 428 (473)). These new social bonds of State desire are the symbolic embodiment in the despot-emperor of the accomplishment of a royal double incest, and the consequent establishment of both a new alliance and a new direct filiation by the despot-emperor. The actions of the despot-emperor are to make the break with the territorial social machine's operation of coding the flows through a complex polyvalent system of alliance and extended filiation (D&G (1984) 192 (210)). It is for the figure of the despot-emperor to launch and undergo a massive solitary decoding and deterritorialisation, driven by the paranoiac madness and zeal to start again from zero. This is not only to break with the alliance and filiation coding of the territorial machine, it is for the despot-emperor himself to physically step outside the tribe and step outside his lateral alliances and extended filiation. The flight to the outside and the stepping outside of all the codings and territories puts the despot-emperor into both a position of exceptionality in relation to the codes, and thereby the position to be able to claim a new unmediated direct relation to God. Whilst the territorial social machine operates to close off the germinal implex and intensive filiation, the despot-emperor ventures back into this intensive field. In this exceptionality and direct relation to God, there is the first marriage to the sister and the first royal incest. The despot-emperor sets out on his solitary deterritorialisation and leaves the tribe for a first marriage with a woman coded as sister. This exogenous and endogenous marriage is both the accomplishment of incest with the sister and the establishment by the despot-emperor of a new alliance focused on this marriage (D&G (1984) 200 (218)). With this new alliance the despot-emperor is able to overcode all the marriages within the tribe and appropriate all of the alliance debt which was previously mobile and finite. On the return to the tribe the despot-emperor enters into a second marriage with the woman coded as mother of the tribe. This second marriage is both the accomplishment of incest with the mother and the establishment of a direct filiation that scrambles all the lineages and connects the despot-emperor to a direct filiation to the deity (D&G (1984) 200–1 (218)). This direct filiation through marriage to the mother of the tribe enables the despot-emperor to assert an accumulation and appropriation of all the filiative stock in the flows and the chains as his own right. This is the new alliance and direct filiation that marks a new social machine beyond that of the territorial social coding of polyvocal alliance and filiation, and it is this new alliance and direct filiation that enables the operation by the State social machine of its defining operation of overcoding all the chains and all the flows. The new alliance directly connects the despot-emperor to the people, and directly links the despot-emperor to the deity. This is the despot's royal incest that aggregates an amorphous intensive zone for the despot-emperor such that he exists as the one who is not bound by the codes for the repression of the intensive germinal field: 'Both marriages are essential to the overcoding, as the two ends of the tie for the despotic knot' (D&G (1984) 201 (219)). The double royal incest is necessary precisely so that the despot-emperor is the one capable of overcoding all the codes of the flows and chains. Both the incests flatten the social field, the incest with the sister removing a spatial dimension of the depth from the representation of the social field, and the incest with the mother removing the temporal dimension from the representation of the social field. Over this flattened social field all the signifying chains and all the social flows, all the detachments from the chains and deductions from the flows, are now overcoded by virtue of the despot-emperor's exceptionality and his imposition of the new alliance and direct filiation on the socius.

Overcoding is the second great inscription of the ecumenon socius. The territorial inscription was the double articulation of alliance and filiation that founded the ecumenon on the basis of the repression of intensive germinative desiring production. The despot-emperor overcodes this inscription with the Imperial individuation of the Urstaat abstract machine and the establishment of the Imperial State social machine. In the self-organisation and emergence of the Imperial State machine there are the connective syntheses of the new alliance, which operate to align all production to the despot-emperor in the State assemblage, and the disjunctive syntheses of direct filiation that call forth a new body of the socius for inscription and the usage of the disjunctive synthesis for the inscription. Despotic overcoding is to operate the exclusive usage of disjunctive syntheses of inscription, because the Urstaat abstract machine is the very idea of the usage of exclusive disjunctive syntheses of inscription for social organisation. The idea to impose a transcendent unity on social organisation is to use the disjunctive synthesis of inscribing the social in an exclusive manner, enabling the operation of a molar organisation in social organisation that allows the molar fold operation on the social field of organising it as a four-dimensional extensive manifold structured from a recessed transcendent dimension. The inscribing molar fold abstract machine draws out a flat plane of transcendent organisation of the body of the despot-emperor. Over this plane the usage of exclusive disjunctive syntheses of inscription, further, forces the distribution of singularities in the social field to become aligned on singularities of the exclusive nature of either cycle or point. In the Imperial State social machine the kernel of in-depth territorial representation is now taken up in the molar fold, taken up in the royal incest of the despot-emperor's new alliance and filiation, and transformed. There is still the three-fold operation structure of territorial representation in depth; there is the repressing representation, the repressed representative, and the displaced represented. In territorial in-depth representation the repressing representation was alliance, the repressed representative in reality the intensive germinal earth, and the displaced represented incest. With the social machine of the despot-emperor incest has now become possible in the exceptionalism and royal incest of the despot-emperor, and the State social machine inscribes the socius and overcodes the socius with the despot-emperor's signifier of the royal incest as the repressing representation (D&G (1984) 201 (219)). Incest has migrated from the displaced representative fundamentally disfiguring what was at stake for desiring production in territorial repression and representation to becoming the new repressing representation. The repressed representative remains what is, was before and will always be: the intensive and desiring production. The displaced represented shifts to be the supposed desire of the despot – to sleep with the sister and the mother, Oedipus – where it will lay in wait to be activated in the capitalist social machine. The new repressing representation in the State social machine has profound effects in terms of the operation of the State representational system and social machine generally and will be discussed shortly, but it is the immediate ratcheting up of socio-psychic repression in the State social machine (D&G (1984) 201–2 (219–20)). The structure of the overcoding in State representation is that there is a prohibition and repression of desiring production and the intensive precisely on the basis that there is the despot-emperor who is one that in royal incest is not subject to the prohibition. Repression becomes more explicit: there exists one who is not subject to the prohibition, therefore all others are completely subject to the prohibition of the despot. Whilst desiring production in the territorial machine was repressed and coded there was flexibility in a double articulation of social production inscription that was not an absolute exclusive use of the disjunctive synthesis. In the State social machine the overcoding inscription on the basis of the molar fold is an exclusive disjunctive synthesis, with desiring production exclusively in the body of the despot, and with complete repression of desiring production for all other members of the socius. The socio-psychic repression of desiring production becomes a general mortification. Further, this repression has now also shifted to a transcendent position of the prohibition, with the result that alongside the repression there was now also a position for the first time of a judgement on life.

As the despotic incest repressing representative bears down on desiring production and represses it, the representation not only represses the flows but it also overcodes the signifying chains and detachments from the signifying chains of territorial representation. Whereas in the territorial social machine there are mobile and flexible detachments, with the despotic repressing representation there is linearisation and flattening of the signifying chains that causes a single detached object to jump out from the signifying chain as a transcendent object which functions along side the repressing representation to structure the signifying chain. In the territorial social machine the detachments from the signifying chain and deductions from the flows were coded partial objects and social flows. In the implementation of an Urstaat social machine a single partial object jumps outside the chain as transcendent. Whilst in the territorial chain there is the independence of the voice of alliance and the graphic body of filiation, with the State machine writing aligns itself on the voice and raises the voice of the despot as the new alliance to a transcendent object. Whilst in the territorial machine there is the system of extended filiation, with the State machine there is the deterritorialised full body of the despot-emperor and his royal incest. These new features of State alliance and filiation in the repressing representation cause a now transcendent partial object to jump outside the chain and structure it alongside the despotic repressing signifier. This transcendent object could be anything (the anus (D&G (1984) 211 (229–30))), but presents itself in State social machines as the 'phallus as voice' (D&G (1984) 210 (229)).

Overcoding is, thus, the operation of the State abstract machine in the molar fold that draws a plane of organisation, effecting a new alliance and direct filiation of a despot-emperor over the territorial machines in a new repressing representation that is a regime of repression even harsher than the previous. The effect of the repressing representation causes a transcendent phallus-voice partial object to jump out of the signifying chain and participate in its structuring. This repressing representation that rises up in the molar fold and universally overcodes the entire unified signifying chain is the despotic master signifier (D&G (1984) 207 (225)).

The despotic signifier of the royal incest and the prohibition of desiring production, in tandem with the transcendent detached object, overcode all the territorial signs in a process of decoding them as territorial signs to be recoded as signifiers in relation to the master signifier and detached object. The molar fold and master signifier, operating as the repressing metaphor, establish the signifying order as a closed, transcendently structured, symbolic order of signifiers. This whole signifying chain depends upon the master signifier and the detached partial object, and the master signifier spreads the effects of signification through the chain. In this signifying order of the State social machine signifiers relate to other signifiers, and it is not a matter of what the signifier represents or designates but rather of the metaphor and metonymy of the signifying chain where the signified is always the effect of the signifiers. The master signifier effects a complete linearisation of the signifying chain into a single chain, removing all connotation exhibited in the previous territorial regime of representation.

The molar fold and master signifier, further, establish the transcendent voice of high of the despot and a consequent centrality of writing in the State social machine. This transcendent point of despotic emission, however, though based on the despotic voice as alliance point of emission, becomes in the signifying system of the State social machine a point of emission of writing. In the State social machine graphism loses its independence from the voice and aligns itself on the transcendent despotic voice. In subordinating itself to the despotic voice, however, graphism falls back on this voice as a new system of writing (D&G (1984) 202 (220)). It is a matter of transcribing the words of the despot-emperor, and of the bureaucratic writing of the despot-emperor's retinue that govern the empire. The despotic voice turns to writing, such that this voice becomes 'a fictitious voice from beyond that expresses itself as a flow of writing of direct filiation' (D&G (1984) 205 (223)).

The despot's master signifier is the despot's law, the prohibition that mortifies desiring production, and consigns all to desiring within a regime of castration, an order of representation for desire structured by the transcendent master signifier and transcendent detached partial object. Within the State social machine desire is, thus, constituted as lack and desire is welded as inseparable from the despot's law. Desire can only function in relation to a transcendent law that declares universal castration, and in a signifying order of representation in which the master signifier distributes lack to all the elements of the signifying chain, and desire passes from signifier to signifier, limited to desiring in relation to the State social machine transcendent detached partial object. In the State social machine this catching of desire within the law of the despot in the signifying order of in-depth and surface Imperial representation is doubled by desire being caught up in an Imperial system of recognition. In the State social machine desire is the property of the despot-emperor (D&G (1984) 199 (217)), whence desire is the desire of the despot, and hence desire becomes caught up in an order of recognition in which desire is the desire of the other.

The establishment of the State social machine also proceeds by way of a massive deterritorialisation and decoding. Whilst ecumenon social machines operate through code and territory, there is a moment in the establishment of the State social machine where there is a massive organisational deterritorialising and decoding (D&G (1984) 196 (214)). The moment for the deterritorialisation and decoding is the moment that the State arrives in a single stroke by the despot's double incest and will to start again from zero. All the territories and alliances of the territorial social assemblages are momentarily put in total deterritorialisation, and all the codes of the connotative double articulation of alliance and filiation are put in total decoding. The massive decoding allows the earth as socius and surface of inscription of the territorial machines to be deterritorialised so that it can be taken up as an object of transcendent unity for the State social machine and transformed into the new socius and surface of inscription of the State social machine. The massive deterritorialisation and decoding also scrambles all the systems of territorial detachments from the signifying chains and deductions from the social flows, reducing them to pure stock and flow for the new socius to appropriate. This deterritorialisation and decoding, though, is only instantaneous, a necessary moment of striating again, because the State social machine then immediately overcodes all the deterritorialised codes and reterritorialises all the deterritorialised flows. This is the overcoding of the despotic master signifier and the constitution of the unified territory of the despot-emperor (although, in the overcoding and reterritorialisation the local level functioning of the territorial assemblages are all left intact).

The body of the despot emerges as the new socius of the State social machine, replacing that of the earth (D&G (1984) 195 (213)). This body of the despot then becomes both the surface of inscription of the social machine and the centre of all productive flows. As surface of inscription this body of the despot is no longer the flexible and relatively open surface of inscription of the earth in the territorial machine. The body of the despot as surface of inscription is organised as a plane of organisation. The molar fold and master signifier operation lay out the body of the socius as a pyramid on the basis of the transcendent organisation of the socius (D&G (1984) 194 (212)). This flat pyramid is drawn on the basis of the four key terms in State social machine representation and inscription: at the peak of the pyramid there is the despot-emperor with the master signifier and the phallus-voice and at the base corners are on one the sister and the other the mother. Alternatively, this pyramid could drag apart the despot's master signifier and the phallus drawing the body of the despot and socius of inscription as a transcendently structured two-dimension plane on which its entire surface of inscription, and therefore possibilities of the social field, would be stretched between the four corners of despotic master signifier, phallus, mother and sister, drawing a plane of transcendent organisation as a kind of despotic Schema R. On this surface of the socius the exclusive usage of the disjunctive synthesis of recording carve up the social field into the hierarchically structured binary arborescent plane of organisation of the State social machine (D&G (1987) 424 (468)).

In the deterritorialisation and reterritorialisation that constitute the body of the despot as the new body of the socius, the despotic social body falls back on all social production and appropriates it entirely for itself as surplus value of the despotic code (D&G (1984) 199 (217)). In the social machine, the body of the despot as incarnation of the abstract machine appears as the cause of the collective conditions of social production and appropriation (D&G (1984) 194–5 (213–14)). All the coded flows, detachments and deductions of the territorial assemblages now aligned on the body of the despot are 'forced into a bottleneck' (D&G (1984) 199 (217)). In the State social machine all the flows now converge in the one great flow of consumption of the despot-emperor.

The Imperial State of the archaic empires are the social assemblages in which the Urstaat abstract machine and State social machine develop the purest and most fully worked-out possibilities of that abstract machine and social machine. In the Imperial State the despot-emperor is the eminent unity at the summit of an organisational and bureaucratic pyramid (D&G (1984) 205 (223)). The Imperial State is a megamachine apparatus of capture both in terms of the social field and in terms of all of social production (D&G (1988) 424 (468)). The State captures the people at the level of the desiring investment of the social field where as the exceptional despot-emperor they knot the people in a new social bond or as jurist-legislator organise the people in the new social machine. In the Imperial State the territorial system of lateral alliances and extended filiation are kept in place, but they are now captured within and subsist in the conditions of the new alliance and filiation of the despot. In the massive deterritorialisation-reterritorialisation the Imperial State captures everything inside its territorial grasp, with subsequent State apparatuses of capture for the land (rent), wealth (money in tax), and the people (profit in public works) (D&G (1988) 437 (483)). The earth and all its production are captured as the object of the higher unity of the Imperial State assemblage.

In the Imperial State assemblages the relation between the people and the despot becomes one of infinite debt. The despot-emperor operation of the imposition of the new alliance and direct filiation appropriates for the despot-emperor all the blocks of alliance debt and all the filiative stock. The Imperial State assemblage technically accomplishes the rendering infinite of all debt to the despot-emperor and converting all mobile finite alliance debt into infinite despot-emperor debt by the introduction into the assemblage of money (D&G (1984) 197 (215)). The Imperial State assemblage introduces money so that taxes can be levied and paid to the despot, thus then introducing a general equivalent that can transform the existing blocks of debt and create a cycle of infinite debt and debt payment to the despot-emperor.

In the territorial assemblages the strategies and practices of warding off the arrival of the State social machine included potlatch and the consumption of excess in feastings and festivals. In the State social machine the function of antiproduction changes completely. With the despot-emperor body of the socius falling back on production and appropriating it entirely, all the flows are aligned on the despot-emperor. The Imperial State assemblage constitutes itself transcendent antiproduction of the social field, whereby the prodigious despot-emperor personal consumption, the consumption of the palace and bureaucracy, and vast public works of monument building, all make up immense projects of antiproduction in the social machine.

In place of collective investment of the organs in the territorial assemblages, the Imperial State social machines entail that all the organs and all the flows are appropriated by the despot-emperor. In the wave of decoding and deterritorialisation in the arrival of the Imperial State machine all of the collectively invested organs of the territorial assemblages are detached from that socius and they undergo an elevation that allows them all to become attached to the body of the despot-emperor as the body of the new socius (D&G (1984) 210 (228)). This is the assemblage operation of the despot's double incest and prohibiting repressing representation, and in it royal incest rediscovers the intensive field of filiation. However, the attaching of all the organs to the body of the despot imposes a massive latency of the people as their desiring production is shut down, and the despot-emperor himself the paranoia that a single organ might flow outside the despotic body (D&G (1984) 211 (229)).

Indeed, the Imperial State assemblage presents to its people not only a latency of desiring production but also a life of social production of crushing machinic enslavement. The despot-emperor is the sole and transcendent public property holder and master of the surplus value of the code. The human beings of the Imperial State assemblage are literally just one part of a social megamachine that assembles together people, tools and animals under the control of a higher organising Imperial unity (D&G (1988) 457 (505)). The people of Imperial State know a real machinic enslavement, with the bonds of the territorial regime overtaken, and the bonds to the despot conditioned by force and enslavement and no question of there being anything approaching subjectivity beyond that, perhaps, of the despot-emperor himself.

In line with the in-depth migrations in Imperial representation and the jumping outside of the transcendent partial object phallus-voice, the Imperial State assemblage's regime of signs changes completely. It does so in two ways. First, of course, is the creation of a transcendently organised signifying order in place of the territorial connotative polyvocal double articulation. Overcoding in this signifying semiotic is fully effected by the despotic signifier and phallus, uniformity of enunciation, uniformity of substance of expression, no designation, and redundant and perpetual referral from signifier to signifier (D&G (1988) 135 (149)). Second, the whole collective assemblage of enunciation of the Imperial State assemblage aligns itself on writing. Central to the signifying regime assemblage is the despot-emperor's transcendent voice. Whilst graphism and the voice were independent in the territorial social machines, in the Imperial State social machines graphism loses its independence by becoming subordinated and aligned on the despot-emperor's voice. However, in becoming aligned the graphism becomes reborn as an Imperial writing as the voice of the despot-emperor must be transcribed, the order of the despot-emperor received and communicated, the ownership of the despot-emperor's land and people be accounted. The territorial magic triangle is broken up, and the assemblage of enunciation centres around writing in tablets, stones and books regarding matters of Imperial law, bureaucracy and accounting.

The Imperial State machine is the age of Imperial law, the Urstaat law, the law of both the magician emperor that knots and binds with the master signifier (S1) of the jurist-priest that governs through pacts and treaties (S2) (S1–S2) (D&G (1988) 351 and 424 (387 and 468)). The Imperial law is defined by the operation of the Urstaat abstract machine in overcoding through the molar fold, transcendence, the master signifier, the unified signifying chain, and the plane of organisation: 'overcoding is the essence of the law' (D&G (1984) 212 (231)). It is the operation of the master signifier, the metaphoric and metonymic necessity of the signifieds, and the arbitrariness of designation, and is 'the juridical form assumed by infinite debt' (D&G (1984) 213 (232)).

Imperial law does not, however, effectuate the Urstaat abstract machine of law in the way law would effectuate later in State social machines. State law comes later to become:

> a guarantee against despotism, an immanent principle that unites the parts into the whole, that makes this whole the object of a general knowledge and will whose sanctions are merely derivative of a judgement and an application directed at the rebellious parts.
>
> (D&G (1984) 212 (231))

Rather, Imperial law was someway from being able to fully overcode its territory, and the despot-emperor's bureaucrats were someway off developing a juridical signified (D&G (1984) 212 (231)). The Imperial State assemblages, beyond the blanket overcoding, left the productions and the reproduction of territorial social assemblages in place. As a result, the Imperial law can only 'govern nontotalisable and nontotalised parts, portioning them off, organising them as bricks' (D&G (1984) 212 (231)). In Imperial law there thus results a paranoiac trait that the formal unity of the Imperial law cannot unite the parts into a whole. Further, Imperial law possessed a syntagmatic logic of sign relating to other signs, but where 'the verdict [has] no existence prior to the penalty, and the statement of law [has] no existence prior to the verdict' (D&G (1984) 212 (231)). The Imperial law 'reveals nothing and has no knowable object' (D&G (1984) 212 (231)). This is the depressive trait of Imperial law, and it would take the Imperial jurists some time to develop a juridical signified for the despot-emperor's law and a paradigmatic axis linking suitable juridical signified to the syntagmatic axis.

Indeed, in the Imperial State assemblages it is the role of the despot-emperor's jurist-scribes that appears central to Imperial law and its new regime of writing. Jurist-priests are always numerous in the despot-emperor's retinue (D&G (1984) 202 (220)), the paranoiac despot-emperor and the perverse reterritorialising jurist-priests (D&G (1984) 193 (210)), the despot monster and the accompanying jurist-priest legislators (D&G (1984) 213 (232)). The jurist-priests spread the despot-emperor's invention of the despotic master signifier and the Imperial law, and develop piecemeal the juridical signifieds for this law. The role of the jurist-priests is to add to the significance of the despot-emperor's voice and signifier an interpretation, supplementing it by adding signified, reimparting signifiers, producing signifiers and reproducing signifiers (D&G (1988) 114 (126)). The assemblage of Imperial law thus develops two crucial aspects of the Urstaat abstract machine, and State social machines are a regime of legality and a regime of discourse as significance and interpretation (D&G (1988) 114 (126)).

The appropriation by the despot-emperor of all the flows and the organs and their attachment to the despot's body as socius, the machinic enslavement, and the nature of Imperial law, mean that the Imperial State assemblage shifts from the regime of cruelty of the territorial machine to a regime of terror. No organ can come detached from the body of the despot-emperor, and no flow can be allowed to escape the overcoding of Imperial law. The whole regime has become a system of latency where desiring production amongst the people has been shut down. The despot-emperor becomes so paranoid at the organ that may detach itself from him, or of the flow he would no longer code, that the despot-emperor enters a realm of unspeakable vengeance against any body that detaches an organ or enters into a decoded flow. Thus, the regime of terror shifts the work of the eye to foreseeing everything and ensuring no organs or flows escape from the despot-emperor's appropriation and overcoding. The eye of the magic triangle is replaced by a collective surveillance of the people of themselves, foreseeing and reporting any detachable organs or decoded flows.

The fate of the State social machine: spiritualisation and conjunctions of flows

There are two other State forms and ages of law in addition to the Imperial States. These two forms are the diverse States that all developed on the Urstaat abstract machine but in very different conditions to those of Imperial States, and the capitalist nation State that has been deployed and developed in the contemporary capitalist social machine. In the diverse States law becomes spiritualised, subjectivising, and turns to topical conjunctions of relatively decoded and deterritorialised social flows (D&G (1988) 448–53 (495–500)). In the capitalist social machine the law becomes the capitalist axiomatic, and the State and its Urstaat legality the model for effectuating the capitalist axiomatic (D&G (1988) 448–53 (495–500)).

The diverse States that effect the State abstract machine do so in assemblages and with undertakings that are novel in relation to the Imperial State social assemblages. The State abstract machine appears in many State assemblages, on very different scales, making alliances with many different forces, entering into mixed social assemblages of State. These diverse States include evolved empires, autonomous cities, feudalism, monarchies, oligarchies and democracies. All the diverse States appear under conditions of relative decoding and deterritorialisation of the flows, this relative decoding and deterritorialisation broadly being the result of the emergence of private property and the privatisation more generally. However, in all the diverse States it is the one Urstaat abstract that structures all States.

All State forms are assemblages of the Urstaat abstract machine and all the State forms refer back to the Imperial State social machine: 'It is always the Urstaat that returns in subsequent State forms under other guises and conditions' (D&G (1984) 220 (240)). All the diverse states come into existence against the absolute background of the Urstaat, and the diverse State forms cannot be thought without the Urstaat as their horizon (D&G (1984) 218 (238)). In all the diverse States there is always 'everywhere the stamping of the Urstaat on the new state of things' (D&G (1984) 218 (238)). Indeed, such is the reach of the Urstaat that capitalism reawakens the Urstaat in the forms of the capitalist State (D&G (1988) 460 (508)). The reach of the Urstaat results in 'it could be that, spiritual or temporal, tyrannical or democratic, capitalist or socialist, that there has never been but one State' (D&G (1984) 192 (209)). This Urstaat abstract machine and the Imperial law is also the background and horizon for all the diverse legalities of the diverse States: 'overcoding is the essence of the law' (D&G (1984) 212 (231)). All State law never fully breaks from transcendence, overcoding, the master signifier, signification and a plane of transcendent organisation.

There are the two poles Urstaat abstract machine and social machine, however, and this has enabled a considerable flexibility and modernisation of the concept and practice of law in many of the diverse States. There is the one pole of the magician-emperor who binds with the master signifier (S1), and there is the jurist-priest who governs through pacts and treaties and is repository of all the juridical signifiers (S2) (D&G (1988) 428 and 460 (472 and 508)). There is thus in the relation S1–S2 across the Urstaat abstract machine, considerable scope for the abstract machine to be instantiated in State assemblages that recess the Imperial S1 in order to organise on the more legalistically developed S2 pole of State legality.

In the diverse States, however flexibly assemblaged, the Urstaat abstract machine still operates as both the image of thought and the desiring investment of the social field. The image of thought and desiring investment of the social field in State thought never break away from transcendence, overcoding, the master signifier, signification and the plane of transcendent organisation. Further, State desire and unconscious identifications never break free from the welding of desire to law in castration and desire as lack, nor the State investment of the social field breaking free from the paranoia and fascism of the despot-emperor or the perversion and neurosis of the despot-emperor's jurist-priests.

In sharing the abstract machine of the Urstaat, a lot of the problematic of social organisation that the diverse States need to deal with is addressed in line with the manner of the State social machine in overcoding and the plane of transcendent organisation. However, in the diverse State assemblages, against the horizon of the receding Urstaat and the impending breaching of the capitalist social machine, there is the problematic of operating the State social machine under conditions of relative decoding and relative deterritorialisation in the flows brought about by the introduction of private property into the flows and circuits of the State forms. Given the inherent difficulty in overcoding all the flows, decoded and deterritorialised flows do emerge across the State socius in private property and private land, circuits of commercial money, emergence of commodity production, and the emerges of classes. Of equal concern for the State form of the privatisation of property was that there was a corollary gradual privatisation of large aspects of the previously public social bond, as social interdependence came to shift onto personal privatised obligations and bonds. In both respects of private property and privatised bonds the diverse States were faced with the emergence of an increasingly large private zone in the State public sphere, with quite high levels of decoding and deterritorialisation. The difficulty was exactly how to deal with these flows within the framework of the State social machine. The State assemblages could no longer overcode coded territories, but would have to deal with decoded and deterritorialised flows and also to innovate in relation to inscribing privatised social bonds.

The answer of the diverse States was two-fold. They would: (i) inscribe privatised social bonds in a spiritualisation of the State form and in centring on State assemblages new processes of subjectification; (ii) inscribe privatised decoded and deterritorialised social flows in topical law conjunctions of recoded flows:

> These are the aspects of a becoming of the State: its internalisation in a field of increasingly decoded social forces forming a physical system; its spiritualisation in a supraterrestrial field that increasingly overcodes, forming a metaphysical system. The infinite debt must become internalised at the same time as it becomes spiritualised.
>
> (D&G (1984) 222 (242))

The spiritualisation of the State was advanced in the evolved empires that fell under the influence of monotheisms, though processes of spiritualisation of the State are very important in the social assemblages of many diverse States (D&G (1984) 217 (236)); (1988) 453 (500)). The spiritualisation of the State needed the spiritualisation of the despotic State form, internalising and spiritualising the despotic infinite debt, and the development of practices of active subjectification. The despotic State's founding structure remained somewhat matriarchal, and monotheism's influence on the State form was to introduce a new primary axis of Father-Son for the structure of the State (D&G (1984) 217 (236)). In this operation the infinite debt owed to the despot that was such a crucial feature of the despotic State assemblage could now be realigned as an infinite spiritual debt, and internalised in the religious practices. The coming together of the monotheisms and the newly spiritualised State form adds a completely new regime of signs to the State social machine and its own despotic signifying regime of signs (D&G (1988) 111 (123)). With the addition of the semiotic, and support in religious practices, the entire system of despotic socio-psychic repression changed. The system of repression became based on a relation to God and infinite debt that operates as a vehicle of an internalisation of a private relation to subjectification. The new assemblages and regime of signs taken from the monotheisms into the newly spiritualised State forms were the personal passional monomaniacal assemblages (D&G (1988) 127 (140)) and the post-signifying regime of signs (D&G (1988) 111 (123)).

The regime of signs and personal assemblages are processes of passional subjectification in a line of flight and a proceeding of subjectification in relation to a point of departure or betrayal (D&G (1988) 127 (140)). The point of departure or betrayal is the point of an object cause of desire in the social field, and the engendering of a passional proceeding of subjectification in relation to this object cause of desire. It is the emergence of consciousness and subjectification as the grounding of the spiritual State form. Whilst the despotic signifying regime operated paranoiacally, the spiritualised State regime of signs is authoritarian, subjectifying in serial proceedings, and, ultimately, the creation of the self-legislating subjects to replace the signifying despot (D&G (1988) 130 (143)). The regime of signs of the post-signifying semiotic has the object cause point of desire and the proceeding of the production of a subject, that subject split between the subject of enunciation and the subject of the statement ($\$ \blacklozenge a$). It is the new collective assemblage of enunciation of the State form, and a process of subjectification as a new State regime of social subjection replacing despotic machinic enslavement, itself the new State system of socio-psychic repression. Adding the passional subjectifying regime of signs to the despotic regime of signs there is obtained the new social bond and discursive structure of the diverse social States between despotism and capitalism: $S1–S2 / (\$ \blacklozenge a)$ (D&G (1988) 125 (138)).

The spiritualisation of the State, the spiritual realignment of infinite debt, and the integration into the State form of monotheistic operations of subjectification, together addressed the problematic of the diverse State forms in a substantial way. Amongst the diverse States, even if it does not proceed through spiritualisaton, the States to cope with relative decoding and deterritorialisation have turned to operations of the subjectification of their populations. However, in addition to operations of subjectification, the novel challenges for the diverse States were by no means over. The diverse States and their law would have to: operate conjunctions of decoded/recoded social flows; ensure the adequation of subjectifications and conjunctions of recoded flows and, so, an adequation of subjectivity and private rights; and, provide a guarantee against the despotism from which the State form and the law arose in order to socially embed private flows, persons and relations (D&G (1984) 212 (230)).

The diverse State needed to invent new codes for decoded and deterritorialised flows of money, private property and commodities (D&G (1984) 218 (237); (1988) 459 (507)). The task of the diverse States is to invent new codes for conjunctions of private decoded flows in topical law recodings of the flows:

> The law in its entirety undergoes a mutation, becoming subjective, conjunctive 'topical' law: this is because the State apparatus is faced with a new task,

which consists less in overcoding already coded flows than in organising conjunctions of decoded flows as such. Thus the regime of signs has changed: in all these respects, the operation of the imperial 'signifier' has been superseded by processes of subjectification; machinic enslavement tends to be replaced by a regime of social subjection.

(D&G (1988) 451 (498))

The diverse State law tends to become topical, whilst not ceasing to carry the entire baggage of the despotic State machine and law as overcoding. New law becomes a set of topics, relating to land, things, people, dealing with private property and bonds of personal dependence. The topical law is not coding or overcoding, but a recoding that is a provisional and relative accommodation of the conjunction of decoded flows. This recoding is in the new topical framework of the diverse States but also framed within the overcoding State image of thought and legality. What is new in diverse State legality is a pragmatic openness to the flows and to private property and relations. The law and the State remain central, however, in all these diverse States, because for there even to be processes of the appropriation of private wealth and processes of subjectification the active intervention of the law and State were necessary.

However, with the emergence of capitalism the State form and the law changes again. It is not a case of diverse States with the topical recoding of decoded and deterritorialised flows in law, and no longer even a State social machine. Social organisation ceases to be an adventure of the ecumenon, and moves to sprawl across the full ontological modality of the social field of ecumenon, mechanosphere and planomenon. With capitalism the State social machine changes entirely, as does the operation of the State and of law:

A new threshold of deterritorialisation. And when capital becomes an active right in this way, the entire historical figure of the law changes. The law ceases to be the overcoding of the customs, as it was in the archaic empire; it is no longer a set of topics, as it was in the evolved States, the autonomous cities, and the feudal systems; it increasingly assumes the direct form and immediate characteristics of an axiomatic, as evidenced in our civil "code".

(D&G (1988) 453 (500))

The capitalist social machine enters with a generalised conjunction of the flows, which overtake topical conjunctions, and brings forward a purely economic organisation of the social field. There is the formal end of the adventure of social organisation in the ecumenon (though not without a welling up of the ecumenon Urstaat abstract machine in the midst of the intensive social field of the capitalist social machine). The law ceases to be topical relating to land, things and people, to become convertible abstract rights expressing the workings of capitalism and its axiomatic. Whilst the modern diverse States were crucial in the capitalist conversion of the social field (colonial regime, public debt, modern taxation and indirect taxation, industrial protectionism, trade wars) (D&G (1988) 454 (501)), the State form is entirely eclipsed by the capitalist social machine as the primary organisation of the social field. In capitalism the State form is recycled as an immanent model of realisation of a capitalist axiomatic of organisation that exceeds the State form (D&G (1988) 454 (501)).

Ecumenon, mechanosphere, planomenon: the adventure of capitalism

The ecumenon social organisations of the territorial social machines and the State social machines proceeded in coding, overcoding, and a plane of transcendence, with processes of territorialisation and reterritorialisation. The capitalist social machine and the adventure of capitalism arrives as the exterior limit of all ecumenon social organisation, and is the 'negative of all social formations' (D&G (1984) 153 (168)). The capitalist social machine is an entirely new adventure in social organisation 'of another species, functioning in an entirely different way' (D&G (1984) 227–8 (247)), beyond ecumenon social organisation, operating, rather, in the intensive morphogenetic field and all the way to a surfacing of the planomenon. The new adventure of capitalism 'is defined by the decoding and deterritorialisation of the flows in capitalist production' (D&G (1984) 244 (265)).

The model of the capitalist social machine has two aspects. One aspect is purely economic and is the abstract machine of capitalism. The second aspect is regulatory and is the social implementation of the capitalist axiomatic which is a necessary corollary to the economic abstract machine.

Capitalism is the event of the general conjunction of abstracted decoded and deterritorialised flows, and constitutes capital as the intensive body of the socius. Capitalism is the intensive and virtual mathematical and physical operation of differential flows, not passing by way of representation. It is a purely economic abstract machine of generalised arbitrage, immanence and differential flows. These differential flows have no assignable exterior limit, with the result that the economic abstract machine of capitalism is systemic crisis. In capitalism surplus value of code becomes surplus value of flows, and antiproduction spreads to become pervasive to all capitalist production. Infinite debt shifts to the banking sector, and the banks and finance come to control the operation of the entire global capitalist system.

However, the capitalist social machine also operates on the basis of a massive supporting and regulatory framework to deal with and compensate for the capitalist economic abstract machine that is decoding and deterritorialisation without end, absence of exterior limits, systematic crisis and the power of the banks. This supporting and regulatory framework is the capitalist axiomatic, nation States as models of realisation of the capitalist axiomatic, and very large-scale operations of recoding and reterritorialisation. This capitalist axiomatic constitutes the only limit that is known to the capitalist social machine as an interior limit, which is constantly surpassed and displaced in relation to severe contractions of systemic crisis.

The nation States, though surpassed by capitalism as the social machine, play an absolutely vital function in the regulatory and supporting framework for the capitalist system. Capitalist decoding and deterritorialisation is always axiomatised, recoded and reterritorialised by the full capitalist social machine. Capitalism as a social machine is the occupation of the intensive morphogenetic field of social organisation, and both the organisation of the intensive field and the primary organisation of the ecumenon is from continuous operations in the intensive field of social organisation: capitalism defines a field of immanence (D&G (1984) 250 (271)). The capitalist interior limit is the relative limit of all social organisation in the capitalist social machine.

For this model of the capitalist social machine to take over the organisation of the social field and for the emergence of axiomatic law a number of processes must eat away at the State social machines and assemblages. There must be a breakdown of all the territorial and State codes that come to bring about a generalised decoding of the social flows. This breaking down and generalisation occur by way of processes of privatisation of flows in the State assemblages: gradual and piecemeal privatisation of organs, of goods, of people, of land and of the means of production. This amounts to processes of the abstraction of the quantity of labour, commodities as units of abstract labour, and the development of rent differentials. The decoding of the flows is accompanied by processes of generalised deterritorialisation of wealth and people. The deterritorialisation takes place in physical developments as well as more processes of privatisation. These include deterritorialisation of land as wealth, commodity production, monopolistic appropriations, new technical machines and the development of industrial capacity. The State itself must decode and deterritorialise somewhat so as to recode and reterritorialise as a State that protects private property and which provides a legal system that supports a system of private property. This involves the development and robust protection of a core of property and contract rights, State finance and public debt, a colonial appropriation regime, industrial protectionism and trade wars (D&G (1988) 454 (502)). Money, introduced in the State social machine as the means for taxation, becomes the abstraction of the decoded flows in monetary quantities, an extensive system of general equivalent for abstracting the flows, and the substitution of money for the very idea of code. In the light of generalised decoding, deterritorialisation, and the monetary abstraction of the flows: 'value suddenly presents as an independent substance, endowed with a motion of its own, in which money and commodities are mere forms that it assumes and casts off in turn' (Marx quoted D&G (1984) 227 (247)).

Beyond the generalised decoding and deterritorialisation of the flows, for the arrival of the capitalist social machine there needs to be a specific new massive deterritorialisation and the conjunction of the two new deterritorialised flows. It is a conjunction of massive deterritorialisation of the decoded flows of production in the form of money-capital and the decoded flows of labour in the form of the deterritorialised worker (D&G (1984 33 (36)). This conjunction of a pure flow of capital and pure flow of labour is a machine: it is the intensive operation of the capitalist social machine that taps forces of self-organisation and emergence for the profit of the capitalist. In the conjunction, capitalism sets together two differential flows and opens up the intensive morphogenetic field for capitalist production and organisation. Capitalism is engendered in the differential relation between the two decoded flows of capital and labour power. The conjunction leads to the enterprise of production for the sake of production, and arrives when industrial capital appropriates production. Capital as finance capital and trade capital existed and operated in the State social machines, but only as a capital of alliance with various activities of the State social machine. At this point the nature of capital changes fundamentally. Capital becomes filiative (D&G (1984) 229 (249)). The capitalist conjunction becomes independent of money and commodities, and capitalism appropriates the production of production, of recording, and consumption.

In the conjunction of decoded capital and decoded labour, capital enters into relations itself, counter-actualising itself becoming intensive, and differentiating itself into the two decoded flows: 'This is the differential relation Dy/Dx, where Dy derives from labour power and constitutes the fluctuation of variable capital, and where Dx derives from capital itself and constitutes the fluctuations of constant capital' (D&G (1984) 227 (248)).

The differential relation is not an indirect relationship between two coded or qualified flows, but it is a direct relationship between decoded flows whose respective qualities have no existence prior to the differential relation itself. The qualities of the flows result solely from their conjunction as decoded flows, and 'outside this conjunction they would remain purely virtual' (D&G (1984) 249 (270)). This differential relation is the self-organisation and emergence of the motor of capitalism, and is precisely a differential relation between a flow of two series of differences in a manifold that has a dynamic distribution of singularities. In the operation of differentiating into itself capital counter-actualises itself to become intensive and virtual, opening up a virtual plane for capital and an intensive morphogenetic field for the economic operation of capitalism: 'the differential relation is the conjunction that defines the immanent social field particular to capitalism' (D&G (1984) 227 (248)). The capitalist surface of inscription is the plane of immanence as plane and body of capital, with no higher dimension than that which flows on it.

This capitalist machinic conjunction, however, is an operation that involves two very different flows being put together in a conjunction on the basis that these two flows actually are equal in the conjunction. The two flows are capital and means of payment, flows of capital measuring economic power and flows of purchasing power measuring income. Yet, in these two flows there is no common measure between the two flows before the conjunction that creates the capitalist economic machine: 'Measuring the two orders of magnitude in terms of the same analytical unit is pure fiction, a cosmic swindle, as if one were to measure intergalactic or intra-atomic distances in metres and centimetres' (D&G (1984) 230 (250)).

There is a dualism of money in capitalism that must be dissimulated. The two flows of capital and flows of purchasing power are incommensurable to each other, and money plays on two boards (D&G (1984) 229 (249)).

However, the capitalist abstract machine that proceeds through decoding and deterritorialisation makes use of an inclusive use of the disjunctive synthesis of recording and inscription, and draws an intensive and immanent plane for the inscription of the socius and new capitalist body of the socius. What defined the social machines of the ecumenon were the exclusive usage of the disjunctive synthesis and the drawing of a plane of organisation, with organisational strategies of coding and overcoding. In the capitalist economic abstract machine the two flows are held in an inclusive disjunction that is immanent, intensive, and where the differences between the two flows are not cancelled out. Indeed, in the capitalist abstract machine the two flows are put into a conjunction at different levels of power: 'That the flow of financing is raised to an entirely different power from the flow of means of repayment signifies that power has become directly economic' (D&G (1984) 229 (249)).

The two flows are held together dynamically in a conjunction where they are immanent to each other, but incommensurable to each other because of the absence of common measure.

In this conjunction of capital and the capitalist abstract machine from its inception it is the banks that play the central role in the capitalist assemblage. They are crucial in two respects. First, the banks lay out the intensive plane of the body of capital and the new body for capitalist inscription. The banking sector creates the first immense deterritorialised flow of capital that constitutes full body of capital (D&G (1984) 237 (258)). When the banks create a debt to themselves they do so as the instantaneous creation of an infinite debt to themselves:

> [the banks] hollow out at one extreme of the full body [of capital] a negative money (a debt entered as a liability of the banks), and projects at the other extreme a positive money (a credit granted the productive economy by the banks).
>
> (D&G (1984) 237 (258))

The full body of capital is drawn, and the infinite debt moves from being owed to the State to being owed to the banks. The second aspect of banking to the capitalist social machine is the control of the relations and conversions between the two flows of money (D&G (1984) 229 (249)). The banks constitute the economic power centres by which the flows of capital enter into immanent but incommensurable inclusive disjunction at a power advantage to capital. The banks, particularly central banks, try and control all the communications, conversions and co-adaptations between the two flows in the capitalist conjunction (D&G (1984) 229 (249)). Given the capitalist social machine's need to dissimulate the incommensurability of the two flows, the control of the two flows in banking is pivotal to the operation of the entire system. Together with the co-operation of the capitalist

State, the banks operate the principle of guaranteed convertibility between the two flows, without which the dissimulation would not be possible. In short, the banks control the entire capitalist machine (D&G (1984) 230 (250)).

In this economic abstract machine of capitalism surplus value of code is transformed into surplus value of flow. The conjunction of the two immanent but incommensurable flows of labour and capital in which the intensive machinic difference is not cancelled out is the surplus value of the flow:

> It is from the fluxions of decoded flows, from the conjunction, that the filiative form of capital, x + dx, results. The differential relation expresses the fundamental phenomenon of the transformation of surplus value of code to surplus value of flux.
>
> (D&G (1984) 228 (248))

This surplus value of flow finds in the immanent but incommensurable differential relation 'the fathomless abyss where surplus value of flow is engendered' (D&G (1984) 238 (259)). There is the flux of capital across the body of capital socius, there is the reflux of purchasing power, and the afflux of raw profit as surplus value of flow (D&G (1984) 238–9 (259)). The capitalist machine, though based on the surplus value extracted from the conjunction of the flows of capital and labour, in its financialisation has found many more ways to extract surplus value of flow from generalised decoded and deterritorialised flows. The abstract machine of capital has developed to become the arbitraging of any two immanent but incommensurable flows. It is the rendering of any two immanent but incommensurable flows into a forced conjunction, where the surplus value of flow can be extracted. These conjunctions of surplus value of flow can be the result of an increase in constant capital in technological machines in which human flows and machinic flows are conjoined in such a way that draws out a machinic surplus value of flow from which capital can extract. A deregulated global financial system finds very many flows that can be placed in an immanent but incommensurable conjunction, extracting surplus value of flow from floating currencies, securitisation and derivatives.

In the capitalist social machine antiproduction, which had been an important balancing function in territorial social machines and a transcendent instance opposed to production of royal antiproduction in State social machines, now becomes a generalised antiproduction pervasive throughout all production, and becomes capable of massive expansion in scope. Antiproduction becomes so central and expanded in capitalism as surplus value of flow must not only be produced and extracted, but surplus value of flow also needs to be absorbed and realised. Antiproduction integrates and realises surplus value of flow (D&G (1984) 234 (254)). Antiproduction is injected into production itself, conditioning the production itself (D&G (1984) 235 (255)): 'Antiproduction apparatus ceases to be transcendent, and pervades all production and becomes co-extensive with it' (D&G (1984) 250 (271)). In capitalism no one escapes participation in the activity of antiproduction that drives the entire productive system. Very many of the activities of the capitalist State realise surplus value of flow in antiproduction in the military apparatus, and commerce realises surplus value of flow in the antiproduction of advertising (D&G (1984) 235 (255)). State and commerce have found great scope for antiproduction in security, and a deregulated global financial system has produced an antiproduction machine capable of swallowing up all productive capitalist activity.

Thus, there are the basics of the capitalist economic abstract machine and plane of recording. It operates through machining conjunctions in decoded and deterritorialised flows. In particular, the capitalist abstract machine is the conjunction of the flows of capital and labour that are incommensurable to each other but connected in an immanent inclusive disjunctive synthesis. The capitalist abstract machine draws a plane of immanence for capital and constitutes the socius as the intensive body of capital. Capital falls back and appropriates all production and inscribes production on the body of capital. Surplus value of flow issues forth from the intensive conjunctions as the intensive difference that is not cancelled out in the conjunction. In the capitalist assemblage, although enterprises physically make the conjunctions, it is the banks that operate this capitalist abstract machine.

The abstract machine of capitalism of the immanent but incommensurable conjunction of the flow of capital and the flow of labour, where difference in intensity is not cancelled out but taken as surplus value of flow, is further characterised by the absence of an exterior relation to that relation. Between immanent but incommensurable differential relations in inclusive disjunctive syntheses of conjunction there are no limits to the relations (D&G (1984) 230 (250)). The differentials are not cancelled out or resolved, and form a fractal line of flight in continuous variation (D&G (1984) 230 (250)), and forms a curve without a tangent (D&G (1984) 231 (251)). The quotient of the two differentials is not calculable, and it remains a deviating line in continuous variation, 'endlessly delayed by accidents and deviations' (D&G (1984) 231 (251)). In this absence of exterior limit to the differential relationship there are, thus, ever increasing waves of capitalist decoding and deterritorialisation and pursuit of production for the sake of production (D&G (1984) 259 (281)).

However, capitalism must pursue this pursuit of production for the sake of production within the determinate mode of production necessary for the continued reproduction of capital. In this respect, in order to enable the survival of capitalism and the reproduction of capital by the capitalist machine, that social machine must produce an interior limit to capitalist decoding and deterritorialisation, so as to be able to have some consistency to the conjunctions of decoded and deterritorialised flows. The interior limits are produced by the capitalist social machine precisely because the absence of an exterior limit to capitalist differential relations poses fatal consequences to capitalist machine's ability to reproduce as decoding and deterritorialisation tends to absolute decoding and deterritorialisation: 'capitalism has no external limit, only an immanent limit that is always displaced in capitalist reproduction of itself' (D&G (1984) 230–1 (250–1)). These interior limits take the form of some level of an axiomatic of the flows and their conjunctions, some level of regulation by the capitalist State, and some level of the recoding and reterritorialisation of economic flows and desiring production. These interior limits are, however, always entirely interior, immanent and provisional. The capitalist machine is always pursuing greater production and extraction of surplus value of flow in the decoding and deterritorialisation of economic and financial flows. However, simultaneously, there must also be a corollary movement of recoding and reterritorialisation in order to avoid capitalism's tendency to absolute coding and deterritorialisation (D&G (1984) 261 (283)). Capitalism is 'continually drawing near to the wall, while at the same time pushing the wall away' (D&G (1984) 176 (192)):

> But all [capitalism] confronts are its own limits (the periodic depreciation of existing capital); all it repels or displaces are its own limits (the formation of new capital, in new industries with high profit rate)…Capitalism confronts its own limits and simultaneously displaces them, setting them down farther along.
> (D&G (1988) 463 (511))

Whenever the capitalist machine systemic crisis reaches an impasse – falling rate of profit, organised demands of labour, acute financial crisis – the existing interior limits are surpassed and displaced.

Thus, the capitalist machine is itself the relative limit of social organisation (D&G (1984) 176 (192)). The relative limit is the moveable immanent interior limits of the capitalist machine in relation to systemic crisis of the capitalist machine. In the capitalist social machine there is systemic crisis and immanent moveable limits that is continuity within the absolute break (D&G (1984) 231 (251)), and 'capitalism engenders itself in this break of a break that is always displaced in the unity of the schiz and the flow' (D&G (1984) 231 (251)).

The interior limit of capitalism and relative limit of social organisation is the capitalist axiomatic, together with the activities of the capitalist nation State. What organises the capitalist machine and all the capitalist social assemblages is the global axiomatic, capitalist nation States, and social operations of recoding and reterritorialisation both large scale and small scale. The axiomatic and associated recodings and reterritorialisations are the displaceable interior conditions by which capitalism can pursue its otherwise unlimited decodings and deterritorialisation whilst reproducing itself and inhibiting its absolute limit. In the capitalist social machine, the organisation of capitalist production and the capitalist social assemblages there are two models of realisation of the axiomatic. At the large scale the model of realisation of the axiomatic is the capitalist State, and at the small scale the model of realisation of the axiomatic is the private family organised by Oedipus. It is the axiomatic that replaces all notions of coding and topical recodings in the capitalist social machine. The axiomatic is made up of modern and contemporary elements, together with many elements that the capitalist social machine recycles from prior social machines. The result of the latter is that the axiomatic is realised in operations of recoding and reterritorialising that are 'artificial, residual, archaic; but they are archaisms having perfectly current functions; our way of "imbricating", of sectioning off, of re-introducing code fragments, inventing pseudo codes and jargons' (D&G (1984) 257 (279)).

The axiomatic works to: (i) stabilise the immanent capitalist and to keep the flows in a bound state on the body of the capitalist socius; (ii) co-ordinate the displacements of the interior relative limit; and (iii) block lines of flight and new desiring abstract machines that do not accord with the logic of capitalism (D&G (1988) 144 (159)). The capitalist axiomatic becomes the new model of law in capitalism, and constitutes the new enlarged system of socio-psychic repression. In the capitalist social machine law changes to become the new immanent global model of law, which operates at the same level as the capitalist economic machine in the intensive morphogenetic social field, although this same immanent axiomatic legality is also realised extensively in the models of the capitalist nation State, the Oedipal family, and other social assemblages of recoding and reterritorialisation.

The axioms of the capitalist axiomatic are operative statements that indicate what is to be done, principles, working assumptions, best practice (they are not theoretical propositions or ideological formulas) (D&G (1984) 251 (272–3)). The axiomatic is part of the capitalist collective assemblage of enunciation, and enters into the material and technological regime of capitalism. The regime of signs in capitalism is decoded flows of expression and decoded flows in reciprocal presupposition that is asignifying. The regime of signs is a pure field of algebraic immanence that the axiomatic enters into to constitute the capitalist collective assemblage of enunciation. These axioms are articulated in the regime of signs to enter into the intensive morphogenetic field of the capitalist material and technological regime of the flows. The axioms effectuate conjunctions and disjunctions of the capitalist flows that directly intervene to direct what is to be done and to apply provisional stratifications on the flows. Axioms as statements are entirely independent of each other, such that the axiomatic can simply add or subtract statements according to the requirements of the co-ordination of the capitalist interior limit (D&G (1988) 461 (509)). The axiomatic is immanent to the capitalist social machine, with a range of capitalist agents involved in the creation and operation of the axiomatic. These agents include national central banks, international organisations such as the Bank of International Settlements, trade block organisations, nation states, private banks and market providers, global law and accountancy practices, international trade associations. At the global level the axiomatic is in need of constant finessing and reworking, whilst at the national level of the State politics is simply the implementation at the local level of the axiomatic (D&G (1988) 461 (509)). Recent global capitalism has explored two versions of the axiomatic. One axiomatic prevailed loosely over the third quarter of the twentieth century with regulation of international capitalism, with State public provision of services, a settlement between capital and labour, and

Keynesian State management of growth. This axiomatic was abandoned by capitalism in the final quarter of the century and into the twenty-first, with the adoption of a neo-liberal axiomatic of deregulation of finance and markets, minimal State, and war of capital against labour. In the neoliberal axiomatic: 'at the limit, the only axioms that are retained concern the equilibrium of the foreign sector, reserve levels, and inflation rate' (D&G (1988) 462 (510)).

In the axiomatic the primary model of realisation is the nation State. The first task of the modern nation State is to order and regulate the social field for the economic interests of capitalist reproduction, and then to regulate decoded flows and axiomatised flows within its sovereign jurisdiction (D&G (1984) 246 (267)). In the realisation of the capitalist axiomatic 'the principal organ is the State' (D&G (1984) 252 (273)). The capitalist nation State finds itself in the position of realising an axiomatic that exceeds them, and they are surpassed as social machines organising social production (D&G (1988) 454 (501)). However, capitalism cannot do without the State form: 'It is the form of the nation State with all its possible variations that the State became the model of the realisation of the capitalist axiomatic' (D&G (1988) 456 (503)). The axiom operates directly and immanently at the global level of the intensive morphogenetic field of capitalism. However, capitalism needed the States from the start to provide the necessary conditions for capitalism. It is only through the framework of the State form that the axioms can be realised extensively in an on the ground implementation. This recycling of the State form in capitalism resuscitates the abstract machine of the State social machine. In order to implement the axiomatic and recode and reterritorialise the capitalist flows, the State with all its features of transcendent overcoding, unities, signification, and image of thought, becomes inseparable from the capitalist social machine and central to the capitalist social field:

> In this sense it indeed completes the becoming concrete that seemed to us to preside over the evolution of the abstract despotic Urstaat: from being at first a transcendent unity, it becomes immanent to the field of social forces, enters into their service, and serves as a regulator of decoded and axiomatised flows.
> (D&G (1984) 252 (272))

Thus, the State is the realisation of the axiomatic in recodings and reterritorialisation, and does so in a transcendent model that is an archaism of the Urstaat, forms that are resuscitated old codes, and the spread of an image of thought. The realisation of the axiomatic and support for the global capitalist machine extends in the modern capitalist States to direct interventions in the capitalist circuits. Modern States not only stand behind the guarantee of convertibility between the two flows, but by way of the central bank funds directly intervene in the markets and coordinate State bail outs of the capitalist system. In all this:

> The social axiomatic of modern societies is caught between two poles, and is constantly oscillating from one to another. Born of decoding and

deterritorialisation, on the ruins of the despotic machine, these societies are caught between the Urstaat that they would like to resuscitate as an overcoding and reterritorialising unity, and the unfettered flows that carry them toward an absolute threshold...They are torn in two directions: archaism and futurism, neo-archaism and ex-futurism, paranoia and schizophrenia.

(D&G (1984) 260 (282))

With the capitalist social machine the 'entire historical figure of the law changes...it increasingly assumes the direct form and immediate characteristics of an axiomatic' (D&G (1988) 453 (500)). The axiomatic abstract machine of legality replaces both State overcoding and diverse States' topical recodings, though of course recycling and maintaining within the new axiomatic abstract machine of legality an even more robust Urstaat abstract machine of legality and of the continued use of topical recodings of decoded flows. Capitalist legality has a double life: first as the immanent axiomatic operating in the intensive morphogenetic social field of capitalism; second as the national level in the implementation of the axiomatic in State law and topical overcoding. The first model of law is a new immanent model of global law axioms, subsuming and cannibalising all existing legalities (D&G (1988) 463 (511)).

The capitalist machine needs an axiomatic to compensate for the tendency of its economic abstract machine to approach absolute decoding and deterritorialisation. This is a problem of the flows of capital, and is addressed with the new model of legality of a global immanent axiomatic and its implementation at a national level in the capitalist State. However, the capitalist social machine also needs to deal with desiring production as the decoding and deterritorialisation that was necessary for the emergence of the economic abstract machine also bears down on previously coded, overcoded, territorialised, reterritorialised desiring production and investment of the social field. The capitalist social machine requires private persons subjectivised ideally in a system of lack, and direct libidinal investments of the economic flows of capitalism. It does the former by way of the application of the whole capitalist axiomatic onto the capitalist family. In both the co-option of the flows of desiring production and the private familial application of the capitalist axiomatic it constitutes a new system of socio-psychic repression.

The capitalist machine is a machine of flows, flows of money, flows of commodities, differential flows within capitalism, and, of course, the flow by which capital creates surplus value. The direct investment of these flows of money is how the capitalist social machine integrates desire and illicits the unconscious investment of the capitalist social field. It is flows and breaks of flows, flows of money, flows of financing, money that makes money, and economic mechanisms that are desired and unconsciously invested (D&G (1984) 104 (114–15)). This investment of the social field is not ideological, but of an immanent desiring production and direct libidinal investment of the intensive and extensive social field (D&G (1984) 239 (259–60)). The desire for flows of capital is not only for the capitalists, but it is a socio-economic complex of the unconscious

(D&G (1984) 245 (266)). The hook of this unconscious investment of the capitalist social field is for even those who are manifestly exploited in capitalism, and this is because the capitalist machine intensively conjoins two incommensurable flows on a basis of convertibility, such that to invest means of payment money is also to invest capital moneys.

The social organisation of the capitalist social machine does not pass through non-economic factors but instead productive activity itself is marked in terms of forces, agents and means of production: 'capitalism has taken upon itself the relations of alliance and filiation' (D&G (1984) 263 (285)). Whilst not suspending the operations of subjectification developed in the spiritualised State and diverse States, and adding a new layer of subjectification by the nation States (D&G (1988) 457 (505)), capitalism now moves to become the point of subjectification in the social field (D&G (1988) 130 (143)). The capitalist subjectification is the application of the capitalist axiomatic to private persons through the capitalist family, reinvoking almost all the operations of subjectification in all previous social machines. Capitalism takes first level images of persons determined in the social field by the conjunctions of the flows that are applied to the family as second level persons in the closed social field of the private family. The familial determinations become the application of the axiomatic (D&G (1984) 264 (287)). From the genealogy of the ecumenon socio-psychic repression complex, capitalist machine moves the State machine displaced represented of desire of Oedipus to become the repressing representation. Desiring production in capitalist decoding and deterritorialisation does not have an exterior limit as it did in ecumenon social machines, and desiring production can tend towards the absolute limit of social organisation in absolutely decoded and deterritorialised desiring production. In order to keep desiring production in a bound state on the body of the capitalist socius the social machine develops a displaceable interior limit to repress desire. From the State social machine the capitalist social machine borrows the displaced represented of Oedipus, and uses this as the new repressing representation. The interior limit of the capitalist axiomatic is applied to the private family as the Oedipal interior limit. The repressing representation no longer separates desiring production from social production, but passes within social production between the first level representation of the capitalist field and the second level representation of the privatised family:

> Father, mother, and child thus become the simulacrum of the images of capital ('Mister Capital, Madame Earth', and their child the worker), with the result that these images are no longer recognised at all in the desire that is determined to invest only their simulacrum. The familial determinations become the application of the social axiomatic.
>
> (D&G (1984) 264 (285))

The Oedipal family is the personal and private territory that corresponds to all of the capitalist social machine's reterritorialisations of decoded and deterritorialised

desiring production (D&G (1984) 265 (286)). This application in displaced represented of the State social machine brings with the capitalist imaginary Oedipus
the entire system of the despotic State, welding desire to castration, law and lack.

Thus, capitalism is always doubled. One side is the economic abstract machine
of decoding and deterritorialisation without exterior limit; and an axiomatic that
stabilises and regulates the economic side through nation States, Oedipus and
reterritorialisation. In this capitalist social machine legality finds a new immanence in a global axiomatic, but it is in the Urstaat abstract machine that the
capitalist social machine finds its pervasive colonisation of the social field as
adjunct to capitalism's intensive economic field. The State sovereignty in capitalism presides over national and international law, the contemporary image of
thought, and the model for contemporary subjectivity and desiring production.

By way of conclusion to the discussion of the capitalist social machine, some
reflection can be added on the contemporary circumstances of the deregulation
and globalisation of banks and financial institutions that have produced an explo-
sion of decoded and deterritorialised conjunctions of financial flows that are
immanent but incommensurable, and not possessing any exterior limits to their
differential relation. Forty years ago these developments in the capitalist social
machine were unknown, though nonetheless all too foreseeable:

> The route taken by the decoded flows is traced by recent monetary history,
> the role of the dollar, short-term migratory capital, the floating of the curren-
> cies, the new means of financing and credit, the special drawing rights, and
> the new forms of crisis and speculations.
>
> (D&G (1984) 245 (266))

In the neoliberal revolution a fundamental shift was effectuated in the organisation
of the capitalist machine. The filiation of capital was passed from industrial capital to finance capital, with resulting implications for capitalism's immanent field
of flows. In order to extract surplus value from flows, the banks and financial
institutions need to massively increase the volume of the flows through credit
creation, securitisation, derivatives and proprietary speculative trading. This is to
massively increase the conjunctions of financial flows in immanent but incommensurable differential relations without exterior limits and to move decoded and
deterritorialised flows from intensive conjunctions towards conjunctions of series
of pure virtual differences. By these global networks of massively increased
and computerised financial flows, the banks and financial institutions draw a real-
time virtual plane of immanence for the capitalist socius precisely as a plane of
financial differences, series of differences, differential relations, diverging and
converging series, conjunctions of differential relations in immanent synthesis,
distributions of singularities, thresholds and bifurcations, lines of continuous
variations, chaos effects, non-linearities, fractal effects and catastrophe effects.

The capitalist principle, though, is that capitalist decoding and deterritorialisation,
and the endless extraction of surplus value from flow, is invincible. The capitalist

social machine will not decode and deterritorialise itself to the absolute and the collapse of capitalist social organisation because capitalism is always a relative decoding and deterritorialisation because the axiomatic recodes and reterritorialises: 'capital appearing as something transcendent' (D&G (1994) 100)). The organisation of capitalism necessarily results in the capitalist machine existing in a state of systemic crisis. However, always whenever the systemic crisis becomes threatening to the very reproduction of the capitalist machine the axiomatic of capital is operated on and the interior limits of capitalism surpassed and displaced. Systemic collapse will always be averted, and absolute deterritorialisation will not come through the efforts of the banks and financial institutions.

Planomenon as ethos: prefiguring a social machine of the absolute limit (nomad social machine)

The planomenon raises the problematic of social organisation beyond the adventure of the ecumenon (coding, overcoding, territorialisation, reterritorialisation, plane of organisation) and beyond the capitalist social machine and its relative decoding and deterritorialisation and axiomatic. This is the problematic of a fourth social machine and fourth legality. It is to establish a planomenon social organisation and legality, and the social organisation and legality of the plane of immanence. It is to establish a social machine that connects the planomenon earth together with the planomenon brain in a social organisation as the planomenon connecting to cosmic forces and tapping cosmic forces as an ethos. It is to establish a social organisation and legality on the basis of a desiring investment of the social field, the earth, thought, and cosmic forces as the forces of immanence and of exteriority. The investment of pure immanence is to live and think on the plane of immanence, to live and think the virtual forces of the cosmos and the outside. It is to live and sense in an intensive morphogenetic field of sensations and affects, and to live in a social machine of minimal extension and stratifications. It is to invest social organisation precisely as a virtual problematic of social organisation, and to invest the intensive problem social field as a problem field of sensations and affects. In all this, to establish a planomenon social organisation is to leave and take flight, to leave the residues of the ecumenon social machines, to leave the plane of the capitalist social machine, and to take a line of flight that traverses the planomenon and an engendering exteriority.

A planomenon social machine is supermolecular. It is a social machine that draws a plane of immanence for social organisation, and that socially organises on the basis of the processes of decoding and deterritorialisation. Supermolecular social machines have very little in common with molar social machines, or with the capitalist social machine that cannot establish a consistent immanent abstract machine for social organisation and must rely upon elements recycled from the molar social machines of an axiomatic, nation States, and Oedipus. A planomenon social machine, as well as drawing a plane of immanence for social organisation, operates an abstract machine of transversal consistency that taps the virtual and intensive exteriority and forces of cosmos on a fractal line of flight. A planomenon social machine has intensive social assemblages of desiring production, and low levels of stratification. The abstract machine of the planomenon social machine is also the image of thought of the social machine. The abstract machine of the planomenon of transversal consistency that taps the virtual and intensive exteriority and forces of cosmos on a fractal line of flight is a war abstract machine, with its relations of exteriority to the other social machines (D&G (1988) 376 (415)). The war abstract machine can inform very many different assemblages. There are assemblages of philosophy, mathematics and music that are war machines; a person can be a war machine; a relationship can be a war machine. All that defines a war machine is its virtual organisation in an abstract machine of transversal consistency that taps the virtual and intensive exteriority and forces of cosmos on a fractal line of flight. Just as the war abstract machine is the abstract machine of exteriority and becoming, the social machines of the war abstract machine are of the outside and the untimely. The war abstract machine at the level of the virtual problematic of social organisation calls for a social machine yet to come, for a people yet to come, for a new earth, but also has found that the conditions of the nomads on the desert and steppe take up the war abstract machine in their social machine of the nomad social machine (D&G (1988) 351 (387)).

The planomenon abstract machine connects with virtual exteriority the nonorganic cosmic forces. The forces of exteriority are the forces of the virtual plane of immanence and of the intensive morphogenetic field. These forces are not the forces of expression-content double articulation of the molar fold (organism) organisation, but nonorganic and cosmic forces that are supermolecular. They are the forces of self-organisation and emergence that are brought forth when decoding and deterritorialisation become absolute. What these cosmic forces issue forth are consistencies of decoded and deterritorialised flows in immanent inclusive disjunctive synthesis. This is the immanent machining of the plane of immanence, in which the play of difference and repetition machine consistencies in virtual multiplicities, dynamically and transversally holding together heterogeneous elements and flows in a self-organising criticality (D&G (1988) 323 (356)). Running through the plane of immanence and all the multiplicities is the fractal line of flight that draws all the multiplicities and the plane of immanence. This is the planomenon, which is earth, brain and also social organisation. It is cosmic surplus value: surplus value of decoding, deterritorialisation, destratification, transversal machinic consistencies, emergent capabilities, fractal lines of becoming.

The planomenon abstract machine of social organisation emerges on the plane of immanence of social organisation: 'it draws a plane of consistency, a creative line of flight, a smooth space of displacement' (D&G (1988) 423 (466–7)). The abstract machine of planomenon social organisation addresses the problematic of what holds something together (D&G (1988) 323 (356)), and machines a virtual diagram of social organisation in a transversal consistency of decoding and deterritorialisation for the virtual multiplicities of the problematic of social organisation.

The consistency is a creative line of flight in continuous variation, existing only in its continuous variations: 'the war machine form of exteriority is such that it exists only in its metamorphosis' (D&G (1988) 360 (397)). The abstract machine, thus, remains flush to the virtual problematic of social organisation and never constituting a theorematic of social organisation. The creative line of flight of the planomenon abstract machine engenders and traverses the very problematic of social organisation, experimenting with the problematic of connecting the planomenon earth and planomenon brain in a dynamic consistency of social organisation that connects to and taps cosmic forces. This transversal machinic consistency in continuous variation finds 'the totality of its conditions only in a properly cosmic plane, where all the disparate and heterogeneous elements are convoked' (D&G (1988) 327 (361)). It is precisely the supermolecular modality of the planomenon abstract machine that means the machine and assemblage is 'molecularised matter, which must accordingly "harness" forces; these forces are necessarily forces of the cosmos' (D&G (1988) 342 (377)).

The abstract machine in addressing the problematic, drawing the plane of immanence, and establishing the transversal consistency, also opens up an intensive morphogenetic smooth space and makes an intensive distribution of people in this smooth space. The abstract machine is 'the drawing of a creative line of flight, the composition of a smooth space and the movement of the people in their smooth space' (D&G (1988) 422 (466)). The abstract machine is image of organisation of exteriority, and is also an image of thought that places thought 'in an immediate relation with the outside, the forces of the outside' (D&G (1988) 376–7 (415)) (schizo thought). In all this, in relation to the other social machines, with the planomenon war abstract machine:

> It is not enough to simply affirm that the war machine is external to the State apparatus. It is necessarily to reach the point of conceiving the war machine itself as a pure form of exteriority, whereas the State apparatus constitutes the form of interiority we habitually take as a model, or according to which we are in the habit of thinking...returned to its milieu of exteriority, the war machine is seen to be of another species, another nature, of another origin.
>
> (D&G (1988) 354 (390–1))

The planomenon war abstract machine in thought and social organisation calls forth 'another justice, another movement, another space-time' (D&G (1988) 353 (390)), and 'a pure and immeasurable multiplicity, the pack, an irruption of the ephemeral and the power of metamorphosis...bear[ing] witness to another kind of justice' (D&G (1988) 352 (388)).

It was the nomads who invented a social machine that instantiated the planomenon: 'Nomad existence necessarily effectuates the conditions of the war machine in space' (D&G (1988) 380 (419)). The nomads create the nomad social machine with the planomenon earth of the desert and the steppe that presents itself as deterritorialisation: 'It is the earth that deterritorialises itself, in a way that provides the nomad with a territory. The land ceases to be land, tending to become simply ground (sol) or support' (D&G (1988) 381 (421)).

The earth puts forward the exterior forces of the cosmos in a deterritorialisation that makes the nomad: the deterritorialised earth connects up with and taps the exterior forces of the cosmos, and draws the plane of immanence for the nomad social organisation: 'The earth assets its own power of deterritorialisation, its lines of flight, the smooth spaces that live and blaze their way for a new earth' (D&G (1988) 423 (467)).

It is a social machine very different from ecumenon social machines, irreducible to the State social machine, outside State sovereignty and prior to its law. The nomad social machine is from the exterior, the cosmic forces and the deterritorialised earth: the plane of immanence for social organisation.

The nomad social machine draws the plane of immanence for social organisation, and it invents a planomenon abstract machine for the drawing a smooth intensive and for distributing people in that smooth space. The nomads invent a vortical social organisation: 'occupying an open space with a vortical movement that can rise up at any point' (D&G (1988) 363 (401)). The vortex is precisely a transversal consistency in a line of absolute deterritorialisation in continuous variation. It is the planomenon idea to the virtual and intensive problematic of social organisation. The war abstract machine results in the nomad social machine reterritorialising on deterritorialisation itself. The social machine operates on a fractal line of continuous variation consistency of deterritorialisation without reterritorialisation. The nomad social machine 'draws a plane of immanence, a creative line of flight, a smooth space of displacement' (D&G (1988) 422 (466)). The nomad social machine draws the plane of immanence, establishes a virtual abstract machine of transversal consistency and metamorphosis, and then forges an intensive morphogenetic field of social organisation: 'the drawing on a line of flight, the composition of a smooth space and of the movement of the people in that smooth space' (D&G (1988) 422 (466)).

The nomad social machine is an intensive social assemblage of speed and absolute movements. The assemblage possesses consistency in its lines of deterritorialisation, and is characterised not so much by a regime of signs, a regime of bodies, a territory, and aspects of deterritorialisation, as by intensive features that cut across regimes of signs and regimes of bodies in an intensive assemblage of deterritorialisation bearing on the problems the assemblage encounters living in the intensive field of social organisation. The nomad social assemblage has intensive spatiogeographical features, an intensive mathematics and topology, and a countersignifying semiotic regime of sensations and affects.

The nomad social assemblage does not lay down a territory as such, but makes and occupies a smooth space dynamically. A smooth space is an intensive space with no extension, where the movements are also intensive. The nomads take from their horses the vectors of speed, and make movements at speed across the smooth space of the steppe and desert in the manner of a vortex crossing smooth space. The smooth space is without boundaries or enclosure (D&G (1988) 381 (420)), smooth space is occupied without being counted or measure (D&G (1988) 362 (399)), and the nomad social assemblage makes a dynamic and intensive distribution of people and animals across the smooth space.

The nomad social assemblage grasps and operates this smooth space in a counter-signifying regime of topology and affects (D&G (1988) 118 (131)). The topology of smooth space allows the numerical and mathematical organisation of the social assemblage and its movements. With the transversal consistency of the war machine virtual multiplicities, the nomad assemblage establishes the numerical organisation of the assemblage: 'For so peculiar an idea – the numerical organisation of the people – came from the nomads' (D&G (1988) 387/8 (428)). On to the lines of alliance and filiation the nomad assemblage adds a numerical organisation, and the assemblage develops a logic of packs of subject groups in movement, not the closed subjugated segregative groups of the State social machine (D&G (1988) 358 (394)). The nomad assemblage does not use the number to count, rather it is an intensive ordinal number – the numbering number – that so the number can operate to move people and things in smooth space (D&G (1988) 118 (131)). The ordinal number is directional and not metric, and in the nomad topology of smooth space; 'it is the number itself that moves through smooth space' (D&G (1988) 389 (429)).

This dynamic mathematical organisation of nomadic distribution in smooth space is social organisation in an intensive morphogenetic social field. This field is populated by sensations, thresholds and metamorphoses. Everything in the nomad social assemblage is in relation to sensations, intensities, affects, events, and becomings animal and woman (D&G (1988) 352 (388)). The intensive social field is where the nomad social assemblage carries out processual desubjectifications, and is the field of the exteriority of intensities and affects. The features of the nomad social assemblage of weapons, jewellery, and secrecy, relate to an exterior field of intensive movements and the exteriority of intensities and affects (D&G (1988) 400–2 (442–5)). The relations in the nomad social assemblage to becoming animal, and to becoming woman, relate to the centrality of relations of becomings in the nomad assemblage (D&G (1988) 352 (388)). Indeed, in the nomad social machine, as in all assemblages that effectuate the war machine, the social assemblage is an assemblage of desiring production.

As such, in relation to the social organisation of the other social machines, in the nomad social machine the image of organisation and the image of legality change very significantly. Legality becomes the operation of a flat dynamic transversal consistency of decoded and deterritorialised flows in continuous variation on a line of flight. Legality is transformed into an immanent emergent law. The nomads 'give evidence of another law, another assemblage, and who sweep everything away in their journey' (D&G (1986) 73), and the nomad social machine 'bears witness to another kind of justice' (D&G (1988) 353 (389)).

In the context of the wider considerations of virtual and intensive social organisation as the planomenon as ethos by giving evidence of another kind of justice, and of law precisely as a flat dynamic transversal consistency of decoded and deteritorialised flows in continuous variation, it is the nomad social machine that points the way to an idea of emergent law and a legality for a new earth. It is the nomad who knows the way to the new earth.

Of course, picking up this line of flight in the contemporary conceptualisation of legality and social organisation, and in the contemporary conditions of legality and social organisation, despite presenting fundamental difficulties in its own right, is deeply challenging because of the dominance of the social machines, abstract machines of legality and thought, and social assemblages, whose genealogy most of the chapter explored.

Chapter 5

Emergent Law

Schizo Lawyer and Vagabond Lawyer

> Beneath the general operation of laws, however, there always remains the play
> of singularities…The domain of laws must be understood, but always on the
> basis of a Nature and Spirit superior to their own laws, which weave their rep-
> etitions in the depths of the earth and of the heart, where laws do not yet exist.
>
> (Deleuze (1994) 25)

> Where one believed there was law, there is in fact desire and desire alone.
>
> (D&G (1986) 49)

> It is no longer a question of imposing a form upon matter but of elaborating
> an increasingly rich and consistent material, the better to tap increasingly
> intense forces.
>
> (D&G (1988) 329 (363))

Introduction

The workshop on social machines and social assemblages, drawing in the prior
two lectures on the earth and the brain, developed the noology of legalities. The
noology of legalities is the deployment of the schizo image of thought in relation
to legality, the virtual problematic of social organisation and legality, the drawing
of a plane of immanence for all legality, and the study of social machines, abstract
machines of legality, and assemblages of legality (both extensive and intensive).
This noology of legalities was linked to the social machine of the people yet to
come and the new earth, and is an investment of the social field in accordance
with this social machine. Chapter 4, 'Four Laws: From the Ecumenon to the
Planomenon', developed the noology of legalities in the discussion of the four
social machines drawn out by Deleuze & Guattari, and of their relations to the
ecumenon, mechanosphere and planomenon. This chapter extends the noology of
legalities in the development of the concept of emergent law as the concept that
best draws out the reach and scope of Deleuze & Guattari's work on social
organisation and legality. The concept of emergent law is legality as a philosophical

and ethical-aesthetic practice and paradigm, and the legality of absolute decoding and deterritorialisation. This extension of the noology of legalities is pursued initially through the fundamental opposition between logos legality and nomos legality that Deleuze & Guattari draw in their thinking about social organisation and legality. There are complex relations and tensions between logos legality and nomos legality on the problematic plane and problem field of legality, although it is in the nomos legality that Deleuze & Guattari find an immanent ontological priority of an emergent law that organises cosmic decoded and deterritorialised forces for social organisation and legality. The extension in the noology of legalities of the concept of emergent law is to establish and develop the concept itself as a philosophical and ethical aesthetic practice and paradigm centred on an abstract machine of the creation of new immanent concepts of legality (D&G (1994)). Emergent law is a virtual and intensive legality, connecting the planomenon earth and planomenon brain directly to the cosmic forces of decoding and deterritorialisation. Emergent law as a practice is both critical and creative. In its critical aspect it is a matter of having done with molar law and molar lawyering, and all that these entail on terms of the State social machine, the State abstract machine and assemblage within the capitalist social machine, and the deployment of Oedipus in the private family (the relation between emergent law and capitalism is considered in the final chapter 'A Legality for a New Earth'). This critical distancing from molar law and molar lawyering is two-fold. There is a 'doing without' of molar law and molar lawyering on the basis of a know how of multiplicities, problematics, abstract machines of legality, assemblages of legality. The noological know how of multiplicities of legality suppleates and replaces molar law and molar lawyering. There is a 'having done with' on the basis of the investment of the abstract machine and immanent social field of the people yet to come and the new earth, with a correlate ability to disinvest the attachments to the State social machine and the investments of the capitalist social field. In its creative aspect it is a matter of establishing the concept of emergent law, drawing its plane, sketching out its abstract machines, intensive assemblages, and the conceptual personae that operate it. The abstract machine of emergent law, drawing on the schizo image of thinking, the war machine, and the nomos, is schizo law, and its conceptual personae is the schizo lawyer. The emergent law intensive assemblage is the machining of the intensive social problem field of problems of sensation, affects and becoming, and the conceptual personae of this intensive assemblage, drawing on vagabond thought, is the vagabond lawyer. Emergent law is the alliance of the schizo lawyer and the vagabond lawyer. Emergent law becomes a philosophical and ethical-aesthetic practice and paradigm, and develops as a social machine of justice, orientated towards a legality for a new earth.

Relationship between logos legality and nomos legality

In Deleuze & Guattari's work on social organisation and legality the terms logos and nomos are each defined and used very specifically, and are related to each other very complexly, in ways that define the highest stakes of their work on social organisation and legality. The starting point to understanding this is: 'In all respects there is an opposition of the logos and the nomos' (D&G (1988) 369 (408)). There are broad similarities between them. Both are the organisation of self-organisation and emergence in the disjunctive synthesis of recording the socius. Both are abstract machines of legality and images of thought. Both are modes of investing the social field and organisation of desiring production. They are both operative on the one plane and field of the problematic of legality. However, in how they achieve these operations there is a fundamental divergence between them.

The logos is the molar and extensive legal organisation, and is marked by a gravitas to its organisation. It is the organisation of legality through an exclusive usage of the disjunctive synthesis of recording the socius, and it imposes a plane of organisation on the body of the social. The logos is the operation of a transcendence in the organisation of legality, establishing a recessed higher dimension from which the plane of organisation is laid out and striated. It is always pursued in social organisation in terms of language, the master signifier, signification and interpretation. The logos is the abstract machine of the molar fold, which organises according to the paradoxical metaphor that constitutes a transcendent overcoding of the social field. It is the organisation of legality through operations of coding and territorialisations. The molar overcoding flows organise everything in the social field into totalities and wholes, and everywhere establishes fixed divisions and boundaries. It is organisation of legality in a hierarchical and arborescent model, where there is a dominance of relations of interiority and identity. In the logos organisation of legality the social field is gridded out on the transcendent plane of organisation and overcoding, and the existence of an intensive social field lost in adherence to hylomorphism. The social space of the logos organisation is striated space, and one occupies space by counting it. The logos organisation produces for this space a subjectivity, which is divided, desires as lack, and is in possession of an unconscious structured and bound by the logos organisation. It produces a machine for ordering fixed states of affairs.

The nomos is the supermolecular and virtual legal organisation, and is marked by a celeritas of speed and movement to its organisation. It is the organisation of legality through an inclusive usage of the disjunctive synthesis of recording the social, and it draws a plane of immanence for the body of the social. The nomos is the operation of immanence in the organisation of legality, creating a high and fractal dimensional flat plane across which pass the speeds and movements of the plane of immanence. It is fundamentally a mathematical way of organising a legality, immersed in manifolds, multiplicities, distributions of singularities, and an arithmetic of the numbering number. The nomos is the abstract machine of the war machine, and it organises in immanent transversal consistencies in continuous variation tapping cosmic surplus value to bring into being the movements of the social virtual plane and intensive field. It is the organisation of legality through operations of decoding and deterritorialisation. The war machine organises everything in the social field through open nomadic distributions, and everywhere there are the shifting dynamic thresholds of different becomings. It is organisation of legality in an open distributed network, with a prevalence of relations of exteriority and the openness to change and becomings. In the nomos organisation of legality the plane of immanence of the socius and its virtual movements opens and play out in the intensive social field where the virtual movements enter into intensive social matters. The social space of the nomos organisation is smooth space, and space is occupied on a vector without counting. The nomos organisation produces for this social space superjects as diverse emergent consistencies of becomings, arraigned in an exteriority of intensities, affects and metamorphosis. It produces a machine for holding together lines of social flight in continuous variation.

Thus the plane and field of the problematic of legality is drawn between the two legalities of nomos and logos. They are the two existent states of legality:

> These two coexistent states of desire are the two states of the law. On the one hand, there is the paranoiac transcendent law that never stops agitating a finite segment and making it into a completed object, crystallising all over the place. On the other hand, there is the immanent schizo law that functions like justice, an anti-law, a 'procedure' that will dismantle all the assemblages of paranoiac law.
>
> (D&G (1986) 59)

There is the logos paranoiac legality and the nomos schizo law:

> One captures desire within great diabolical assemblages, sweeping along in almost the same movement servants and victims, chiefs and subalterns, and only bringing about a massive deterritorialisation of man by also reterritorialising him, whether in an office, a prison, a cemetery (paranoiac law). The other movement makes desire take flight through all the assemblages, rub up against all the segments without settling down in any of them, and carry always farther the innocence of a power of deterritorialisation that is the same thing as escape (schizo law).
>
> (D&G (1986) 60)

With these two co-existent logos and nomos states of law there are the corresponding two modalities of lawyers and lawyering:

> Hence another possible formulation of an inverse relationship: there would be something like two groups, the psychotics and the neurotics, those who do not tolerate Oedipalisation, and those who tolerate it and are even content with it and evolve with it. Those on whom the Oedipal imprint does not take, and those on whom it does… It is the recording of desire on the increase body

without organs, and the familial recording on the socius, that are in opposition, the schizoid eccentric circle and the neurosis triangle.

(D&G (1984) 124 (135))

There are the logos molar legality and molar lawyers, and there are the nomos schizo legality and the schizo lawyers. Both are co-existent unconscious deliriums and investments of the social plane and field. Individual assemblages of legality will tend to one or the other of these poles, though assemblages of legality may also swing between these poles in becomings fascist and becomings anarchic.

Indeed, there are movements by which there is a take over of a nomos machine and assemblage of legality by the powers of the logos legality:

As a general rule, a smooth space, a vectorial field, a nonmetric multiplicity are always translatable, and necessarily translated, into a 'compars': a fundamental operation by which one repeatedly overlays upon each point of smooth space a tangent Euclidean space endowed with a sufficient number of dimensions, by which one reintroduces parallelism between two vectors, treating multiplicity as though it were immersed in this homogeneous and striated space of reproduction, instead of continuing to follow it in an 'exploration by legwork'. This is the triumph of the logos or the law over the nomos.

(D&G (1988) 373 (411))

Further, where there is the triumph of the logos, and the ascendency of molar law and molar lawyers, the powers of molar law and molar lawyers are always blocking and bearing down upon the merest indications of the forces of the *I*, expunging it as a creative source of legality (D&G (1986) 50).

However, this logos legality is only ever a thickening and striation of the nomos legality plane of immanence (D&G (1986) 50), and 'beneath the general operations of the law [logos] there always remains the play of singularities [nomos]' (Deleuze (1994) 25). The forces of decoding and deterritorialisation of the nomos legality are stronger than the coding and territorialising powers of the logos legality (D&G (1988) 373 (411)), and 'the war machine is a nomos very different from the "law"' (D&G (1988) 360 (397)). Molar legality gives way to immanent nomos legality: 'paranoid law gives way to schizo law...the transcendence of duty in the social field gives way to a nomadic immanence of desire that wanders all over this field' (D&G (1986) 73). Transcendent logos refers to an immanent nomos legality: 'the transcendence of the law was an abstract machine, but the law exists only in the immanence of the machinic assemblage of justice' (D&G (1986) 51), and there is 'an unlimited field of immanence instead of an infinite transcendence' (D&G (1986) 51).

Thus, the two co-existent states of law, the nomos and the logos, are not the bipoles of the plane and field of the problematic of legality. Rather, the nomos is the monopole of the plane and field of the problematic of legality. It is out of this monopole that the logos legality collapses as a loss of virtual and ontological symmetry. The nomos, the war machine, has an ontological superiority of forces in relation to the logos legality, is in direct relation to and taps cosmic forces, and is of 'an entirely different nature...[and] takes place outside' (D&G (1988) 375 (413–14)). Thus, the virtual immanent plane and field of the problematic of legality have a law: 'Speed and absolute movement are not without their laws, but they are the laws of the nomos, of smooth space that deploys it, or the war machine that populates it' (D&G (1988) 386 (426)).

This nomos legality is a virtual organisation of legality:

> The nomos came to designate the law, but that was originally because it was distribution, a mode of distribution. It is a very special kind of distribution, one without division into shares, in a space without borders or enclosure. The nomos is the consistency of a fuzzy aggregate...
>
> (D&G (1988) 380 (420))

This organisation of the inclusive disjunctive synthesis links the nomos legality directly to the forces of the schizo movement of thinking and desire, making the nomos legality always a schizo law:

> It becomes nevertheless apparent that schizophrenia teaches us a singular extra-Oedipal lesson, and reveals to us an unknown force of the disjunctive synthesis, an immanent use that would no longer be exclusive or restrictive, but fully affirmative, nonrestrictive, inclusive. A disjunction that remains disjunctive, and that still affirms the disjoined terms, that affirms them throughout their entire distance, without restricting one by the other or excluding the other from the one, is perhaps the greatest paradox. 'Either... or...or,' instead of 'either/or.'
>
> (D&G (1984) 76 (84))

It is legality as a line of flight of nomos schizo law from molar legality and molar lawyering:

> The other movement makes desire take flight through all the assemblages, rub up against all the segments without settling down in any of them, and carry always farther the innocence of a power of deterritorialisation that is the same thing as escape (schizo law).
>
> (D&G (1986) 60)

In the noology of legalities and in emergent law, this ontological superiority of nomos legality is the basis for the drawing of a plane of immanence for all legality, on which to think the entire field of legality between molar law and emergent law.

Emergent law

From the perspective of emergent law, the noology of legalities is part of emergent law. Emergent law is the philosophical and ethical-aesthetic practice and paradigm of the social machine of the planomenon problematic of social organisation and legality. Emergent law is the legality that connects the planomenon earth and the planomenon brain in an immanent emergent consistency that directly connects and taps the forces of the cosmos for social organisation and legality. The noology of legality of the schizo image of thinking, the problematic of social organisation and legality, the drawing of the plane of immanence for all legality, abstract machines of legality, intensive and extensive assemblages of legality, the conceptualisation of legalities in the survey of social machines, and the ontological priority of nomos legality are all necessary parts of emergent law practice and social machine. Emergent law, in addition to all the elements developed in the noology of legalities, is the operation by which the line of flight of emergent law can be taken, the creation of concepts of legality, and the creation of its own concept of emergent law.

The operation by which emergent law line of flight becomes available is the 'having done with' molar law and molar lawyering. Despite the ontological priority of nomos legality, it is the logos concept of law that has been taken up in State social machine and in the capitalist social machine. The power and dominance of the molar image of legality, molar law and molar lawyering, is near overwhelming. This power and dominance of the molar image of legality has been for a very long time and has become pervasive to all aspects of the social field. The State social machine has nurtured and developed this image of molar legality, and done so precisely as the State image of thought, and implemented this abstract machine across the plane of organisation it imposes on the entire social field. Although surpassed as a social machine by the capitalist social machine, the molar image of legality, molar law and molar lawyering, are the mode of implementation of the capitalist axiomatic in nation States, trade blocks and international organisations. It is the State molar image of law that is deployed in the Oedipal operation by which the capitalist social machine applies its axiomatic to subjectify persons in the private family, and by which it ties the molar image of legality to desire and the unconscious.

For emergent law it is not really a matter of arguing the merits and demerits of the molar image of legality, molar law and molar lawyering. There are those people who take the molar image of law and the molar image of thought, who tolerate the State social machine and Oedipus, and who are even content with it and evolve with it (D&G (1984) 124 (135)). These are people with deep unconscious investments of the State social machine, its image of thought, its interiority, its sexuality. There are those people who deeply invest in the capitalist social machine and all its flows, who happily combine this investment of the capitalist social field with their investment of all the archaisms of the State social machine and subjectification (the defining cynicism and piety of the modern social field: 'The extreme spiritualisation of the despotic State, and the extreme internalisation of the capitalist field, define bad conscience' (D&G (1984) 268 (291))). There is nothing to say about emergent to such captures of desiring production by the capitalist and State social machines and such investments of the social field. Indeed, Professor Challenger and his colleagues were employed from the start to drive such people from the discussions at hand. It is a matter of those people on whom the capitalist social machine does not take, on whom Oedipus does not take, on whom the molar image of thought does not take, on whom the molar legality does not take fully (the decoded and deterritorialised). The issue here is, thus, the leaving of molar law and molar lawyering, of leaving the capitalist social machine, of leaving the State social machine, of leaving the State image of thought, and of leaving subjectivity, desire structured by law, desire as lack, desire as the desire of the other. Emergent law is for those people who want to leave molar law, molar lawyering and the capitalist social machine (schizo lawyers, vagabond lawyers). Thus, with emergent law the first task is to make the emergent law line of flight from molar law and molar lawyering available to those who want to leave molar law and molar lawyering (the relation of emergent law to the capitalist social machine is pursued in the next chapter).

Making the emergent law line of flight available is a matter of laying out the conditions for a 'having done with' molar law and molar lawyering. It is a matter of getting rid of the despot's paranoiac social delirium and the abstract machine of the Urstaat, the theology of absence, and the dream of fascist transcendent unity and authority. A matter of getting rid of the fundamental structuring of everything in the overcoding operation of paradoxical instance of exception, the recessed transcendent dimension, the master signifier and the detached partial object. A matter of giving up all thought of transcendence, totalities and identities, hierarchies, representation, signification, interiority and subjectification. No more a matter of the desires, dreams and unconscious of the State philosopher and the royal lawyer, the love of molar law and the fidelity to molar law, and the endless interpretation, exegesis, hermeneutics, analysis and signification. No more the molar lawyer: 'signification, interpretation, subjectification: the three fundamental neuroses of the human being' (D&G (1988) 134 (148)).

Emergent law can 'have done' with molar law and molar lawyering and pursue the line of flight of emergent law on the basis of two operations, the first a 'doing without' and the second a 'having done with'. Both are operations of suppleation (Harari (2002); Thurston (2004); Ragland and Milovanovic (2004); Murray (2005)).

There is the operation of 'doing without' molar law and molar lawyering on the basis of a know how of multiplicities, problematics and machining. The noology of legalities reveals that molar law and molar lawyering are not a universal legality, but simply one among others, with its own genealogy. Molar law and molar legality are not necessary for social organisation or social individuation, as there are other legalities, and, indeed, new legalities can always be created. It is not the case that there is either molar law and molar lawyering or there is social chaos, social break down, and mute daughters. Molar law and molar lawyering are not the only possible arrangement of legality for social machines and social assemblages. Molar law and molar lawyering are not the only image of organisation and image of thought, and they are not the only way of investing the social field, they are not the only way of organising an unconscious, and they are not the only way of organising a subject or individuation. In short, the operation is to simply replace molar law and molar lawyering with the noology of legalities and emergent law. You don't need molar law and everything else that comes with it ('a motley painting of everything that has ever been believed' (D&G (1984) 267 (290))), on the basis of a know how of the schizo image of thought in relation to legality, the virtual problematic of social organisation and legality, the drawing of a plane of immanence for all legality, and the study of social machines, abstract machines of legality, and assemblages of legality (both extensive and intensive).

The second operation is the 'having done with' molar law and molar lawyering. Emergent law can only call forth people on this operation, call forth lawyers yet to come. Unconscious investments of the social field can be profoundly deep and fixed. Yet what emergent law calls forth is becoming of 'having done with' molar law and lawyering on the basis of a disinvestment of the molar social machines, abstract machines, assemblages and subjectivity on the basis of the investment in the social machine yet to come, in the nomos legality, in cosmic forces of decoding and deterritorialisation, in the schizo image of thinking, in lines of flight, escape and becomings. In this, emergent law turns against molar law and molar lawyering, as indeed did the noology of legalities the moment a plane of immanence is drawn for all legality. Faced with the State social machine, emergent law becomes a war machine against State thought and legality. It is 'a field against the constructions of the law' (D&G (1986) 86), and it is 'a furor to bear against sovereignty, a celerity against gravity, secrecy against the public, a power against sovereignty, a machine against the apparatus' (D&G (1988) 352 (388)). Emergent law becomes 'a "procedure" that will dismantle all the assemblages of paranoiac law' (D&G (1986) 59), it 'unties the bond just as it betrays the pact' (D&G (1988) 352 (388)), and it is a matter of escape from the machines and assemblages of molar law (D&G (1986) 60).

In this second operation there is for emergent law a consideration that cuts across the dominance of the State molar machines in the social field and of the deep capture of desiring production in this social field. Capitalism produces prodigious decoding and deterritorialisation of the social field, with capitalism stripping away at all the codes and territories that are needed to support the molar investments. It is the case that the capitalist axiomatic reapplies the codes and territories, and these are done so in Oedipus in the private family. However, capitalist decoding does produce people upon whom molar law 'and all that' has not taken fully, and it produces the decoded and deterritorialised as outsider (D&G (1984) 245 (266)) or as minority (D&G (1988) 469–71 (518–20)). Capitalism creates the milieu for the emergence of lawyers who have done with molar law and molar lawyering.

Having done with molar law and molar lawyering, or at least at the best it could possibly be done, emergent law turns to the creative task of conceptualising the abstract machine and intensive social assemblage of the emergent law social machine, and to its conceptualisation of itself as a philosophical and ethical-aesthetic practice of the problematic of legality. Emergent law is the schizo law abstract machine and the vagabond lawyering intensive assemblage. They replace the molar law abstract machine and the molar lawyering extensive assemblage.

Abstract machine: schizo law and the schizo lawyer

Schizo law is the abstract machine of emergent law, and it is a philosophical process and practice. It is a philosophy of difference and repetition, multiplicities, machining consistencies, and the practice of creating concepts of legality as machinic consistencies. It is the process of the operation of the schizo image of thinking continuously in relation to the virtual problematic of legality and social organisation. It is the know how of multiplicities and virtual machinic consistencies: 'It is the process in itself, the tracing of the field of immanence' (D&G (1986) 56). Schizo law draws the plane of immanence for all legality, and is the engendering of the problematic of legality within legality as a continuously self-positing virtual and intensive problematic. It is to re-activate the nomos legality as the war machine legality, the legality of the inclusive disjunctive synthesis, the decoded and deterritorialised legality, and the planomenon abstract machine. Schizo law is the transversal consistency in continuous variation in the virtual problematic of legality and it is the creation of concepts of law as transversal consistencies in continuous variation concepts. It is a legality that taps immanent nonorganic forces of organisation, and taps the surplus value of immanent self-organisation and emergence in the problematic of legality. Schizo law is the concept and practice of the conceptualisation of the virtual consistency of legality that connects the planomenon earth and the planomenon brain precisely in the connection of cosmic forces. This virtual consistency legality is in continuous variation both as concept and practice on a fractal line of becoming. In schizo law the conceptualisation of law becomes a tapping of cosmic forces of decoding and deterritorialisation in transversal consistencies in continuous variation on a fractal line that draws the plane of immanence of legality. Schizo law is the practice of creating new concepts of legality precisely in keeping this schizo law concept of law in continuous variation.

The operator of the abstract machine of schizo law is the schizo lawyer. The schizo lawyer is created in the concept of schizo law as its conceptual personae. The schizo lawyer bears and operates all the features of the noology of legalities and schizo law. The schizo lawyer is the one who has successfully 'had done with' molar law and molar lawyering. 'Having done with' is one of the defining features of a schizo conceptual persona: 'For what is the schizo, if not first of all the one who can no longer bear "all that": money, the stock market, the death forces, Nijinsky said – values, morals, homelands, religion, and private certitudes?' (D&G (1984) 341 (374)).

The schizo lawyer is the one that leaves molar law and molar lawyering, to move into the pure exteriority of legality, so as to break the bonds and betray the pact of the molar image of legality. In this exteriority of legality the schizo lawyer operates the schizo image of thinking, and, drawing close to the nomos, draws the plane of immanence for all legality. This counter-actualises all legalities into a virtual problematic of social organisation and legality, and discovers for legality the problematic of connecting the earth and the brain in a social organisation that connects to cosmic forces as the problematic of social organisation and legality. The schizo lawyer in the noology of legalities counter-actualises all legalities into abstract machine and assemblage multiplicities, and populates the plane of immanence of the problematic of legality with abstract machines of legality, and conducts operations of exploration and transformation upon these abstract machine multiplicities. This is the schizo lawyer's operation of the creation of immanent concepts of legality and the schizo conceptualisation of all legality. In conceptualising all legality the schizo lawyer creates new concepts of law, creates and operates the concept itself of emergent law, and in conceptualising taps creative processes of decoding and deterritorialisation in thinking for the conceptualisation of law and the creation of new nonorganic social relations (D&G (1988) 423 (466)). Alongside these concepts, the schizo lawyer invents conceptual personae for these concepts of law, so that the intensive morphogenetic fields of the concepts can be sensed in their intensities. Having had done with the State social machine, it is the schizo lawyer who calls forth and invests the social machine yet to come, the social machine that is virtually there and sustains all of schizo thinking and emergent law.

The investment of the social machine to come has both features of resistance to the present and an orientation and investment of the future. The resistance to the present is the 'having done with' molar law and molar lawyering, and all the schizo escapes are resistances to the present. In relation to resistance to the capitalist social machine, the schizo lawyer takes up a position at the absolute limit of capital so as to explore the legalities of the relative limits of capital:

> The schizophrenic deliberately seeks out the very limit of capitalism: he is its inherent tendency brought to fulfilment, its surplus product, its proletariat, and its exterminating angel... In the schizo, the two aspects of *process* are conjoined: the metaphysical process that puts us in contact with the 'demoniacal' element in nature or within the heart of the earth, and the historical process of social production that restores the autonomy of desiring machines in relation to the deterritorialised social machine.
>
> (D&G (1984) 35 (38))

The investment of the future, though, is where the work of the schizo lawyer is most deployed. There are two aspects, but in both what the schizo lawyer connects to are 'the virtual movement that is already real though not yet in existence' and the schizo lawyer is 'not a mirror to the social field but a watch that is running too fast' (D&G (1986) 83). One aspect is to explore the virtual and intensive problematic of legality, to explore all the virtual and intensive movements of abstract machines of legality and of assemblages of legality, so as to think: 'when can one say that a statement is new? When can one say that a new assemblage is coming into view?' (D&G (1986) 83). The other aspect is the core investment of the future, is to think legality for a new people, a new society, to connect legality and social organisation to the virtual and the intensive, and to connect a conceptualisation of emergent law to an ecology of the virtual and intensive earth and brain planomenon.

Intensive assemblage of legality: vagabond lawyering

The emergent law assemblage of legality is an intensive assemblage of vagabond lawyering. The vagabond lawyer is the lawyer who wanders from place to place, at home in the courts but by no means a State lawyer, a great fixer of legal problems precisely by the possession of a 'wild' mercurial logic of the legal problem that comes from outside the State machine, molar law and molar lawyering. The vagabond intensive assemblage of legality is the assemblage the vagabond lawyer avails themselves of in their vagabond lawyering. The vagabond assemblage of legality emerges between the logos legality and the transcendent plane of organisation it draws for legality, and the nomos legality and the plane of immanence that it draws for legality. The vagabond assemblage of legality is between the two planes of legality, much in the way that metallurgy has found itself between the plane that the nomad social machine draws and the plane the Imperial State machine draws (D&G (1988) 415 (458–9)). The vagabond lawyer is always a hybrid, an alloy, and a twin formation moving between two legalities and making in the in between an intensive assemblage of legality that is novel in relation to the molar assemblage of legality and the creator from intensive social problems of new equitable and legal rights.

What makes the vagabond lawyer and vagabond assemblage of legality is an ambivalence and ambulance in relation to the exclusive or inclusive disjunctive synthesis of recording. It is the exclusive or inclusive usage of this synthesis that distinguishes the organisation of logos legality and nomos legality. The vagabond lawyer and assemblage of legality are ambivalent to this distinction, and is ambulant on the plane of organisation of legality and on the plane of immanence of legality at will, and is able to be ambulant between the planes. The vagabond lawyer does not reside on the plane of organisation of legality all the time, nor does the vagabond lawyer reside on the plane of immanence of legality, but they are aware of both of them, and face and connect to both planes of legality. This itinerancy of the problematic of legality gives the vagabond lawyer the advantage of two contrast spaces in relation to the problematic of legality. However, what is crucial to the vagabond assemblage of legality is that it discovers between the two planes of legality an intensive morphogenetic field of social problems of legality and organisation, and all the intensive immanent resources of an immanent intensive morphogenetic social field. The vagabond assemblage of legality operates with the intensive flows of matter-movement of the social field and intensive problems of legality and social organisation. This matter-movement is of sensations, intensities, abilities to affect and be affected, events, becomings and metamorphoses in the flows of social matter-movement across the intensive social field. These flows of social matter-movements and the connections and conjunctions in the intensive flows that constitute intensive social problems present themselves to the vagabond assemblage of legality as problems to be addressed. These intensive problems are real immanent problems of desire and power that populate the intensive social morphogenetic field (D&G (1986) 50). Whilst these intensive problems may not be thought or addressed by molar law and molar lawyers due to their hylomorphism, these problems do present themselves to the vagabond assemblage between the planes. Thus, there opens up a new legal jurisdiction of intensive problems, that are beyond the jurisdiction of the State assemblages of legality, and which supplements the molar jurisdiction of legal problems with a jurisdiction of exteriority and another logic of the legal problem.

The circumstances of vagabond lawyers and the vagabond assemblage of legality go further still than the simple availability of intensive social problems of legality and the new jurisdiction of the intensive morphogenetic field. The intensive morphogenetic field of matter-movement is laden with singularities, consistent multiplicities, dynamic thresholds, abstract machines to operate, abilities to trigger affects, becomings to initiate and metamorphoses to enchain. It is the intensive machinic phylum of the intensive social field of social problems. All of these resources are available in the intensive social field to be taken up within the vagabond assemblage of legality. The vagabond lawyer and the vagabond assemblage of legality address and work with an 'intensive materiality possessing a nomos' (D&G (1988) 408 (451)), and engage with the materiality of the social flows and intensive social problems.

The vagabond lawyer and vagabond assemblage of legality is associated with three sets of operations: operations centred around a prospecting of the social flows; operations centred around processes and events; and, operations of cases of solution without precedent and the creation of new rights.

Vagabond lawyering does not impose a set form on matter, but works with the intensive social flows and the emergence of intensive problems in those flows. There is thus no option for vagabond lawyering other than simply to follow the social flows, and vagabond lawyering becomes an itinerant prospecting of the social flows (D&G (1988) 409 (452)). Vagabond lawyering explores the intensive social field, and investigates the nonorganic life proper to the matter of intensive social organisation. This investigation of the intensive flows and nonorganic life in social flows entails sensitive and sensible evaluations, the ability to intuit singular and ordinary points in intensive flows, discerning of intensive traits of expression, sensing the points of affect and being affected, and eliciting the intensive conditions of events. Vagabond lawyering is a detective work of intensive social problems and events that any sleuth would recognise ("What Happened?" D&G (1988) 192 (212)).

Through occupying the intensive machinic phylum of social organisation and legality the vagabond assemblage of legality has learnt and incorporated intensive actions that can produce or change events. Such events may or may not entail an actual change or event, but do entail that there is a change or event in intensity in the flows and arrangements of the morphogenetic social field and a change or event in the arrangement of all the virtual multiplicities and consistencies of the plane of immanence. In social assemblages statements and order-words play a fundamental role in the assemblages' collective regime of enunciation because statements, given the pragmatic context in which they are employed, are able to enter directly into the regime of materiality and bodies and effect incorporeal transformation events by which there is a shift in virtual, intensive and actual arrangements. The pragmatic context that is so crucial to the operation of order-words is the relevant arrangements of forces and powers in the intensive morphogenetic problem field. The machinic phylum of the social field is scattered with little abstract machines for the effectuation of incorporeal transformations, for effecting little intensive social individuations through the arrangement of intensities and affects, and eliciting particular events and transformations in bodies or the social field. The vagabond assemblage of legality learns and incorporates all these intensive operations of the intensive social field, and operates on problems of desire or power not with the clunky extensive tools of a molar lawyer but with all the tricks and ruses of the vagabond lawyer and their machinic phylum of legality and their nonorganic life of sociality, and which makes the vagabond lawyer have something of the alchemist-sorcerer to them (D&G (1988) 411 (454)).

However, perhaps the most far-reaching operation of the vagabond assemblage of legality is the development of cases of solution without precedent to intensive social problems and otherwise irresolvable legal problems. In the intensive morphogenetic social field real immanent problems of desire and power present themselves as deadlocks and problems in the flows of social matter-movement. It may be that these deadlocks and problems in the flows of social matter-movement have already been before the molar law and the solution was inadequate, or it may be the intensive problem is entirely presented in the intensive social field. The vagabond assemblage of legality self-organises and emerges precisely in relation to the intensive self-positing of intensive problems of desire and power in the intensive social field, and the assemblage must fashion something for the treatment of these intensive social problems. The vagabond assemblage of legality operates outside the molar assemblage of legality, and so, in principle, without any of the problem-solving resources of molar law and lawyering. The vagabond assemblage of legality, of course, turns to the resources of the machinic phylum of legality. The greatest resource of the machinic phylum of the matter-movement of social organisation and legality is the abstract machine of the nomos that the materiality of the intensive social field possesses (D&G (1988) 408 (451)).

This abstract machine is of transversal consistency of decoded and deterritorialised flows in continuous variation. In the intensive materiality of the field of the vagabond assemblage of law the intensive problems present themselves in terms of complexes of sensation, intensities, ability to affect and be affected, dynamic thresholds and events. In response to these problems, the vagabond assemblage of legality machines a case of solution without precedent to the intensive social problem as a case that is unique as it responds to the unique circumstances of the problem before the assemblage. The case of solution without precedent is the machined transversal consistency in continuous variation of a composed block of sensations, intensities, affects, dynamic thresholds and events, and now also transformations, becomings and metamorphoses. These composed intensive consistencies are composed little unique assemblages that answer the intensive problem and are intensive cases of solution. The vagabond assemblage of legality deploys an immanent justice taken from the self-organisation and emergence of the machinic phylum of legality, and is the creation of new immanent rights in the jurisdiction that the vagabond assemblage of legality carves out at the exteriority of the State social machine, molar law and molar lawyering.

Indeed, in all the operations of the vagabond assemblage of legality there is the assemblage of legality no doubt closer to how real problems of social organisation and legality are tackled and resolved than the molar image of law and assemblage of legality, and so all the more easier to do without them. From their discussion of legality and justice in *Kafka*:

> The important thing is not what happens in the tribunal or the movements of the two parties together but the molecular agitations that put into motion the hallways, the wings, the backdoors, and the side chambers...The important things are always taking place elsewhere, in the hallways of the congress, behind the scenes of the meeting, when people confront the real, immanent problems of desire and power – the real problems of justice...The contiguity of offices, the segmentation of power, replaces the hierarchies of instances and eminence of the sovereign.
>
> (D&G (1986) 50)

Occupying the intensive field between the plane of organisation of State molar legality and the plane of immanence of nomos legality, the vagabond assemblage may enter into relations with either the State molar legality or the schizo legality of the plane of immanence. The relation, though, with the State molar legality is one of individual vagabond lawyers moving into the State molar legality as mavericks that are needed for certain jobs but are only barely tolerated: 'even going so far as to propose a minor position for them within' the system and privilege of molar law (D&G (1988) 373 (411–12)). There are times in which the State molar lawyers cannot stand the vagabond assemblage of legality, and shut it down or stamp their molar lawyering all over the assemblage. However, the vagabond assemblage of legality is exterior to the State social machine and molar law, and a concept and social machine of emergent law would join the schizo lawyer and the vagabond lawyer in an alliance of juridical creativity.

Emergent law (refrain)

Emergent law, of course, includes all of the noology of legalities. Emergent law is the sum total and practice of all the know how of the problematics of legality and the know how of all the multiplicities and consistencies of the legalities and assemblages of legality. Emergent law is also the 'having done with' of molar law, capitalist social machine, and all Oedipal familiarity and correlated investments of the social field. Emergent law operates with an 'orphan unconscious… "beyond all laws"…where the question of Oedipus can no longer even be raised' (D&G (1984) 81–2 (90)). It is precisely in this leaving that emergent law engenders thinking in legality and engenders the birth of a mutant legality within legality. Emergent law is further defined as by the following: an openness to the future and continuous variation; a machine of desire and justice; a war machine for legality and a new social machine; the alliance of the schizo lawyer and the vagabond lawyer; a philosophical and ethical-aesthetic practice and paradigm; and the investment of the social machine of a society yet to come.

In emergent law there is an openness to the new and to transformations, together with continuous variation in emergent law. Emergent law is to live in the virtual and intensive problematic of social organisation and legality and its continual respecifications. Emergent law is, of course, not a set of fixed normative laws, but rather continuous processes of know how to organise things in relation to the problematic of legality, organising processes and events through immanent processes and events. It would be a matter of continuous openness to the future, of thinking and sensing attractors, multiplicities, and events, that are active in the immanent social field in the vicinity of actualised social organisation: 'listening for murmurings of new assemblages of desire, of machines and of statements, that insert themselves into the old assemblages and break with them' (D&G (1986) 83). Emergent law in its openness to transformations would be 'the sound of a contiguous future' (D&G (1986) 83), it would be 'less a mirror than a watch that is running fast' (D&G (1986) 59), and it would be 'a thought that appeals to people instead of taking itself for a government ministry' (D&G (1988) 378 (417)). In sum, emergent law is to diagnose becomings in social organisation, and invent new nonorganic social relations:

> …not to contemplate the eternal or reflect on history but to diagnose our actual becomings…The diagnosis of becomings in every passing present is what Nietzsche assigned to the philosopher as physician, 'physician of civilisation', or inventor of new immanent modes of existence.
>
> (D&G (1994) 113)

In emergent law, desire, justice and schizo law replace molar law, and emergent law develops as a practice of desire, justice and the creation of concepts of legality. Emergent law is a machine of desire and justice: 'where one believed there was law, there is in fact desire and desire alone. Justice is desire and not law' (D&G (1986) 49). Emergent law is immanence, desire, real problems, a field of justice, and a line of escape (D&G (1986) 50–1), and it is: '...the machinic assemblage of justice – that is the mutual immanence of decoded law and deterritorialised desire...it is the process itself, the tracing of the field of immanence' (D&G (1986) 52).

Emergent law is the nomos war machine of legality. It is the abstract machine of legality that emerges in relation to the virtual problematic of social organisation and legality and the drawing of the plane of immanence for legality. Emergent law is: the image of legality of schizo law; the abstract machine of legality of schizo law and the schizo lawyer; the intensive assemblage of vagabond lawyering; the regime of signs of topology, multiplicities and affects; the regime of content and bodies of vagabond law; and, its juridical territory is absolute deterritorialisation and the plane of immanence. Emergent law connects together the planomenon earth and planomenon brain in a war machine legality that directly connects the legality to the forces of the cosmos, and the eternal return enters directly into legality.

Against a background of a dying socius, the schizo lawyer and the vagabond lawyer address each other (Tarkovsky, 1966). I will paint icons. I will cast bells. I will create diagram concepts of legality. I will compose consistencies of sensation and affect of legality. Emergent law is the alliance of the schizo lawyer and the vagabond lawyer: 'AXIOM III. The nomad war machine is the form of expression, of which itinerant metallurgy is the correlative form of content' (D&G (1988) 415 (458)).

The emergent law machine has schizo law as its form of expression with its substance of expression as virtual smooth space, and has vagabond lawyering as form of content and its substance of content as the intensive morphogenetic field. In this it is a philosophy and ethical aesthetical practice and paradigm of the virtual and intensive problematic of legality, creating new concepts and composing consistencies of sensation, affects, incorporeal transformations and becomings. Emergent law is to make legality a philosophical and ethical aesthetic practice and paradigm. It becomes the legality of desiring a social machine that invests and calls forth the people yet to come, and that works to create a new earth.

Chapter 6

A Legality for a New Earth
Ecology of the Virtual and Intensive Earth

It is only after matter has been sufficiently deterritorialised that it itself emerges as molecular and brings forth pure forces attributable only to the Cosmos.

(D&G (1988) 347 (382))

We lack resistance to the present. The creation of concepts in itself calls for a future form, for a new earth and people that do not yet exist...the constitution of an earth and a people that are lacking as the correlate of creation.

(D&G (1994) 108)

There will have to be a massive reconstruction of social mechanisms if we are to confront the damage caused by Integrated World Capitalism. It will not come about through centralised reform, through laws, decrees, bureaucratic programmes, but rather through the promotion of innovatory practices, the expansion of alternative experiences centred around a respect for singularity, and through the continuous production of an autonomising subjectivity that can articulate itself appropriately in relation to the rest of society.

(Guattari (2000) 59)

Introduction

This final chapter considers the relation of the concept of emergent law to contemporary conditions. This is to consider the status of emergent law as a potential social machine. The chapter draws out two aspects of contemporary conditions that particularly touch upon the status of the concept of emergent law as a potential social machine. These two aspects are general processes of virtualisation of social organisation, and advanced crisis in capitalist social organisation. It was one of Deleuze & Guattari's persistent claims that at the exterior limit of processes of virtualisation and of the capitalist social machine that a new earth would emerge as a new socius. If processes of virtualisation and the capitalist social machine approach this exterior limit and the drawing of a new earth, the concept of emergent law can be evaluated as a social machine and legality for the new earth. The final part of the chapter turns to characterise how emergent law would develop as a social assemblage, and proposes that it would develop a legality very different from that of the State social machine and the axiomatic of the capitalist social machine. Whilst the concept of emergent law makes of legality a philosophical and ethical-aesthetic practice and paradigm of the schizo lawyer and vagabond lawyer, the development of emergent law as a social machine would make law an ecology or ecosophy (Guattari (2000)). Emergent law would be the practice and paradigm of an ecology of the virtual and intensive earth, massively extending the reach of ecology presently understood, and opening up to a creative autonomy in relation to subjectivity, social organisation and the environment, heralding an ethical and ecological creativity and sustainability.

The first contemporary condition that touches on the status of emergent law as potential social machine is what Pierre Levy has conceptualised as the emergence of processes of virtualisation of many aspects of social organisation. If Levy's diagnosis of general processes of virtualisation of social organisation is taken as compelling, the concept of emergent law as a potential social machine becomes of clear interest as it is one model of a social machine and assemblage that operates in the virtual and intensive registers of social organisation.

Pierre Levy has developed from Deleuze & Guattari's work the argument that contemporary conditions are increasingly being defined by processes of virtualisation (Levy (1998); Levy (1999)). The idea of virtualisation is that social production, economic production and social organisation are no longer organised actually and extensively, but rather becoming organised intensively and virtually. The virtual is not only a philosophical ontological modality but where we increasingly live:

> A general movement of virtualisation has begun to affect not only the fields of information and communication but also our physical presence and economic activities, as well as our collective framework of sensibility and the exercise of intelligence. The process of virtualisation has even affected our modalities of being together, the conditions of a collective 'we' in the form of virtual communities, virtual corporations, virtual democracy. Although the digitalisation of messages and the extension of cyberspace play an important role in this ongoing change, the wave of virtualisation taking place extends far beyond the field of information technology.
>
> (Levy (1998) 15)

Levy considers that social life is undergoing major transformations as a result of the development of global capital networks, technological innovation, a transformation in the nature of labour, a transformation in the nature of communication, and a general intensification of all social, economic and cultural processes. Computerisation and the development of new communications technology have enabled a new global mode of economic arrangements, and enabled new forms of intellectual, collective, and institutional working and communicating.

Economic conditions and technological developments have resulted in new levels of intensification and virtualisation of social and economic arrangements. Levy argues that this evolution involves a shift to a heightened mode of social existence: '...a displacement of the centre of ontological gravity of the object considered. Rather than being defined principally through its actuality (a solution), the entity now finds its essential consistency within a problematic field' (Levy (1998) 26).

Virtualisation '...transforms an initial activity into a particular instance of a more general problematic' (Levy (1998) 27). It is a 'transition to the problematic' that results in a space of exploration and experimentation in knowledge and thinking, with a necessary focus not on laws and institutions but upon dynamic events and processes (Levy (1998) 27).

Virtualisation results in the emergence of a new knowledge space. A space is produced whenever people interact, and these spaces comprise the participants, their messages and actions, and a reflexive grasp of the emergent whole of the interactions. Thus, knowledge space is not a geographical territory, institution or State, but rather an 'invisible space of understanding, knowledge and intellectual power', and a 'qualitative, dynamic, living space of a humanity in the process of inventing itself through the creation of its world' (Levy (1998) 143).

Levy terms the emergent subject of this knowledge space as collective intelligence. Virtualisation is accelerating both the capacities and capabilities of collectively intelligent communities, and it is these communities that are forging, working, and populating the knowledge space, exploring problems and producing solutions and more knowledge. The emergent subject of collective intelligence will, for Levy, develop from knowledge techno-machines such as cyberspace to increasingly become the co-ordinating agency of social production and organisation generally as the knowledge space expands (Levy (1998) 128).

Thus, there is with Levy the argument that we are living through places and times where social organisation itself has entered into the virtual, with the opening up of the virtual social problem field, where new intellectual agents and operations are required to work this virtual problem space.

The second contemporary condition is the relationship between emergent law and the capitalist social machine, and particularly the contemporary conditions of capitalist system that can be characterised as systemic financial crisis, psychic disorder and environmental degradation. The Deleuze & Guattari contention was that there would be a point at which the capitalist social machine would hit an exterior limit that it would not be able to cross, and a point at which social organisation would have to metamorphose. This limit for Deleuze & Guattari was the schizo process of desiring production and thinking and the emergence of a new earth as absolutely decoded and deterritorialised body of the socius. Emergent law is a concept and model of the Deleuze & Guattari ideas of the schizo process and the new earth social organisation at the exterior limit of capitalism, and, as with the processes of virtualisation, the concept and model of emergent law should be evaluated in relation to the contemporary proximity of this exterior limit.

There is in the relation of emergent law and the capitalist social machine some level of confluence in that they share an immanent milieu of emergence and development: 'Modern philosophy's link with capitalism, therefore, is of the same kind as that of ancient philosophy and Greece: the connection of an absolute plane of immanence with a relative social milieu that also functions through immanence.' (D&G (1994) 98).

However, emergent law draws the absolute plane of immanence for social organisation that capitalism will not do. Thus, within the capitalist social machine emergent law necessarily exists in relation to capitalism as the forces of a resistance to the present. The assemblages of emergent law, the intensive assemblages of desiring production of the problematic of legality, the practices of the schizo lawyers and vagabond lawyer, to the extent they are able to thrive, stand opposed to the capitalist organisation of the legality and the social and economic field.

However, in the relation of emergent law as a social machine to the capitalist social machine there is the potential point at which they meet not just in opposition but when the emergent law social machine surpasses the capitalist social machine as operating the problematic of legality and social organisation.

It is in conditions of absolute decoding and deterritorialisation that emergent law can emerge as a social machine after capital and State. In this respect, the relation between the emergent law social machine and the capitalist social machine is the two sides of the exterior limit to social organisation, with emergent law invoking the beyond of the limit, and the capitalist social machine warding off the exterior limit with its displaceable relative interior limit:

> Philosophy takes the relative deterritorialisation of capital to the absolute; it makes it pass over the plane of immanence as movement of the infinite and suppresses it as interior limit, turns it back against itself so as to summon forth a new people, a new earth.
>
> (D&G (1994) 99)

This relation between emergent law and the capitalist social machine as either side of the exterior limit is heightened and the stakes raised in immediate contemporary conditions as the capitalist social machine appears intent upon pushing its displaceable relative interior limits into the zone of the absolute exterior limit of social organisation.

It is necessary for the reproduction of the capitalist social machine that there be a distinction in the capitalist social machine between its displaceable relative interior limit and its absolute exterior limit of absolute decoding and deterritorialisation. However, there are contemporary respects in which the distinction becomes difficult to draw. The clear problem areas for capitalism are systemic financial crisis and ecological degradation, although proliferation of absolutely decoded and deterritorialised lines of flight from capitalist subjectivity also push the relative interior limit ever closer to the absolute limit of desiring production. The neo-liberal project of rendering financial capital filiative, and of operating with an extreme minimal axiomatic on flows of capital, banking, shadow banking, and creation of credit and creation of arbitraged flows in financial flows such as floating currencies, securitisation and derivatives, has brought global finance capitalism to a stage at which the system has pursued such high levels of decoding and deterritorialisation that the distinction between capitalism's interior relative limit and the absolute exterior limit has become indiscernible. It is the same with regard to environmental degradation, it has become indiscernible whether the relative interior limits that the capitalist social machine places on environmental usage are in fact the absolute limit, even perhaps the surpassing of the absolute limit, of what the planet is capable of in supporting capitalist reproduction. In capitalist subjectivity, which of course is the application of the capitalist axiomatic, the indiscernibility of the distinction between the relative and interior and the absolute exterior limit of social organisation allows very considerable scope for lines of flight from capitalist subjectivity and from the investment of the capitalist social field. Anti-capitalist social movements do attest to lines of flight in desiring production, and the gathering of people in intensive social assemblages linked to the investment of new social machines and assemblages, and the calling forth of a people and a new earth of the exterior limit of capitalism and social organisation.

In accordance with the operation of the capitalist social machine, if the exterior limit is always avoided by the relative interior limits, and there is always a difference between the relative interior limit and the exterior absolute limit, no matter how minimal, conflicted, or indiscernible, the dominance and survival of the capitalist social machine is assured. However, contemporary capitalism seems to be doing a very good job itself driving the relative interior limit towards the absolute exterior limit, and there are people intensively assemblaging at the absolute exterior limit of capitalism and social organisation.

Therefore, the relation of emergent law to the capitalist social machine is that in addition to resistance to the present, the relation of emergent law to the capitalist social machine is to make ready in case. If the relative interior limits of capital were to coincide with the exterior absolute limits of the capitalist social machine and of social organisation itself, then there would be absolute decoding and deterritorialisation of the capitalist social machine and social organisation itself. At this absolute point, there is the emergence of the social machine of the people yet to come, of the society yet to come, and of the emergence of the new earth as the new socius: 'But the earth asserts its own powers of deterritorialisation, its lines of flight, its smooth spaces that live and blaze their ways for a new earth' (D&G (1988) 423 (467)).

At this absolute exterior limit the organisation of the new earth begins to directly connect to and tap cosmic nonorganic forces: 'It is only after matter has become sufficiently deterritorialised that it itself emerges as molecular and brings forth forces attributable only to the Cosmos' (D&G (1988) 347 (382)).

At this absolute exterior limit desiring production becomes autonomous in the socius and directly productive of the new earth, and the plane of immanence presents itself as the surface for the inscription for social organisation and desiring production. There is absolute decoding and deterritorialisation of the socius, the absolute limit is attained. When deterritorialisation becomes absolute there is the connection of all the lines of flight, and the raising of all of them to the power of an abstract line that draws a plane of consistency (D&G (1988) 510 (561)). An abstract machine covers the entire plane of consistency (D&G 1988) 11 (12)), and we leave behind the territorial assemblages in order to enter the age of the cosmic machine (D&G (1988) 342 (377)), the immense mechanosphere that is 'the plane of cosmicisation of the forces to be harnessed' (D&G (1988) 343 (378)). From the absolute deterritorialisation there is the creation of a new earth, a cosmic earth (1988) 346 (381): 'Earth consolidated, connected with the Cosmos, brought into the Cosmos following lines of creation that cut across it as so many becomings' (D&G (1988) 510 (562)).

At this absolute limit of the creation of the new earth it is the eternal return that enters into the earth, the brain and social organisation. Emergent law is the legality for a new earth, and the articulation of the eternal return in social organisation and legality. As Caprica had explained, with the eternal return:

> It is not being that returns but rather returning itself that constitutes being in so far as it is affirmed of becoming and that which passes. It is not some one thing that returns but rather returning is the one thing which is affirmed of diversity or multiplicity. In other words, identity in the eternal return does not describe the nature of that which returns, but, on the contrary, the fact of returning for that which differs.
>
> (Deleuze (1983) 48)

Emergent law connects the cosmic earth as eternal return and the cosmic brain as eternal return in thinking. This cosmic schizo brain is eternal return no less than the cosmic earth, always tending towards an elaboration of 'a [virtual and intensive] material of thought in order to capture forces that are not thinkable in themselves' (D&G (1988) 342 (377). It is the eternal return that engenders thinking in thought, such that:

> We will think the past against the present and resist the latter, not in favour of a return but in favour, I hope, of a time to come (Nietzsche), that is, by making the past active and present to the outside so that something new will finally come about, so that thinking, always, may reach thought.
>
> (Deleuze (1988b) 119)

This eternal return in the connection of cosmic earth and cosmic brain is the refraining of the refrains of earth and brain: 'Let us recall Nietzsche's idea of the eternal return as a little ditty, a refrain, but which captures the mute and unthinkable forces of the Cosmos' (D&G (1988) 343 (378)).

The refraining of the refrain is the abstract machine of the plane and field of immanence that selects only eternal return (D&G (1988) 165 (183)), and it is a refraining of the refrains that connects and creates the cosmic line of flight to a new earth as 'the memory of an angel, or rather the becoming of the cosmos' (D&G (1988) 350 (386)). At the absolute limit emergent law arises as the legality of eternal return and as the dark precursor abstract machine of a new earth.

There thus arises the new earth as the new global immanent socius, and the creative tasks of a noology of legalities are activated. At the absolute limit of exteriority of the capitalist social machine and all social organisation, is installed the schizo lawyer, making ready in case:

> The schizophrenic deliberately seeks out the very limit of capitalism: he is its inherent tendency brought to fulfilment, its surplus product, its proletariat, and its exterminating angel… In the schizo, the two aspects of *process* are conjoined: the metaphysical process that puts us in contact with the 'demoniacal' element in nature or within the heart of the earth, and the historical process of social production that restores the autonomy of desiring machines in relation to the deterritorialised social machine.
>
> (D&G (1984) 35 (38))

The schizo lawyer can cross the barrier between molar forces and supermolecular forces (D&G (1984) 322 (354)). The absolute limit of social organisation is attained when desiring production breaks through in all the decoded and deterritorialised flows and establishes an immanent socius and social organisations of immanent consistencies. At capitalism's absolute limit the deterritorialised socius gives way to the immanent socius, and the decoded flows throw themselves into desiring production (D&G (1984) 382 (417)). Capitalism and schizophrenia take us to the end, where desiring production functions at the limit of social production determined by the conditions of capitalism: 'The end of history has no other meaning' (D&G (1984) 130 (142)). It is our 'own "malady", modern man's weakness' (D&G (1984) 130 (142)). At this end of history, two meanings of process meet, the capitalist movement of social production that goes to the very extremes of its deterritorialisation, and the schizophrenic movement of metaphysical production that carries desire along with it and reproduces it in a new earth. The schizo lawyer is the harbinger of death of the capitalist social machine and the arrival of a virtual social plane and field that doubles history (D&G (1984) 331 (371)). At capitalism's limit the deterritorialised socius gives way to the new earth, and the decoded flows throw themselves into desiring production of the brain (D&G (1984) 139–40 (153)).

Thus, at the absolute exterior limit the conditions for an emergent law social machine are present. The emergent law social machine pursues absolute decoding and deterritorialisation, going much further in the direction of social organisation by decoding and deterritorialisation than the capitalist social machine ever aspired (D&G (1984) 340 (373)). The regime of social production and the regime of desiring production become a single fractal line (Deleuze (1988b) 44) drawing the immanent becomings of the new earth. The schizo lawyer draws the plane of immanence for the emergent law social machine, and the schizo law abstract machine and the vagabond lawyer intensive assemblage organise the social plane and field. There is the development of a legality for a new earth.

In thinking of emergent law as a new social machine and legality for a new earth, rather than thinking of it in terms of being more or less like State legality and social machine, or more or less like the capitalist axiomatic social machine and legality, or even in terms of the nomad war social machine of which it shares many features of abstract machine and intensive assemblage, it should be thought of as a novel social machine and legality whose closest existing enterprise would be ecology, although a massively deepened, extending, rhizomatic ecology (Guattari (2000); Bonta and Protevi (2004); Halsey (2006); Herzogenrath (2009); Cullinan (2011)).

Emergent law is a machinic ecology of the earth, the brain, social organisation and cosmic forces (Guattari (2000) 66). It is an ecology of subjectivity, social relations, the environment, and all the relations between and across them. It is a social ecology, a mental ecology and environmental ecology (Guattari (2000) 28). Informed by an ontology rhizomatic process, it is an ecology where there is an inseparability of earth, brain and social organisation: 'It is quite wrong to make any distinction between action on the psyche, the socius and the environment' (Guattari (2000) 41). It is an ecology that also spans all the ontological registers and their relations. It is an ecology of the ecumenon actualised earth and subdued cosmic forces, the ecumenon State brain and Oedipalised subjectivity, and the molar State social organisations and capitalist axiomatic of the capitalist social machine. It is an ecology of the intensive mechanosphere earth and openness to cosmic forces of self-organisation and emergence, the capitalist economic machine, intensive thinking and individuations of sensation and affect, and the emergent intensive assemblages of desire and becomings. It is an ecology of the planomenon virtual new earth, the planomenon virtual brain and the noology of images of thought, the war abstract machine of transversal consistencies of absolute decoding and deterritorialisation in continuous variation, and of the direct connection to and tapping of cosmic forces and the eternal return. This ecology extends across all the inter-relations of these modalities of ecology in the intensive rhizomatic machinic phylum that connects everything, and in the virtual plane of immanence that draws and creates everything in eternal return. The ecology is, most of all, an ecology of making and living on the planomenon as an ethos, as the new earth, and the eternal return ecology of selecting that which creates greater connections, that which creates greater intensities, and that which sets out becomings of exploration and experimentation:

> Environmental ecology, as it exists today, has barely begun to prefigure the generalised ecology that is advocated here, the aim of which will be to radically decentre social struggles and ways of coming to one's own psyche... Ecology in my sense questions the whole of subjectivity and capitalist power formations.
>
> (Guattari (2000) 52)

This ecology of the virtual and intensive earth as global social machine is nothing less than the task of 'the reconstruction of human praxis in its widest possible terms' in the wake of the capitalist social machine and the State social machines (Guattari (2000) 49). Emergent law is this ecology of the virtual and intensive earth in that it is the philosophical and ethical-aesthetic practice and paradigm of this reconstruction of the human praxis in its widest possible terms. The ecology of the virtual is the philosophical practice of the creation of concepts of earth, brain, social organisation and cosmic forces, concepts of the relations and becomings between the earth, brain, social organisation and cosmic forces, and of the maintaining of a noological ecology of thinking and thought. This ecology of the virtual is the operations of the schizo thinkers and schizo lawyers conceived in the emergent law social machine. The ecology of the intensive is the vagabond ethical-aesthetic practice's intensive existential assemblages in social ecology, mental ecology and environmental ecology (Guattari (2000) 41). The ecology of the intensive is the organisation of individual and collective ventures in terms of sensations, affects and becomings, interventions in individual and collective psychical proceedings, and experimentation and innovative practices in intensive processual assemblages and compositions (Guattari (2000) 39). The ecology of the intensive is the operations of vagabond thinkers and vagabond lawyers conceived in the emergent law social machine. The problematic and problem field of legality and social organisation leave behind State legality and thought and capitalist axiomatic organisation to become a continuous ecology of the virtual, the intensive and actual as the social organisation that connects the earth, the brain and the forces of the cosmos. It becomes an ecology of the virtual and intensive earth, based in the noology of thought and the noology of legalities (now, of course, themselves understood as ecology of thought and ecology of legality), turning on the virtual problematic of social organisation and legality connecting the earth and the brain in a transversal consistency in continuous variation that directly connects the socius to the forces of the cosmos, establishing a creative autonomy in relation to subjectivity, social organisation and environmental ecology, heralding an ethos of ethical and ecological creativity and sustainability.

Bibliography (Vagabond)

> There is no difference between what a book talks about and how it is made.
> Thus a book has no object either. As an assemblage, a book only has itself, in
> connection with other assemblages and in relation to other bodies without
> organs. We will never ask what a book means, as signified or signifier; we will
> not look for anything to understand in it. We will ask what it functions with, in
> connection with what other things it does or does not transmit intensities, in
> which other multiplicities its own are inserted and metamorphosed, and with
> what bodies without organs it makes its own converge. A book exists only
> through the outside and on the outside.
>
> (Deleuze & Guattari, *A Thousand Plateaus*, p.4)

The book has been written as much as an experimental book about complex and
experimental thought, as than an academic book about complex and academic
thought. I don't think an introduction and commentary on the work of Deleuze
and Guattari can have been anything other. As such, a style of composition developed that did not place description and referencing as central. However, of
course, very many things did go into the book, and the book could not have been
produced without all the texts that directly inform it. This vagabond bibliography
(the book's machinic phylum) was drawn up by going through all the books and
copies of articles I had at home or at work, and of each item I asked the question
'has reading this directly informed the book?', with a positive answer getting it on
the list. I have also included in the bibliography a select few references to music,
cinema and TV drama. These references are to pieces of lyrics, music, images and
drama that persistently pulled forward my thinking on this book project.

Alliez, E. (2004) *The Signature of the World: What is Deleuze & Guattari's Philosophy?*
London: Continuum.

Alliez, E. (2006) '*Anti-Oedipus* – Thirty Years On (Between Art and Politics)', in Fuglsang,
M. and Sorensen, B. (eds) (2006) *Deleuze and the Social*. Edinburgh: Edinburgh
University Press, 135–68.

Ansell-Pearson, K. (1999) *Germinal Life: The Difference and Repetition of Deleuze*.
London: Routledge.

Ayler, A. (2004) *Holy Ghost*. Revenant Recordings.

Bateson, G. (2002) *Mind & Nature: A New Unity*. New Jersey: Hampton Press.

Bell, J. and Colebrook, C. (eds) (2009) *Deleuze and History*. Edinburgh: Edinburgh University Press.

Bergson, H. (1992) *The Creative Mind: An Introduction to Metaphysics*. New York: Citadel Press.

Bonta, M. and Protevi, J. (2004) *Deleuze and Geophilosophy*. Edinburgh: Edinburgh University Press.

Buchanan, I. (2008) *Deleuze & Guattari's Anti-Oedipus*. London: Continuum.

Buchanan, I. and Thoborn, N. (eds) (2008) *Deleuze and Politics*. Edinburgh: Edinburgh University Press.

Capra, F. (1996) *The Web of Life*. London: Harper Collins.

Chesters, G. and Ward, I. (2007) *Complexity and Social Movements: Multitudes at Edge of Chaos*. London: Routledge.

Coltrane, J. (1965) *A Love Supreme* (Antibes Live version), Impulse issue (2002).

Coveney, P. and Highfield, R. (1995) *Frontiers of Complexity*. London: Faber and Faber.

Crary, J. and Kwinter, S. (eds) (1992) *Zone 6: Incorporations*. Cambridge, MA: MIT.

Cullinan, C. (2011) *Wild Law: A Manifesto for Earth Justice*, Totnes: Green Books.

Dean, K. and Massumi, B. (1992) *First and Last Emperors*. New York: Semiotext(e).

DeLanda, M. (1991) *War in the Age of Intelligent Machines*. New York: Zone Books.

DeLanda, M. (1992) 'Nonorganic Life' in Crary, J. and Kwinter, S. (eds) (1992) *Zone 6: Incorporations*. Cambridge, MA: MIT, 129–67.

DeLanda, M. (1997) *A Thousand Years of Non-Linear History*. New York: Zone Books.

DeLanda, M. (2002) *Intensive Science and Virtual Philosophy*. London: Continuum.

DeLanda, M. (2006) *A New Philosophy of Society: Assemblage Theory and Social Complexity*. London: Continuum.

Deleuze, G. (1983) *Nietzsche and Philosophy*. London: The Athlone Press.

Deleuze, G. and Parnet, C. (1987) *Dialogues*. London: The Athlone Press.

Deleuze, G. (1988a) *Spinoza: Practical Philosophy*. San Francisco: City Lights Books.

Deleuze, G. (1988b) *Foucault*. London: The Athlone Press.

Deleuze, G. (1989) *Coldness and Cruelty*. New York: Zone Books.

Deleuze, G. (1991) *Empiricism and Subjectivity*. New York: Columbia University Press.

Deleuze, G. (1992) 'Ethology: Spinoza and Us' in Crary, J. and Kwinter, S. (ed) (1992) *Zone 6: Incorporations*. Cambridge, MA: MIT, 625–33.

Deleuze, G. (1993) *The Fold: Liebniz and the Baroque*. London: The Athlone Press.

Deleuze, G. (1994) *Difference and Repetition*. London: The Athlone Press.

Deleuze, G. (1995) *Negotiations*. New York: Columbia University Press.

Deleuze, G. (1998a) *Bergsonism*. New York: Zone Books.

Deleuze, G. (1998b) *Essays Critical and Clinical*. London: Verso Press.

Deleuze, G. (2001) *Pure Immanence*. New York: Zone Books.

Deleuze, G. (2003) *Francis Bacon: The Logic of Sensation*. London: Continuum.

Deleuze, G. (2004a) *The Logic of Sense*. London: Continuum.

Deleuze, G. (2004b) *Desert Islands*. New York: Semiotext(e).

Deleuze, G. and Guattari, F. (1984) *Anti-Oedipus*. London: The Athlone Press.

Deleuze, G. and Guattari, F. (2004) *Anti-Oedipus*. London: Continuum.

Deleuze, G. and Guattari, F. (1986) *Kafka: Towards a Minor Literature*. Minneapolis: University of Minnesota Press.

Deleuze, G. and Guattari, F. (1988) *A Thousand Plateaus*. London: The Athlone Press.

Deleuze, G. and Guattari, F. (2004) *A Thousand Plateaus*. London: Continuum.
Deleuze, G. and Guattari, F. (1994) *What is Philosophy?* London: Verso Press.
Deleuze, G. and Parnet, C. (2002) *Dialogues II*. London: Continuum.
Duffy, S. (2004) 'Schizo Math', *Angelaki*, 9:3 199–215.
Duffy, S. (ed) (2006) *Virtual Mathematics: The Logic of Difference*. Manchester: Clinamen Press.
Evans, E. (2000) 'Math Anxiety', *Angelaki*, 5:3 105–15.
Fuglsang, M. and Sorensen, B. (eds) (2006) *Deleuze and the Social*. Edinburgh: Edinburgh University Press.
Gaffney, P. (ed) (2010) *Deleuze, Science and Philosophy*. Minnesota: Minnesota University Press.
Genosko, G. (1996) *The Guattari Reader*. Oxford: Blackwell.
Genosko, G. (2002) *Felix Guattari: An Aberrant Introduction*. London: Continuum.
Golder, B. and Fitzpatrick, P. (2009) *Foucault's Law*. Oxford: Routledge.
Goodchild, P. (1996) *Deleuze & Guattari*. London: Sage.
Goodrich, P. (1986) 'Law and Modernity', *Modern Law Review*, 49:5 545–59.
Guattari, F. (1992) 'Regimes, Pathways, Subjects' in Crary, J. and Kwinter, S. (eds) (1992) *Zone 6: Incorporations*. Cambridge, MA: MIT, 16–37.
Guattari, F. (1995a) *Chaosmos: An Ethico-Aesthetic Paradigm*. Sydney: Power Publications.
Guattari, F. (1995b) *Chaosophy*. New York: Semiotext(e).
Guattari, F. (1996) *Soft Subversions*. New York: Semiotext(e).
Guattari, F. (2000) *The Three Ecologies*. London: The Athlone Press.
Guattari, F. (2006) *The Anti-Oedipus Papers*. New York: Semiotext(e).
Guattari, F. (2009) *Soft Subversions: Texts and Interviews 1977–85*. Los Angeles: Semiotext(e).
Guattari, F. (2011) *The Machinic Unconscious*. Los Angeles: Semiotext(e).
Guattari, F. and Alliez, E. (1996) *Communists Like Us*. New York: Semiotext(e).
Gutting, G. (ed) (2005) *Continental Philosophy of Science*. Oxford: Blackwell.
Halsey, M. (2006) *Deleuze and Environmental Damage*. Aldershot: Ashgate.
Harari, R. (2002) *How James Joyce Made His Name*. New York: The Other Press.
Hardt, M. (1998) 'The Withering of Civil Society' in Kaufman, E. and Heller, J. (eds) (1998) *Deleuze & Guattari: New Mappings in Politics, Philosophy, and Culture*. Minneapolis: Minnesota University Press, 23–39.
Hardt, M. and Negri, A. (1994) *Labor of Dionysus*. Minneapolis: University of Minnesota Press.
Hardt, M. and Negri, A. (2000) *Empire*. Cambridge, MA: Harvard University Press.
Hardt, M. and Negri, A. (2004) *Multitudes*. London: Hamish Hamilton.
Harvey, D. (2007) *The Limits to Capital*. London: Verso.
Harvey, D. (2011) *The Enigma of Capital and the Crises of Capitalism*. London: Profile Books.
Henry, S. and Milovanovic, D. (1996) *Constitutive Criminology: Beyond Postmodernism*. London: Sage.
Herzogenrath, B. (ed) (2009) *Deleuze/Guattari and Ecology*. London: Palgrave MacMillan.
Holland, P. (1998) 'From Schizophrenia to Social Control' in Kaufman, E. and Heller, J. (ed) (1998) *Deleuze & Guattari: New Mappings in Politics, Philosophy, and Culture*. Minneapolis: Minnesota University Press, 65–76.
Holland, P. (1999) *Deleuze & Guattari's Anti-Oedipus: Introduction to Schizoanalysis*. London: Routledge.

Jefferson Airplane (1968) *After Bathing at Baxters.*

Johnson, D. and Post, D. (1996) 'Law and Borders: The Rise of Law in Cyberspace', *Stanford Law Review*, 48 1367.

Johnson, D. and Post, D. (1997) 'And How Shall the Net Be Governed? A Meditation on the Relative Virtues of Decentralised, Emergent Law', in Kahin, B. and Keller, J. (eds) (1997) *Coordinating the Internet.* Cambridge, MA: MIT, 62–91.

Kaufman, E. and Heller, J. (eds) (1998) *Deleuze & Guattari: New Mappings in Politics, Philosophy, and Culture.* Minneapolis: Minnesota University Press.

Kauffman, S. (1995) *At Home in the Universe.* Oxford: Oxford University Press.

Kahin, B. and Keller, J. (eds) (1997) *Coordinating the Internet.* Cambridge MA: MIT.

Lacan, J. (1998) *Seminar 20: The Limits of Love and Knowledge.* London: W.W. Norton.

Lacan, J. (2006) *Ecrits: The First Complete Edition in English.* London: W.W. Norton.

Lacan, J. (2007) *Seminar 17: The Other Side of Psychoanalysis.* London: W.W. Norton.

Lambert, G. (2006) *Who's Afraid of Deleuze & Guattari?* London: Continuum.

Land, N. (2011) *Fanged Noumena.* Falmouth: Urbanomic.

Lefebvre, A. (2005) 'A New Image of Law: Deleuze and Jurisprudence', *Telos,* 2005:130 103–26.

Lefebvre, A. (2008) *The Image of Law: Deleuze, Bergson, Spinoza.* Stanford, CA: Stanford University Press.

Levy, P. (1997) *Collective Intelligence: Mankind's Emerging World in Cyberspace.* New York: Plenum Trade.

Levy, P. (1998) *Becoming Virtual: Reality in the Digital Age.* New York: Plenum Trade.

MacIntosh, R., MacLean, D., Stacey, R. and Griffin, D. (eds) (2006) *Complexity and Organisation.* Oxford: Routledge.

Marazzi, C. (2010) *The Violence of Finance Capitalism.* Los Angeles: Semiotext(e).

Marks, J. (ed) (2006) *Deleuze and Science.* Edinburgh: Edinburgh University Press.

Massumi, B. (1992) *A User's Guide to Capitalism and Schizophrenia: Deviations from Deleuze & Guattari.* Cambridge, MA: MIT.

Massumi, B. (1998) 'Requiem for Our Prospective Dead: (Towards a Participatory Critique of Capitalist Power' in Kaufman, E. and Heller, J. (eds) (1998) *Deleuze & Guattari: New Mappings in Politics, Philosophy, and Culture.* Minneapolis: Minnesota University Press, 40–64.

Massumi, B. (2002) *Parables for the Virtual.* London: Duke University Press.

May, T. (2005) 'Gilles Deleuze, Difference and Science' in Gutting, G. (ed) (2005) *Continental Philosophy of Science.* Oxford: Blackwell, 239–57.

Milovanovic, D. (1992) *Postmodern Law and Disorder.* Liverpool: Deborah Charles.

Milovanovic, D. (1997) *Chaos, Criminology, and Social Justice: The New Orderly (Dis) Order.* London: Praeger.

Milovanovic, D. (1997a) 'Visions of the Emerging Orderly (Dis) Order' in Milovanovic, D. (1997) *Chaos, Criminology, and Social Justice: The New Orderly (Dis) Order.* London: Praeger.

Mitchell, M. (2009) *Complexity: A Guided Tour.* Oxford: Oxford University Press.

Moore, R. (2003–9) *Battlestar Gallactica: Re-Imagined.*

Murray, J. (2005) 'Sinthome Law: Theoretical Constructions on Lacan's Concept of the Sinthome', *Law & Critique,* 16:2 201–30.

Murray, J. (2006) 'Nome Law: Deleuze & Guattari and the Emergence of Law', *International Journal of the Semiotics of Law,* 19:2 127–51.

Mussawir, E. (2011) *Jurisdiction in Deleuze: The Expression and Representation of Law*. London: Routledge.

Negri, A. (2005) 'Postmodern Global Governance and the Critical Legal Project', *Law & Critique*, 16 27–46.

Nicolis, G. and Prigogine, I. (1989) *Exploring Complexity: An Introduction*. New York: W.H. Freeman.

Nigianni, C. and Storr, M. (eds) (2009) *Deleuze and Queer Theory*. Edinburgh: Edinburgh University Press.

Parr, A. (ed) (2005) *The Deleuze Dictionary*. Edinburgh: Edinburgh University Press.

Patton, P. (2000) *Deleuze and the Political*. London: Routledge.

Patton, P. (2006) 'Order, Exteriority and Flat Multiplicities' in Fuglsang, M. and Sorensen, B. (eds) (2006) *Deleuze and the Social*. Edinburgh: Edinburgh University Press, 21–38.

Patton, P. (2010) *Deleuzian Concepts: Philosophy, Colonisation, Politics*. Stanford, CA: Stanford University Press.

Prigogine, I. (1996) *The End of Certainty*. New York: Free Press.

Prigogine, I. and Stengers, I. (1984) *Order Out of Chaos*. New York: Bantam Books.

Ragland, E. and Milovanovic, D. (2004) *Lacan; Topologically Speaking*. New York: The Other Press.

Raunig, G. (2010) *A Thousand Machines*. Los Angeles: Semiotext(e).

Saber, N. (1999) *Speculative Capital*. London: Pearson.

Serres, M. (1995) *The Natural Contract*. Michigan: University of Michigan Press.

Serres, M. (1997) *Genesis*. Michigan: University of Michigan Press.

Sun Ra (1973) 'Space is the Place' from the album *Space is the Place*.

Tarkovsky, A. (1966) *Andrei Rublev*.

Thurston, L. (2002) *Re-Inventing the Symptom*. New York: The Other Press.

Virno, P. (2004) *A Grammar of the Multitude*. New York: Semiotext(e).

Wuensche, A. (2012) www.ddlab.borg

Williams, J. (2003) *Gilles Deleuze's Difference and Repetition*. Edinburgh: Edinburgh University Press.

Young, N. (1973) 'After the Goldrush' from the album *After the Goldrush*.

Index

absolute limit: organisation 63, 84, 85, 86, 89, 125, 127–32, 154, 155, 156
absolute survey at infinite speed 39, 40, 41
abstract machines: of legality 56, 61–2, 64–7, 70, 73, 82, 84, 86; in noology 38, 86; virtual ontology 2, 4; virtual ontology of the earth 13, 16–17, 18–19, 20, 27, 31, *see also* conceptual personae; fractal abstract machines; molar abstract machines; Urstaat abstract machine
abstraction 46, 47, 116
actual(ised) brain 33, 34
actual(ised) social organisation 56
adventure of capitalism 89, 115–27
adventure of the ecumenon: State social machine 97–115; territorial social machine 89, 90–7
to affect and be affected 15, 16, 17, 27, 29, 36, 40, 51, 78, 145, 147
affect-events *see* sensation-intensity-affect-events
affects: forces and 2, 28, 58, 64
agencies: assemblages of 68
agents: capitalist 122
alliance: capitalist social machine 125; Imperial state machine 102; schizo and vagabond lawyer 149; territorial social machine 90, 91, 94, 96, *see also* filiation; incest; memory of alliances
alliance debt 91, 93, 96, 97, 102, 107
ambivalence: vagabond thought 48, 49, 52
analogy 46
analytical judgements 46
anti-capitalist social movements 154
anticipation-prevention 62
AntiOedipus 1, 3
antiproduction 61, 96–7, 107–8, 115, 119–20

apparatus of capture: of State social machine 62, 63, 107
arbitraged flows 62, 119, 154
arborescent analytical method 46, 47
arborescent model/structure 21, 22, 74, 106, 135
archaism(s) 101, 107, 124, 139
arrival of God 20, 73
articulation: of expression 23–4, *see also* double articulation
astronomy 43, 99
attractors 15, 16, 28, 29, 30, 36, 49, 64
axioms: as statements 122

banking sector 115, 118–19, 122, 126
battle of forces 28, 50, 56, 68, 76, 79
becoming(s) 58, 89, 90, 134, 136, 137, 145, 147, 148; fractal line of 13, 17, 32, 142; intensive social assemblages 77; virtual ontology 4; virtual ontology of the earth 13, 19, 20, 27, 28, 30
beliefs: State thought 47
Bergson 2
betrayal: point of 113
bifurcation thresholds 15, 16, 29, 30, 36, 65
binary distinctions 100
biocosmic memory of filiation: repression of 90
biological strata 24
block consistencies 79
bodies: machinic assemblage of 69; regime of 67, 68, 69, 71, 74–5, 90, 93, 94, 95, *see also* social bodies
bodies-technologies: multiplicity of 78
body of the despot 106–7, 108
body inscriptions 93, 94, 95, 96, 97